VOLUME II

REMINISCENCES

OF

ADMIRAL CHARLES DONALD GRIFFIN

U.S. Navy (Retired)

U.S. Naval Institute
December, 1975

Preface

Volume II of the Reminiscences of Admiral Charles Donald Griffin contains the transcript of eight interviews (numbers 10 through 17). These were held in the Admiral's home in Washington, D.C. over a period of time ranging from November, 1970 to January, 1972. All these interviews were conducted by John T. Mason, Jr. for the Oral History program of the U.S. Naval Institute.

Admiral Griffin made corrections to the original transcript from the tapes and these are incorporated into the re-typed version. A subject index to the text is included at the end of the volume.

The Admiral's 7th Fleet Command, his duty as Deputy CNO for Fleet Operations and Readiness, his CincUS NAVEUR Command and his CincSOUTH (NATO) Command are covered in this volume. They all highlight his innate wisdom, his decisiveness and his diplomatic skill.

An Appendix at the very end of the volume contains some records and speeches of much historical value. Included are the following:

1. Record of Admiral Griffin's trip to Turkey in August 1966. His conversations with General C. Tural, Chief of the Turkish General Staff.

2. Admiral Griffin's trip to Iran, Oct. 1966, in an effort to further coordination between NATO and CENTO. His conversations with the Shah of Iran.

3. Admiral Griffin's final report as Cinc SOUTH at SHAPE Headquarters in Belgium (Oct. 1967).

4. Admiral Griffin's notes on his visit to Spain in November, 1967. His remarks at the East Coast Sectional Meeting of the Navy League in Madrid.

John T. Mason, Jr.
Director of Oral History,
U.S. Naval Institute

December, 1975

ADMIRAL CHARLES DONALD GRIFFIN, UNITED STATES NAVY, RETIRED

Admiral Charles Donald Griffin, U. S. Navy was Commander in Chief, Allied Forces, Southern Europe, from March 1965 until relieved of active duty, pending his retirement, effective February 1, 1968. Prior to that assignment, he had served from June 26, 1963 as Commander in Chief, U. S. Naval Forces, Europe (CINCUSNAVEUR) and as U. S. Commander, Eastern Atlantic (USCOMEASTLANT), with headquarters in central London on Grosvenor Square. As such he had command of all United States Naval forces and activities afloat and ashore in the European and North African areas, including the U. S. SIXTH Fleet in the Mediterranean Sea.

Although he was born in Philadelphia, Pennsylvania, on 12 January 1906, Admiral Griffin was raised in Washington, D. C. He was graduated from Central High School in Washington in 1923 and the same year entered the U. S. Naval Academy at Annapolis. He was graduated in 1927 and commissioned an Ensign. In 1930 he won his wings as a naval aviator and received orders as scouting aircraft pilot on board USS CHESTER, a heavy cruiser. During this tour of duty he was commended by the Secretary of the Navy for excellence in gunnery.

Subsequent service included extensive staff duty ashore and afloat in both the Atlantic and the Pacific and in Washington. In major assignments at sea Admiral Griffin commanded the aircraft carriers USS CROATAN (CVE 25) and USS ORISKANY (CVA 34), Carrier Division Four and the U. S. SEVENTH Fleet. He also served on the Joint War Plans Committee of the Joint Chiefs of Staff, as Special Assistant to the Chairman of the Joint Chiefs of Staff, as Director of the Navy's Strategic Plans Division, and most recently as Deputy Chief of Naval Operations for Fleet Operations and Readiness.

Admiral Griffin received a Master's Degree in Aeronautical Engineering from the University of Michigan in 1937 and was also graduated from the National War College in 1951. He is active in the Episcopal Church and has served as a vestryman at St. Alban's Episcopal Church in Washington. His hobbies include reading, golf and photography. In earlier years, he was a member of the Navy's Leech Cup Tennis Team.

Admiral Griffin was married to Camilla Yvonne Ganteaume, who died in 1963. Their children are Linda Louise, now the wife of Major Harry Collins, II, USMC, and Lieutenant Charles Donald Griffin, Jr., USN, a 1962 graduate of the Naval Academy and submariner. In November 1964 he married Mrs. Marion Hopkins Schaefer of Washington, D. C., a widow. She has one daughter, Mrs. Richard J. Lewis.

4 March 1968

ADMIRAL CHARLES DONALD GRIFFIN, UNITED STATES NAVY, RETIRED

PROMOTIONS:

Ensign, June 1927
Lieutenant (junior grade), June 1930
Lieutenant, July 1936
Lieutenant Commander, September 1941
Commander, September 1942
Captain, March 1945
Rear Admiral, February 1955
Vice Admiral, January 1960
Admiral, June 26, 1963

DECORATIONS AND MEDALS:

Distinguished Service Medal
Gold Star in lieu Second Distinguished Service Medal
Bronze Star Medal, Combat "V"
Presidential Unit Citation Ribbon, two stars (USS ESSEX and USS YORKTOWN)
American Defense Service Medal, Fleet Clasp
American Campaign Medal
Asiatic-Pacific Campaign Medal, one silver star (five engagements)
World War II Victory Medal
Navy Occupation Service Medal, Europe Clasp
National Defense Service Medal with bronze star
Korean Service Medal
United Nations Service Medal

CITATIONS:

Distinguished Service Medal: "For exceptionally meritorious service ...as Deputy Chief of Naval Operations (Fleet Operations and Readiness) from December 1961 to June 1963. Admiral (then Vice Admiral) Griffin displayed a high degree of imagination and foresight while involved in the personal direction of much of the Navy's operations incident to the Cuban Quarantine. The readiness and proper deployment of U. S. Navy forces were a major concern of Admiral Griffin, and his keen perception and thorough understanding, both of possible measures available to our forces, and of the likely response to be expected of our adversaries, enabled him to discharge his responsibilities during this period of grave crisis with outstanding skill and resourcefulness. Recognizing the need for centralized coordination of policies and procedures throughout the Navy, (he) was instrumental in effecting the establishment of the Office of the Assistant Chief of Naval Operations (Training). Under his leadership, the concept of specially trained counterinsurgency teams was developed and in January 1962 the first

Adm. C. D. Griffin, USN, Ret.

Sea Air Land (SEAL) Teams were established. He was also a driving force in the incorporation into the Fleet of such important contributions as the Automatic Air Intercept Control Computer, the Drone Antisubmarine Helicopter (DASH) weapon system, the P3A (ORION) patrol plane, and the Fleet Computer Programming Centers..."

Gold Star in lieu of the Second Distinguished Service Medal: "For exceptionally meritorious service...as Commander in Chief, Allied Forces, Southern Europe, from March 1965 through January 1968. Serving in this key post of international significance, during a period of unrest, conflict and heightened tensions, Admiral Griffin made outstanding contributions to the security interests of the United States and considerably enhanced the security posture of the North Atlantic Alliance. As a result of his able direction and his skill in coordination, the security and operational readiness of the multinational forces committed to his command were improved significantly. Admiral Griffin continuously demonstrated a high degree of resourcefulness, a keen and perceptive insight, and sound judgment in the achievement of Allied objectives, furthering at the same time, a mutual understanding and respect among the civil and military elements of the NATO countries in his area of responsibility. He was greatly instrumental in the successful achievement of multinational peacetime agreements which would meet the critical test of wartime requirements. Admiral Griffin's efforts in materially enhancing the military readiness and overall effectiveness of Allied Forces, Southern Europe, coupled with his unique contribution in the furtherance of military integrity and general security within Allied Command Europe, was of immeasurable benefit to the mission of the North Atlantic Alliance..."

Bronze Star Medal: "For meritorious achievement as Air Officer of the USS ESSEX in the Pacific War Area from September 1943 to January 1944. Having previously commissioned, organized and trained Air Group NINE while serving as its commander, (he) contributed largely to the success of this group in an attack on Japanese shipping in Rabaul Harbor on November 11, 1943, as well as the defense of the Task Group when subjected to a determined counterattack on that date by approximately 300 Japanese aircraft..."

Presidential Unit Citation (USS ESSEX): "For extraordinary heroism in action against enemy Japanese forces in the air, ashore and afloat in the Pacific War Area from August 31, 1943 to August 15, 1945..."

Presidential Unit Citation (USS YORKTOWN): "For participation with Task Force 58 in the occupation of the Marshall Islands and raids on Truk and the Marianas."

Letter of Commendation (SECNAV): "For high fixed gunnery score, heavy cruiser class, U. S. Fleet."

Adm. C. D. Griffin, USN, Ret.

FOREIGN DECORATIONS:

Medal of Pao Ting by China
Order of the Double Rays of the Rising Sun by Japan
Philippine Legion of Honor (Commander)
Order of Military Merit Taeguk with Silver Star by Korea

CHRONOLOGICAL TRANSCRIPT OF SERVICE:

Jun 1927 - Jun 1928	USS FLORIDA
Jun 1928 - Oct 1929	USS COGHLAN
Nov 1929 - Jun 1930	Naval Air Station, Pensacola, Florida (Flight Training)
Jul 1930 - Jun 1933	Scouting Squadron Nine (Pilot aboard USS CHESTER)
Jul 1933 - Jun 1934	Patrol Squadron Six
Jul 1934 - Jun 1936	Naval Postgraduate School, Annapolis, Maryland
Jun 1936 - Jul 1937	University of Michigan, Ann Arbor, Michigan
Jul 1937 - Jun 1940	Scouting Squadron Six (Operations Officer aboard USS ENTERPRISE)
Jul 1940 - Jul 1942	Naval Air Station, Anocostia, D. C., (Flight Test Officer)
Aug 1942 - Sep 1943	Carrier Air Group Nine (Commanding Officer, aboard USS ESSEX)
Sep 1943 - Dec 1943	Air Officer, USS ESSEX
Dec 1943 - Mar 1944	Commander, Carrier Division Three (Operations Officer, aboard USS YORKTOWN)
Mar 1944 - Sep 1945	Joint War Plans Committee, Joint Chiefs of Staff (Naval Aviation Member)
Sep 1945 - Jan 1946	USS CROATAN (Commanding Officer)
Feb 1946 - Sep 1946	Staff, Commander, EIGHTH Fleet (Operations Officer, aboard USS FRANKLIN D. ROOSEVELT)
Sep 1946 - Sep 1947	Staff, Commander in Chief, Atlantic Fleet (Assistant Chief of Staff, Plans)
Sep 1947 - Jul 1948	Staff, Commander, Fleet Air Wing Two (Chief of Staff and Aide)
Jul 1948 - Sep 1948	Staff, Commander, Air Force, U. S. Pacific Fleet, (Plans Officer)
Oct 1948 - Aug 1950	Office of the Chief of Naval Operations (Head of the Aviation Liaison and Special Projects Section, Strategic Plans Division)
Aug 1950 - Jun 1951	National War College (Student)
Jul 1951 - May 1953	Staff, Commander in Chief, U. S. Pacific Fleet (Assistant Chief of Staff, Plans)
Jun 1953 - Aug 1954	USS ORISKANY (Commanding Officer)
Sep 1954 - Apr 1955	Deputy Chief of Naval Operations, Air (Special Assistant for Special Studies)
Apr 1955 - Jun 1956	Director, Long Range Objectives Group, Naval Operations

Adm. C. D. Griffin, USN, Ret.

Jun 1956 - Nov 1957	Joint Chiefs of Staff (Special Assistant to Chairman)
Nov 1957 - Nov 1958	Commander, Carrier Division Four
Dec 1958 - Feb 1960	Office of the Chief of Naval Operations (Strategic Plans Division Director)
Mar 1960 - Oct 1961	Commander, SEVENTH Fleet
Jan 1962 - Jun 1963	Deputy Chief of Naval Operations (Fleet Operations and Readiness)
Jun 1963 - Mar 1965	Commander in Chief, U. S. Naval Forces, Europe and U. S. Commander, Eastern Atlantic
Mar 1965 -	Commander in Chief, Allied Forces, Southern Europe
1 Feb 1968	Transferred to the Retired List of the U. S. Navy

CINCUSNAVEUR
2 December 1964
Revised (OI-430)
4 March 1968

DECLARATION OF TRUST

The undersigned does hereby appoint and designate as his (her) Trustee herein, the Secretary-Treasurer and Publisher of the United States Naval Institute to perform and discharge the following duties, powers, and privileges in connection with the possession and use of a certain taped interview between the undersigned and the Oral History Department of the United States Naval Institute.

1. Classification of Transcript.

   (✓)a. If classified OPEN, the transcript(s) may be read or the recording(s) audited by the qualified personnel upon presentation of proper credentials, as determined by the Secretary-Treasurer of the U. S. Naval Institute.

   ( )b. If classified PERMISSION REQUIRED TO CITE OR QUOTE, the user will be required to obtain permission in writing from the interviewee prior to quoting or citing from either the transcript(s) or the recording(s).

   ( )c. If classified PERMISSION REQUIRED, permission must be obtained in writing from the interviewee before the transcribed interview(s) can be examined or the tape recording(s) audited.

   ( )d. If classified CLOSED, the transcribed interview(s) and the tape recording(s) will be sealed until a time specified by the interviewee. This may be until the death of the interviewee or for any specified number of years.

2. It is expressly understood that in giving this authorization, I am in no way precluded from placing such restrictions as I may desire upon use of the interview at any time during my lifetime, nor does this authorization in any way affect my rights to the copyright of my literary expressions that may be contained in the interview.

Witness my hand and seal this 28th day of June 1973.

_____

I hereby accept and consent to the foregoing Declaration of Trust and the powers therein conferred upon me as Trustee:

_____

Interview # 10

Admiral Charles D. Griffin, USN, Ret.   by John T. Mason, Jr.
Washington, D. C.   November 3, 1970

Mr. Mason: We meet again on this rainy election day when you have no vote, being a resident of the District of Columbia.

Let us start on chapter ten. I think you'll have some more to say about your tour of duty as Commander of the Seventh Fleet.

Admiral Griffin: Yes. I'm terribly sorry that people in the District of Columbia don't have the full franchise. We do have the right, as of this year, to elect a non-voting delegate to the U. S. Congress. When the people in Washington will get the full franchise, I'm not prepared to say. There's considerable opposition to it in many fields and the probability is it will be some time in the future. However, this has little to do with my tour of duty in the Seventh Fleet.

One of the items that I've mentioned before in connection with my tour of duty in the Seventh Fleet had to do with visitors coming out to that Fleet. It was apparent to me on many occasions that there was little appreciation of the vast distances involved out in the Western Pacific.

The area of interest for the Seventh Fleet, which I would call my parish, was in fact one-fifth of the entire world. It ran from Guam in the Pacific Ocean to the middle of the Indian Ocean.

On many occasions we would get a telegram from Washington suggesting that certain people come out. And they would want to see four or five different types of ships, see Tokyo, see Hong Kong, see Manila, and perhaps Taiwan. They would have about two or three days at the most to do this. There was little or no appreciation of the vast distances involved.

Mr. Mason: This was a Public Relations thing, was it not?

Admiral Griffin: This was a Public Relations thing, but also I thought it was a little deeper than that.

There was little appreciation on the part of many people in the United States, most of them were very highly educated, as to just the plain distances involved, to go from Tokyo to Hong Kong or to Singapore or what have you.

We think largely in terms, and this is naturally a way to think, of the size of the United States in it's relationship to Western Europe. The size of the Atlantic Ocean therefore becomes a measure. The Pacific is so large in comparison to the Atlantic as to defy all reason.

This leads really into another thing: the lack of understanding of the people of the United States to the Oriental. This is something that we worked on very hard in the Fleet, and I will comment on that later.

In connection with this, I made a trip to Guam as part of my parish. And there had an opportunity to see a magnificent shell collection, which had been gotten together by Mr. Nucker, who at that time was the High Commissioner to the Trust Territories of the Pacific.

The reason I was particularly interested in this was that several years back I had had some disc trouble in my back and for about three months was unable to swim, to play golf or tennis. I took up as a hobby walking the beaches of Hawaii and picking up shells off the reefs. I think this is a very interesting hobby and one which I have unfortunately not been able to carry out very much in recent years, but nevertheless I'm still interested in.

Mr. Mason: Have you preserved a collection?

Admiral Griffin: I do have some that are left. Unfortunately the case in which I had my best shells disappeared in one of my shipments and I don't have the faintest idea where it went. This was a nice wooden case with about sixteen trays in it of shells, and they were all filled with fine shells.

I had mentioned before also the fact that I was quite interested in golf. Usually when we were in the Yokosuka area I played golf at Atsugi.

On one occasion Rear Admiral Sutherland, who was the Commander Fleet Air Western Pacific, a classmate and very good friend of mine, and I were invited to attend the ceremonies incident to the opening of a new golf course outside of Tokyo. The people who were principal members of the cast of this ceremony, which included eighteen holes of golf, were Arnold Palmer and Gary Player.

Admiral Sutherland and I were following Arnold Palmer. On about the third hole he suddenly turned around and walked over to us and said, "I understand that you two are rather avid golfers." We allowed as how we were.

To make a long story short: We went around with him and he talked with us for practically the rest of the round. You could certainly see why he has Arnie's Army with him most of the time because he's an absolutely fascinating individual.

I gather that his public relations department had sort of cased the joint, so to speak, and found out that there were two American Admirals out there who loved to play golf, and he was briefed before he came to Tokyo and remembered this. As he was playing he asked one of his associates, one of the Japanese with him, whether the two American Admirals might be in the group witnessing his exhibition match. This chap turned around and recognized us, pointed us out, and so Palmer came over and talked to us. He didn't miss a trick.

Mr. Mason: Very effective.

Admiral Griffin: Very very effective, absolutely. We could use a lot more of that around the world.

An item that gave me a great deal of pleasure had to do with a maid in our house, our household in Yokosuka. We had a lovely young Japanese girl named Taiki-San. I believe that she was just about as pretty as any Japanese woman I had ever seen in my life. She was my wife's maid.

She became interested in a young Japanese man, who was a very talented electronic technician, and on the man's side of the house probably just as attractive as she was. These two made a perfectly splendid couple.

Taiko-San was a Roman Catholic, which is rather unusual for a Japanese, she was a convert.

When the time came for them to make their plans to get married Taiko-San, who did not have a father living, asked me if I would be so kind as to give her away at the wedding.

Then she went to her Priest, and the Priest informed her since I was an Episcopalian it would not be possible for me to serve in that capacity at her wedding.

Taiko-San was not to be deterred in this thing, and she went to the Bishop. The Bishop was very understanding and overruled the Priest and made a determination that I would be permitted to act in this capacity at the wedding.

My wife, in the meantime, was outfitting Taiko-San with an absolutely beautiful trousseau.

The wedding took place as scheduled and I gave Taiko-San away. We drove to the wedding in my car and attracted quite a bit of attention in the city of Yokosuka. It was a thoroughly delightful occasion and I never shall forget it. We have some wonderful pictures of the wedding.

After the wedding there was a reception given at one of the fine restaurants in Yokosuka. In this reception Taiko-San and her party were in typical Japanese formal dress. When the party was about half over they left and changed into appropriate western dress. It was quite an affair. I'll never forget it.

On this particular time when in-port at Yokosuka too, I made a presentation to all the Navy wives in the area. We spent only about twenty-five percent of our time in Yokosuka, which was the home port of the flag ship. The rest of the time we were underway on official visits, or for exercises at sea. I felt that the wives should have a full understanding of everything their husbands were doing while they were away that seventy-five percent of the time.

This was a very successful series of presentations. I then determined to recommend to my successor that he keep this up on a sort of annual basis.

Mr. Mason: And what were they, educational in nature?

Admiral Griffin: Educational in nature, that's right. Just to let them know in somewhat more detail than they undoubtedly had as to just what we were doing and what the objective of all this was.

Mr. Mason: You were pretty adept at Public Relations too, weren't you?

Admiral Griffin: I don't know about that.

Mr. Mason: This is somewhat similar to what you did on the carrier?

Admiral Griffin: That's right. It was a follow through on the same general idea.

Also during this trip, this particular stay in Yokosuka, I was the guest of honor at a very fine luncheon given by General Genda. General Genda was the Chief of Staff at that time of the Japanese Air Self Defense Force. I had gotten to know him quite well.

He, as in the case of many of the senior officers in the Japanese Air Self Defense Force, had been a naval aviator in World War II, and was the individual given the major credit for planning the attack on Pearl Harbor. Of course, since then he has been to the U. S. on several occasions.

Mr. Mason: Yes, the Naval Institute knows very much about that.

Admiral Griffin: Shortly after this we went on a return visit to Taiwan. I wanted to mention, in this connection, there were several affairs given.

One was a luncheon given for me by Major General S. K. Hu, who was the Gimo's interpreter. He was a Michigan graduate and his wife was a Michigan graduate. This was a luncheon given in my honor, to which had been invited all the people in Taipei who held degrees from the University of Michigan. There were almost fifty people there, very very unusual.

On this particular visit also, it was made possible for us to visit the Island of Kinmen, one of the off-shore islands. It was the island on which the CHinese had their headquarters. We flew to an air strip on the east side of the island and had a very fine visit, which included inspection of all the defense activities and a look at the mainland through high-power glasses. The mainland was less than five miles away.

Mr. Mason: You say they had the headquarters there, naval headquarters?

Admiral Griffin: The defense headquarters for the off-shore islands.

Following this visit to Taiwan we left Keelung for Saigon. My flag Captain, Captain Maurer, was relieved by Captain Schneider.

We proceeded to South Vietnam and up the Mekong River to Saigon. This was a very interesting trip up the river. The channel in this river changes frequently and is heavily silted from time to time. It requires up to date, by that I mean daily, knowledge on the part of the pilots who take ships up there. It's rather swift, with a current of about five or six knots.

I mentioned the fact that Captain Schneider had just relieved because when we got to Saigon, in order to turn the ship around in the channel he had to put the bow into a mud bank and then allow the stern to swing with the current. The mud bank became the anchor.

He was in the very unusual position of having to run his ship aground on the first trip that he made newly in command of the ship something that's very rarely ever done in the U. S. Navy. Running your ship aground is not looked upon with great enthusiasm.

Mr. Mason: But he wasn't subject to a court of inquiry.

Admiral Griffin: No, he was not, no indeed.

This was a very interesting visit to Saigon. Ambassador Durbrow was the American Ambassador there at the time, an old friend of mine and whom I still see from time to time.

Also there on that particular occasion was Admiral Sir David Luce, who was the Commander-in-Chief Far East Station, British. He later on became the First Sea Lord of Britain, and he and his wife, Mary, became very close friends of ours. His number two in command was a Rear Admiral Sir Michael Le Fanu, a very brilliant officer who in turn became the First Sea Lord of Britain. I got to know these two very well - wonderful people.

On this occasion of the visit to Saigon I had President Diem aboard to visit. This proved to be an extremely interesting visit. I had met President Diem before on many occasions, and I had always been very much impressed with him.

He was an individual who, as in many cases, liked to talk quite a bit. He was no slouch at this, he could talk for hours on end. But sifting through much of the talk came out a lot of good common sense. He also was the only individual whom I think our authorities felt was in any way capable of bringing together all of the very diverse elements in Vietnam.

Mr. Mason: That was a fairly correct estimate.

Admiral Griffin: It certainly was. And I can't help but feel that our great hope in Vietnam for any sort of a peaceful settlement was to keep him in power and control him, and I believe that he could have been controlled. His brother and his brother's wife became very much in evidence, but I'm still convinced that this could have been handled.

Later on when I was in London I told my staff this when we were having a briefing one day about the situation out there. I told the staff at the time that, "If we ever permit anything to happen to this little fellow Diem, we're headed for an awful lot of trouble in that area." This was about two or three weeks before he was murdered. And there's been nothing but grief there since.

This was very interesting, in fact I have a picture of his visit aboard the ship. This was the last time that I saw President Diem and it retains a place in my memory that I shall cherish.

We went to Hong Kong after this. Also Admiral Luce followed in his flag ship. At that time the Consul General in Hong Kong was Mr. Julius Holmes, who became a very fine friend of mine and was Ambassador to several countries.

During this particular visit to Hong Kong also, Senator Hugh Scott of Pennsylvania came aboard to serve two weeks of active duty time. He was a Captain, Naval Reserve.

I mention this because a little bit later on he was transferred from the ST. PAUL to a carrier when we were operating at sea. He was flown off the carrier in a COD aircraft, which had an emergency landing down on an island south of Tokyo. THis island didn't have an airfield on it. The pilot put the plane down in a dry river bed, but unfortunately there were an awful lot of rocks in this dry river bed so the plane was damaged somewhat. However, the important thing was that the engines had to be changed because of sudden stoppage of the propellers hitting the rocks. We got Senator Scott out of there all right, and fortunately he suffered no injuries.

One interesting item in connection with this however, which I got a big chuckle out of: He and the crew were being taken from the river bed to the closest village. Of course a big crowd collected around. He just couldn't restrain himself and stood up in back of the truck and gave a nice fine political talk, which I thought was just wonderful.

Mr. Mason: Which nobody understood.

Admiral Griffin: That's right. However, he had an interpreter there; someone who could act as an interpreter. So the gist of what he said was translated to the crowd.

The crowd was very wonderful. All the villagers came out and lifted rocks off the river bed and made a usable runway. About a week later, by the time we changed engines and everything else and got the airplane ready and lightened it up quite a bit, we flew it out of there. We got away with that one all right, without hurting the Senator, who now of course is the minority leader in the Senate.

We went on back to Yokosuka. Christmas season was the usual round of parties, which we enjoyed very much. Always, however, keeping a very close eye on the mainland of China and in the Sea of Japan for any unusual activity.

Mr. Mason: Were there any flareups at that time when you were there?

Admiral Griffin: There were none at this particular time.

We did have one flareup which turned out to be not as serious as I thought it was going to be at the time. That came on New Year' Eve. I got the key members of my staff together; most of us were actually at a New Year's Eve party at the Club. We went to the fla ship. I had a carrier in Sasebo, together with the supporting shi of the group. The situation appeared to be such that it would be wise to get this group underway. We got them underway and headed them south. Actually when we got them down in position and flew th Air Group up so that the radars on the mainland could paint the air craft all the activities that we had observed on the mainland sub- sided so it turned out to be not as serious as we thought it might have been.

Mr. Mason: What were these sudden flareup activities? Were they baiting the people on Taiwan?

Admiral Griffin: You didn't know, in some cases probably yes.

Much of the information that we obtained on this particular occasion however was obtained by highly classified intelligence mea It involved movements of troops and movements of aircraft down into a position where they could be used to support an attack against th off-shore islands. THat was the type of activity which we generall noted during this particular period.

During the Christmas season it was our custom to have a Christ party for all the enlisted personnel and my staff, then have anothe party for all the office personnel and staff. Then on New Year's Day I would have an open house for callers at my quarters in Yokosuka.

A highlight after the Christmas period, on my next return to Yokosuka, was a visit to the flag ship by Mr. Roy Crane, who is the cartoonist who draws BUZZ SAWYER. Mr. Crane's daughter was married to a naval officer. His trip was really two fold: It was to come out to get information from various Commanders, and also to see his daughter who was expecting her first child.

I found the interview with him very interesting, and I found out later that he had used information that he obtained from me. He gave me this credit, I am told, at a speech which he made in New York. Information which I had given him provided the basis for about three months of the BUZZ SAWYER story. It was very interesting; he's quite an interesting man.

We went next over to Korea. I think I mentioned going over there and seeing President Posun Yun. So I won't comment on that any further.

Following the visit to Korea we started down south. On the 8th of May we made an official visit to Malaya. We went through the Straits of Molucca and back up on the west coast of Malaya and anchored at Fort Snettenham.

Mr. Mason: Is that for Kaula Lumpur?

Admiral Griffin: Yes, that's the seaport for Kuala Lumpur.

At that time Mr. Baldwin was the American Ambassador to Malaya and he had just arrived. Mr. Baldwin's sister was married to the editor of the WASHINGTON POST. He was not a career diplomat, this was his first ambassadorship. So he was most interested in talking to me about the country, the area, the general problems of protocol. And I was most happy to be able to assist him by using my band to play at a big party which he was giving. It was the first party he'd given since he'd been there. My Public Relations people helped his people, and it all worked out very well. He was a very fine man

The first government official I met there was Tun Razak. He was a Deputy Prime Minister, a rather young man, very much on the ball I would say. His boss, of course, the Prime Minister, was Tunka Abdul Rahman. He was the big boy there for a long time and has, as a matter of fact, not too long ago turned over the reins of government to Razak, who is now the Prime Minister.

We also met the Sultan of Selangor.

Mr. Mason: Was he the top Sultan?

Admiral Griffin: Let me put it this way: he was the Sultan in that area. There is some difference of opinion as to which one woul be the top sultan.

Mr. Mason: Don't they select one from the six or seven on a periodi basis?

Admiral Griffin: That's right, and he was at this time the top Sultan. The reason why they rotate it is that they could never agree that one was it on a continuing basis. At least that's what I was told.

Rahman is a very interesting individual, and I thought was one of the most impressive men that I had met in all of my visits around.

Mr. Mason: Actually he's the George Washington of Malaya.

Admiral Griffin: He's the George Washington of Malaya, no question about it. Feet solidly on the ground, and he knew exactly what he was talking about.

Just before we left there they had a very bad earthquake and slide up in the northern Malaya not far from the coast. I offered to keep the ship there and move it up to be of assistance. This was appreciated very much by the Malayan government, but they said they didn't need any assistance at that time. However, the crew of the ship took up a collection and donated a very considerable amount of money.

Mr. Mason: Do other navies in the area perform in similar fashion, in terms of natural disasters?

Admiral Griffin: If they're in a position to do so, yes.

This finished our visit to Malaya, and we went back to Yokosuka where I had a visit from Governor Meyner of New Jersey. I must say quite frankly I was not impressed by him. Of all the top people that came out and visited I think he impressed me the least. He left me with the impression that he was overly impressed with himself. Everyone else that came out there leaned over backwards to get away from the business of, "I'm the Governor," or "I'm the Senator," or "I'm the Ambassador." He was the single exception to that.

Mr. Mason: Did he have his lovely wife with him?

Admiral Griffin: His wife was with him, that's correct. I suspect it might have been better if she'd been the Governor.

We next paid a visit up to Hokkaido. Hokkaido is a most interesting island. It's more like New England than Japan. As you drive around the countryside it reminds you very much of driving throughout New England. Of course, the winters there are very severe. The Winter Olympics are going to be held there in '72.

Mr. Mason: The population is fairly sparse compared to Japan proper.

Admiral Griffin: The population is fairly sparse, that's correct.

There are some tribes up there which the Japanese are trying to maintain. They are very old ethnic tribes, which are gradually deteriorating. The Japanses are trying to maintain them because of their historical ethnical value.

I don't think it's of any useful purpose to repeat many of the other visits which I made. They were all in a sort of a set pattern

I will comment that in my farewell visits to several of the countries I used my aircraft because time did not permit the ship to go. I flew to Taiwan, to the Philippines, to Korea, to Okinawa, and then back to Japan.

I was very pleased to have been presented medals by Chiang-kai-shek in Taiwan, by General Park in Korea, who relieved Posun Yun as the President and is still the President of South Korea, by Lieutenant General Cabal who was the Chief of the General Staff of the Philippines on behalf of the Philippine government, and by the Minister of Defense in Tokyo on behalf of the Emperor of Japan.

Mr. Mason: May I ask: during your tour of duty, what sort of reports of long time value were sent back, in terms of intelligence or hydrographic or what?

Admiral Griffin: Let me say that: reports were sent back on a continuing basis. They were largely intelligence reports.

Mr. Mason: Which covered a wide range of political relations?

Admiral Griffin: Covered a wide range of political, military, and economic conditions found, analyses of these in relation to other reports that existed, and conclusions and recommendations. These were sent back pretty much on a continuing basis.

Mr. Mason: What proportion of them were requested? Special studies or something of that sort - were there any of those?

Admiral Griffin: Yes, very few. If I had not sent them in I'm sure that many of them would have been requested. I had a pretty good idea what our government was looking for, what the Navy Department was looking for, and answered those things on a continuing bas[is]

Mr. Mason: So that actually our government policy vis-a-vis the Far East leans heavily on some of the products of the Seventh Fleet

Admiral Griffin: Yes, it did at that time. You must recall that at this time we didn't have satelite communications. Some times th[e] ability of Washington, or of Pearl Harbor for that matter, to communicate with me could be impaired by unusual atmospheric condition[s]. Therefore in contrast to the situation which exists now, and relatively speaking, we certainly were more on our own than they are no[w].

It's inevitable as communications improve and the power of weapons increases that the decisions will increasingly accrue to t[he] seat of government. This certainly has happened.

I wouldn't go so far as to say that the commanders in the fie[ld] have to get permission to blow their nose or something like that, but some times and with certain people in positions of responsibil[ity] this came awfully close to being the case. I don't think that thi[s] is all to the good, but however I can understand it. Something lik[e] this is almost inevitable, when you take into consideration the po[wer] of modern weapons. No Chief of State is going to permit a militar[y] official, a military commander, unlimited authority in this field, not at all.

At that time we didn't have the present sure communications. Some times it was most difficult to get through. However, this didn't disturb me too much because I felt that I knew precisely what the objectives of my government were. I knew what they wanted to do. I knew what to do under certain circumstances, and I'd been put in this position of responsibility. My government undoubtedly knew that I wasn't damn fool enough to go off half cocked. So all in all I didn't feel encumbered very much by not having positive communications all the time.

Mr. Mason: By virtue of the mobility of the Fleet, you in effect became the senior intelligence gatherer for the U. S. government out there, didn't you?

Admiral Griffin: That's correct.

Mr. Mason: Because the State Department people were stationed, but you were mobile.

Admiral Griffin: That's correct.

And I also had really under my command, although the basic orders came from Washington, much of the intelligence gathering activity on the part of aircraft and ships.

When the PUEBLO incident blew up and the EC-21 incident came: these things had been going on for many years and we had obtained lots of very good information from these sources. It was my responsibility to protect them, and I did protect them while I was there.

Mr. Mason: Just a word about your personal manner of communication in former times I'm aware of the fact that the Commander of the Asiatic Fleet communicated with CNO by personal letter. Did you engage in any of that?

Admiral Griffin: Only largely to give my own comment on individual in other words officers.

When it came to matters of intelligence interests and other things like that, these went in the form of dispatches.

Speaking of the Chief of Naval Operations, one of the big jobs that he has to do is to make decisions and recommendations. One of the toughest fields for him is in the evaluation and assignments of officers, particularly flag officers.

So I would write to the CNO and give him my personal opinion of the performance of certain flag officers. Almost all the personal correspondence, the written correspondence, was in this field. The rest of it went by dispatch. I didn't put the other in dispatches because too many people read the dispatches, and this was a matter of personal communication between me and the CNO.

Mr. Mason: And whatever your command, be it Far East or Mediterranean, or what, this is a major matter, isn't it, the placement of senior officers?

Admiral Griffin: That's right. It's a very very difficult job and one which, in order to do a good job, the CNO needs advice from his trusted assistants.

Most of the written correspondence was in this field, on the official side.

I was relieved of Command of the Seventh Fleet by Vice Admiral Bill Schoech. The Japanese, most of the people out there, just simply couldn't understand how you could spell a word that way and pronounce it "Shay." This was one of the difficulties I had when people would ask me who was going to relieve me.

Incidentally Bill Scheoch was an old friend whom I'd known for a long long time, and I was very happy to have someone of his caliber to relieve me.

After I was relieved, my wife and I drove up to Tokyo. This was on the 28th of October in 1961. We spent the week-end in Tokyo. I mention this because when we left the hotel in Tokyo on Monday morning we went down to visit in the vicinity of Atusgi for several days before going to Yokohama and take our ship to go back to San Francisco. We got about half way down to Atsugi and suddenly my wife said, "Incidentally, as a matter of interest and curiousity, how much was the hotel bill?" I said, "Good Lord, I didn't pay it."

I hadn't paid a bill since I'd been in Command of the Fleet, because I kept my Aide furnished with enough money and he paid all of my bills. So I called the hotel in Tokyo and told them that I was not trying to run out on them and I sent them the amount of the bill.

We sailed from Yokohama on the PRESIDENT CLEVELAND, one of the President Line ships. Admiral Nomura came all the way down from Tokyo to see us off. I was very very touched with this because at that time he was quite elderly. As I said before his daughter-in-law took him around every place. They came all the way down from Tokyo to see us off. That's the last time that I saw the old gentleman.

I think to just comment briefly overall on my tour of duty out there: Of course the objectives of having this Fleet out there were to maintain control of the seas in that area, to use for our purposes and for the purposes of our Allies and in time of any conflict to deny it to any enemy. I think this was accomplished.

Mr. Mason: We had no real challenge at that point?

Admiral Griffin: We had no real challenge, no. We had no real challenge from the sea, that is correct. But the sea-based forces were in a position to take any action that would have been required in the event there had been a challenge, and the other side knew it.

Mr. Mason: What units of the Russian Navy were anywhere near?

Admiral Griffin: There were units of the Russian Pacific Fleet in the Sea of Japan, and occasionally were down in the southern area. But mostly they were congregated up around the Northern Sea of Japan, north of Hokkaido or up in the vicinity of Alaska. They stayed pretty much up north. They, at that time, were making very few visits. They visited North Korea and occasionally would stop in to Hong Kong. They would stop in at Singapore. But outside of that they stayed pretty much close to home.

Mr. Mason: Did you make a visit into the Sea of Okhotsk?

Admiral Griffin: No, that was considered at that time to be too provocative, and I think this was correct.

Another objective which the Fleet was ordered to do was to prevent the Chinese communists from incursions or taking over the off-shore islands or Taiwan. This was certainly accomplished.

We used the Fleet also to try to keep the Chinese communists somewhat off balance. By that I mean some times to force them to move some of their forces into positions that they normally would otherwise not have moved them. This cost them in terms of maldeployment in logistic costs of moving and so forth.

Mr. Mason: If they had actually attempted to make a landing on the off-shore island, were they equipped with landing ships?

Admiral Griffin: They had lots of landing craft. They could have used the craft that they used for just normal coastal trade, sampan types of things.

Incidentally, a lot of those sampan types are awfully difficult to sink. They're wooden. You put bullets through them and they swell up. They're sort of self sealing in many respects. I've seen wooden ships hit by strafing attacks, for example, and just literally make like a swiss cheese still floating. So they were very difficult to sink, a lot of them.

They had plenty to use for that purpose. But the combination of the Nationalist Chinese defences on the Island and the presence of the U. S. Seventh Fleet were deterrents which kept them from trying anything.

Another objective of course is to enhance and to further the U. S. objectives and prestige abroad. I think the Seventh Fleet was very successful in this, particularly as relates to the "People to People Program."

This was really an Eisenhower program, and one of the things President Eisenhower wanted very much to do. This thing works two ways: Our people aboard the ships go ashore in foreign ports. The people in these foreign ports see these Sailors and Marines, so they learn a little bit about America from them. On the other hand, the Sailors and Marines learn a lot about the country itself. And they will write home to their families. In this way the people in the United States learn a lot more about foreign countries.

We stressed this element of the objectives and duties of the Fleet very strongly out there. And I felt that we had some absolute magnificent Ambassadors of the United States who went ashore. I kept records and in a one year period we had about one and a half million liberties. By liberty, I mean one man going ashore one time Out of one and a half million liberties we had six cases of people who were tried ashore for offences. I thought that this was a pretty doggone good record for Americans.

The British were just amazed at the way our Sailors behaved themselves. They said, "How do you do it?"

It takes a lot of time and effort and understanding and education in order to do it. And when you tell the people what you are trying to do the kids will come through. You tell them what you are trying to do and they'll do it. I was particularly happy with this particular aspect of it.

In summation, I would say that my experience out there in Command of that Fleet left me with a very strong reiteration of my feeling that the Fleet was well worth the investment that the United States had in it.

Mr. Mason: Would you be willing to attach some sort of a forecast: The future attitude and position of the Russian Navy in that area, since the Russian Navy is becoming far more agressive in various parts of the world, would you forecast that it will do so in that part of the world?

Admiral Griffin: I think so, without any question.

The Russians have had the example of the Sixth Fleet in the Mediterranean and the Seventh Fleet in the Pacific so much in their eyes and in their minds. When you combine that with a rather disastrous, from their point of view, failure in Cuba, they really learned a lesson.

They found out in order to project their power overseas, to enhance their ability to achieve their overall goals, which I feel very strongly they still have, of world domination, they must have a fleet which is capable of being employed at any place in the world.

Traditionally their fleet had been to protect the shores of their own country, close in protection. Then they started moving out. They started in early 1960 moving forces into the Mediterranean on a short term basis, largely to permit them to do some operating down there in warmer water than they had particularly up north.

Mr. Mason: This for specific missions?

Admiral Griffin: This for specific training missions. Then they would go back and then for months there'd be no one there.

As the years went on they increased in the Mediterranean, for example, they increased many fold. Now they have more ships in the Mediterrancean than we do in the U. S. Sixth Fleet.

I'll get into that, however, later on in somewhat greater detail.

Mr. Mason: Actually this is predicated on the ability to have adequate bases, isn't it?

Admiral Griffin: Adequate bases or the ability to sustain themselves at sea. They saw what the U. S. had done, in the way of underway replenishment and things like that. So they have developed means of doing that. Not the sophisticated means that we have by any stretch of the imagination, but they do have the ability to go to sea and stay at sea.

The submarines on which they had paid so much attention in the past, and particularly the nuclear submarines, they are now having much greater success with them than they did at first. At first many of their submarines would break down. We have a number of pictures of them being towed back into port. They have cured a lot of these difficulties. So they are developing very rapidly their ability to move to distant waters and to operate there doing whatever the Russian government wants them to do.

In terms of total sea power they're moving ahead very very rapidly. They're building more surface ships than we are. They're building more submarines than we are. I'm talking about combatants. And they're building many more in the field of merchant marine than we are. So they're building up in all respects.

And the obvious objective of this is to put Russian ships on the seas of the world. They recently, not too long ago, had a world-wide exercise in which ships of the Russian Navy were being exercised in practically all the major waterways of the world at the same time.

Mr. Mason: Do we not deem it important to keep pace with this?

Admiral Griffin: Yes, so far as the Navy is concerned we certainly do. There comes a time, however, when there's a question of priority.

We are in a period right now, I don't know whether this is the time to go too deeply into this at this time, but we have terrific difficulties on the domestic side.

This is also a period, for one reason or another, when the fortunes and prestige of the military departments are at a low ebb.

Defense is not a very popular subject now. People want money for health, for welfare, for education, or anything that's domestic The obvious plucking boy is the Defense Department. So the budgets are being cut and cut rather sharply.

People in the country simply have to understand that if you don't have a defense capable of maintaining your position in the world, then all of these other things that are put out for educatio and health and welfare and so forth are absolutely meaningless beca the country will be taken over by some one else. And there you are

The Defense Department is not the bottomless barrel as some people think it is. Actually even holding the Defense budget constant would mean a very considerable reduction in the number of uni that you can get because of inflationary rise in cost of all this equipment.

I don't want to go too deeply into this because I'll comment on it later, but we have so many ships in the Navy that are obsolet not only obsolescence but obsolete, it isn't even funny. The Navy is having a devil of a time right now to meet commitments.

To get back to the question you asked: Most assuredly the Russians are building up. They recognize the fact that in order to be a truly great world power they have got to have the ability to project themselves overseas and make their influence felt. The way you can do this, the only way you can do it, I do not mean it's the only element that is used, but unless you have the ability to contr the seas you can't do it no matter what else you have.

Mr. Mason: Since you did comment on the future of the Russian Navy in the Far East and the position of the Seventh Fleet, perhaps you would add an addendum and forecast what may happen with the Japanese Navy, whether that will be another element in the whole picture?

Admiral Griffin: I think it certainly will be an element in this picture. I think as a concomitant of a reduction on the part of U. S. forces, I'm thinking particularly Navy forces now, there's also going to be a very significant reduction of all U. S. overseas forces of naval, air, and land, there must be an enhanced ability on the part of our friends and allies to protect themselves because our forces have been overseas to do this job, to assist in doing this job. As ours are cut down, theirs must be built up or else we'll run into a very unfavorable balance situation.

On the part of the Japanese: I think that the Japanese have been very careful in their handling of this whole situation. After the war was over and during the occupation years, the Japanese people had a long time to let soak into their minds a thought which was expressed by some and usually by those who did not have the best interest of Japan at heart.

The basic thought was: These guys in uniform, they're the guys that got us into all this trouble. They're the guys who got us defeated. They're the guys who got us occupied, and by golly we're never going to let them get away with anything like that again.

This is why when the first of the Japanese para-military forces came along, they were called Defense Forces. The element of defense was stressed time and time again. No submarines would be built, no attack carriers would be built, and so forth. They had the Air Self Defense Force, the Ground Self Defense Force, and the Naval Self Defense Force. They had a great deal of difficulty getting their service academies started because of this same feeling on the part of the people.

Mr. Mason: And it's really emotional, isn't it?

Admiral Griffin: It's emotional, but it was carried on so long that it became a part of the people themselves.

So the Japanese defense element has to move very very cautious in this field. But I think that they have played their part so well and have endeared themselves so much to the people of Japan that th are now in a position to increase the size of their military establ ment. And therefore, prevent the formation of a gap into which som other non-friendly country might move.

They have the ability. They have the know how. They can buil ships and they can build aircraft. They have the technical ability They have the manufacturing ability. In the field of electronics, for example, they are unsurpassed in the world. They can build the ships and they can operate these ships.

They are very very fine sailors. They are fine aviators. And they do an extremely fine job.

So I expect them to have their budgets increasing and to take over an increasing percentage of their own defense and area defense out there.

They've had to move very slow in the area business too because the people in the Philippines and other parts of the Far East don't easily forget the Japan Co-prosperity Sphere of influence and so forth back before World War II and being overrun by Japanese forces.

Mr. Mason: Will their task become easier, in respect to these other nations, when the Russian units become more numerous?

Admiral Griffin: I think so.

Mr. Mason: Because there's no basic trust on the part of all these other peoples for the Russians, is there?

Admiral Griffin: No, but likewise there isn't very much for the Japanese. This is something that has to be played very carefully and the Japanese know it. In my opinion they are playing it quite well.

We had a very fine trip back to the West Coast. This was the first time that I'd been on a merchant ship in many years. I was told that I could come back by ship if I wanted and part of it would take the place of leave. So I came back by ship and let it count as leave.

At the time I came back I reported to Washington for duty in the Office of the Chief of Naval Operations. It wasn't exactly certain at that time what job I was going to have.

Mr. Mason: Who was CNO then?

Admiral Griffin: George Anderson was CNO when I came back.

In connection with that, he had the Sixth Fleet at the same time I had the Seventh Fleet.

At the time that Arleigh Burke was being relieved and before he was relieved NEWSWEEK had a two or three page article including a chart which showed the odds of who the next CNO would be. There were about ten of us listed. They had racing terms alongside of eac of us, post positions, or something like that. I think I was listed as four to one, or something like that. Anderson was two to one.

Mr. Mason: The selection was to be made by President Kennedy?

Admiral Griffin: The selection was to be made by John Connolly and Kennedy. Anderson, whom I had always thought would be the CNO, was selected.

When I got back there I walked in to Andy and he pretty much gave me my choice. Although he said he would prefer to have me as Op-03, I could also have the job of Director of Joint Staff (of the Joint Chiefs of Staff) which was the Navy's turn to have, if I wante it, which is a job rotated among the services.

Mr. Mason: Is that the job that Count Austin had at one time?

Admiral Griffin: He had it at one time, that's correct, when Radfor was there.

The upshot of this was that Herb Riley, who was acting as Op-03, went down and became the Director of the Joint Staff and I relieved him as the Deputy Chief of Naval Operations for Fleet Operations and Readiness.

One of the first impressions that I had in the job of Op-03 was the influence of McNamara. This became very apparent early in the game.

Mr. Mason: No blushing violet.

Admiral Griffin: No, not in the slightest.

It became very apparent that decision making was being taken over not by people who had experience backed up by sound studies, but by young PhDs who were experts in so-called cost effectiveness, and who generally speaking had very little experience at all in practical operations of any type.

Mr. Mason: The popular appellation was "whiz kids."

Admiral Griffin: The popular appelation was "whiz kids," that's correct. That of course stemmed from the fact that after World War II McNamara and this group offered their services to Ford and were taken on as the so-called "whiz kids."

Mr. Mason: Many of them were with Ford while McNamara was there?

Admiral Griffin: Yes, then they spred around to various places, but they were the so-called "whiz kids."

To come from Fleet Command, which so far as I'm concerned is the highlight of any career in the Navy, back into this atmosphere was quite shocking.

Mr. Mason: It was quite in contrast with what you'd known in the Department before?

Admiral Griffin: Almost completely in contrast to what I had known before. Generally speaking before when you were asked to speak to a subject you were asked to because you were an expert and had a lot of experience in that field and you were listened to. Your recommendations were not always taken, but at least you were listened to.

In this atmosphere of McNamara and company, it was quite apparent that you might talk, but you weren't listened to.

I was also impressed with another thing. The longer I stayed there, the stronger this feeling got. I had the impression that the McNamara system of doing things so often involved first making a decision, and then studying to see what had to be done to fill in all the cracks so that the historical record would show that everything had been done to guarantee making an accurate decision. He had a battery of lawyers that were involved in doing just that.

Mr. Mason: Interesting to hear you say that, sir. It's in my experience almost a consensus of what I've heard people say.

Admiral Griffin: Absolutely, there's no question about it to my mind.

At the time I came back there I don't think that the Congress had hoisted this all aboard yet, because if they wanted to find out something they would still call up an Admiral or a General and say, "Would you mind coming over and giving us a little run down on this or that or the other thing." Under McNamara you couldn't do that. Or at least if you did, you had to report that fact to McNamara - that you were going over.

Mr. Mason: What did this do to the morale of you people who had been so accustomed to command?

Admiral Griffin: It didn't help at all. It made you feel even more frustrated than you normally would have in the Washington atmosphere.

Mr. Mason: Was this changed policy dependent entirely upon the personality of McNamara?

Admiral Griffin: Entirely on McNamara. He put out a series of well over a hundred studies. He established a program planning system of doing things. If a change, which you recommended, the Navy Department recommended, would involve a certain amount of money, then the decision had to go to McNamara for a personal decision on it.

I'll give you an example: If something involved more than a hundred men, it had to go to McNamara for decision. This meant that since the U. S. had some two hundred and eighty destroyers, if you changed the manning level of a destroyer by one, if you increased it by one, it had to go to McNamara for personal decision because that would be two hundred and eighty people.

Mr. Mason: This was a man who couldn't delegate authority.

Admiral Griffin: It was absolutely terrible. It was quite a show.

I had seen many many Secretaries of Defense. The general feeling among the Secretaries of Defense when they left office, the ones that I saw, that included Charlie Wilson, Tom Gates, McElroy, pretty well expressed by many of them in writing was sort of a littl apologetic, "If I only had had a little more power I could have done a better job."

Charlie Wilson was a good example of that. He, I think, considered that he just simply didn't have the ability to make a decision as to whether or not the Army should get more divisions or the Navy should get more carriers or the Air Force should get more wings. A major decision in this field was almost impossible for him Therefore he would never make a decision that involved a shift of more than about three percent.

Mr. Mason: Why was it impossible for him? He certainly had the backing of the President in this, urging that he should make up his mind in this.

Admiral Griffin: That's right, but he felt he didn't know.

A lot of the rest of them felt the same way. That's why they all felt, "If I had a little more power I could make more decisions or better decisions."

McNamara figured out how to get it. And he got it. He got control by controlling every nickel that was spent in the Defense Department. That's how he got it.

Mr. Mason: The cliche of "the power of the purse."

Admiral Griffin: That's right, "the power of the purse," no question about it.

He got it that way and he set up his whole organization around that. Of course the powerful group which he set up first as just a little study group caused the effectiveness of his regime. That was built up by Allan Entoven until he had a position there secondary only to the Under Secretary of Defense.

Mr. Mason: He was a kind of a budgetary man?

Admiral Griffin: Completely, cost analysis.

A story was told, as a matter of fact this was attributed to Tom Moorer, which I thought was just absolutely magnificent, but the people down in DOD didn't think it was very funny at all.

The story went on: Arnold Palmer, just to use figures, had an average score of seventy strokes for every round of golf for a whole year. He made seventy thousand dollars during that year. During this time he used his two iron so many times, his driver so many times, his putter so many times, his six iron so many times, and his wedge so many times. You take this and analyze it from the viewpoint of cost effectiveness and you can show very definitely what Palmer should do: Take his two, three, five, and seven irons and throw them away and get three more putters.

The boys down in DOD didn't think that was very funny at all. But the story went all over theplace. I think it was Tom Moorer who told it first.

Mr. Mason: With this increased centralization of power with the Secretary, it naturally meant that the power of the components, the Admirals and the Generals and so forth, had to be diminished.

Admiral Griffin: No question about it, diminished entirely.

Probably the most frustrated people in the world were the people in the Joint Chiefs of Staff.

Tom Gates, for example, would go over and sit with the Joint Chiefs of Staff on important subjects. They would arrive at a mutually accepted decision in regard to a very tough subject and it would be fine.

But McNamara very rarely sat with them. Certainly all during these early years he didn't at all. Usually the only person he would speak to was the Chairman.

Part of the time the Chiefs felt simply that, "This is a bad situation." Max Taylor was the Chairman, he was brought up and put in the job. This was something President Eisenhower was very mad about too. It was questionable to the minds of many many people as to whether or not Taylor reflected accurately the views of the Chiefs when he talked to McNamara.

We have a splendid war that's now being cranked down in South Vietnam, which I think of all people Taylor had more to do with than any other single guy, because of his association with Kennedy, and McNamara was a close second.

Mr. Mason: The purpose of the Joint Chiefs, their raison d'etre, changed considerably under McNamara?

Admiral Griffin: That's correct. The objective, the reason the Joint Chiefs of Staff existed as stated in the law wasn't being ignored, because McNamara knew what the law was. But he would always have enough contact with the Chiefs, so that when queried he could say, "After consultation with the Joint Chiefs of Staff I made this decision." In many of the cases the decision was made before he even said anything to the Chiefs.

Mr. Mason: I suppose it's interesting just to note the fact, the parellel fact, that the traditional position of the Cabinet changed drastically too, simultaneously.

Admiral Griffin: Exactly right. And the National Security Council, to all intents and purposes, went out of existence. McNamara had an awful lot to do with this too because Kennedy thought very very highly of McNamara.

Before on problems of national importance the National Security Council had ground out position papers that were considered to be national policies. These were put out by the President. They were national policy in these fields for the edification and guidance of officials and subordinates in government, whether military or non-military.

All of a sudden these were just completely done away with and, "What is national policy?" Well, it's what the President says in his speeches. Literally, that's what it was.

Many people said, and he did, that Ike ran a general staff sort of a headquarters. But it's a type of a set up that pretty much guarantees nothing big is going to fall through the cracks too.

Mr. Mason: It seems a bit more compatable perhaps to democracy.

Admiral Griffin: Yes, right, absolutely.

One of the important features of my job as the Deputy Chief of Naval Operations for Fleet Operations and Readiness was in preparing and defending the ship construction budget for the Navy.

This meant setting it up originally, clearing it through the Navy Department, clearing it through the Department of Defense, clearing it through the Budget, and then through four committees of Congress: the two Armed Services Committees for authorization and the two Appropriations Committees for funding.

This was the time that the Navy had been having small ship construction budgets for too many years. As a consequence, we rapid were getting to a point where major portions of the Fleet were very much obsolescent. We had prepared study after study on it on the general subject of block obsolescence and had testified to Congress on this on many occasions and written letters to Defense on the subject. In order to demonstrate it rather vividly I ordered a couple of our newest ships up to the Washington Navy Yard and a couple of our World War II comparable ships that were still operating in full strength in the Fleet up to the Washington Navy Yard and set them side by side. And we had people in the Bureau of the Budget, people in the office of the President, people from Defense, people from the Senate and the House go aboard these ships. We kept them up there for a week. This had a very fine effect because people could see what the score was. They were visual aides first class. I think it did a lot of good.

Just as a matter of interest, the fellow who was the Division Commander of this division of newest ships was Ike Kidd. He came up and did his usual very wonderful job of telling everybody what it was all about.

Mr. Mason: Was Congress reluctant to consider a new building program?

Admiral Griffin: The Senate was a little bit lukewarm on it. And of course they had to be, shall we say, very hot on it in order to overcome pressures against it from the White House and from McNamara in the Department of Defense.

This was a time when McNamara was also saving a lot of money. He saved money by delaying overhauls, postponing them, lengthening the period between overhauls, and actions which meant that ships in commission were just simply going downhill right and left.

Mr. Mason: Where was the major emphasis, on the domestic programs?

Admiral Griffin: On domestic programs.

I wrote and talked on the subject of obsolescence on many occasions and convinced Mendel Rivers, who in my opinion was a great American, that this was something we had to have. Ever since then he has done more to get an adequate Navy shipbuilding program than any other single individual.

At this time of course we had also some discussions in not too unanimous agreement on the subject of nuclear power for surface ships. There was no question about nuclear power for submarines. There was some question of nuclear power for surface ships in the minds of some people.

There were people who would argue, "We need so many ships. Are we better off to take one nuclear ship than to take three conventional powered ships under these circumstances? We can have only so much money to get them."

Of course the advantages of nuclear power were so tremendous that it wasn't quite like putting all your eggs in one basket. Granted you could get fewer ships, but here we were having developed nuclear power to a state where it was fantastically successful, and then reluctant to use it. We could still get many ships.

I supported getting more nuclear ships because I felt among other things the more we got the cheaper the cost per units would be. The operational advantage of nuclear power was absolutely tremendous, which was proved time after time in studies that we had made.

This brings up another thing about McNamara. I don't want to carp all the time on McNamara, but if he didn't like something or didn't want to do it and would have no basic arguments against it at the time, he'd have the problem studied and then send it back for further study. He had some things studied to death.

The CVA-67, the nuclear powered aircraft carrier, ended up by costing about two hundred million dollars more than if we had built it when it was first recommended, rather than study it again.

Mr. Mason: Was there an argument also on the advisability of building smaller units, in light of the fact that Russians were concentrating on submarines, and larger units would be all ones' eggs in one basket, and that meant they'd be more vunerable?

Admiral Griffin: Yes, that's right. This was also part of the general discussion.

Connected with this discussion of nuclear power was also the subject of Rickover, which is one I think known to many many people.

As Op-03, it was my job to, shall we say, handle Rickover. This came about as follows: I was the one responsible for putting in requests for ship visits to many ports through the Commander-in-

Chief of the Fleets. In the case of nuclear powered ships we had a series of very strict instructions which had to be followed. And we had to certify that these things had been done, these studies had been made, before you could get authority to move a nuclear powered ship into a port. That authority would have to be gotten from the Atomic Energy Commission.

The Atomic Energy Commission section that dealt with that was the Nuclear Reactor Section, headed by Rickover in his hat on the AEC side of the fence. On the other side of the fence was Rickover as the Assistant Chief of the Bureau of Ships, at that time for nuclear propulsion.

Time after time we would have a hassle and the request would come back disapproved. I got into this thing very heavily and I found out that one of the basic troubles in this field was that the people in Op-Nav, and Op-03 in particular, were not doing the job properly. Every time a request was turned down we had not done some thing that we were supposed to do, and since Rickover knew it, that was it.

So the first thing I did was to clean my own house, and I cleaned it real good. I got it so that when a request went over, the only grounds on which he could turn the request down was that his product was not safe. I kept him in that position all the time, and I ended up getting along great with him.

I went over, I'd known him before, and I said, "Now look Rick, I'll tell you exactly what I've done." And I outlined for him what I'd done.

I said, "You're not going to get any requests that are not bona fide and that are strictly in accord with regulations any more. You take what action you want to, but I'm just telling you. You can yell all you want to, I don't care. I can yell just as loud as you can. But I want to tell you, our shop is going to be clean as a whistle on this business."

I didn't have any trouble with Rickover, I didn't have any trouble with him at all, not in the slightest.

Among other things I found out also that the CNO on occasions would have a group of people in, some of the Deputy Chiefs, to discuss a problem connected with nuclear propulsion. I went to Andy and said, "I think it's ridiculous. Here we are having a meeting to discuss nuclear propulsion and we don't have Rickover there. He's the expert in this country on this subject. Just because of personality clashes and fights in the past, there's no reason why we should continue this." So he was called, and he responded pretty well to this.

Mr. Mason: To use it in a literal sense - he'd been beyond the pale.

Admiral Griffin: That's right, absolutely.

They started to ask him to come on over and sit in on these things and contribute to them, and this all helped.

I don't condone, by any stretch of the imagination, any of the personal habits he had that were brought out in interviews with young officers and some of the other things that he'd done. But at the same time, and in this particular field, I ended up getting along with him quite well.

Mr. Mason: How do you explain the sources of his power with the Congress, his backing in the Congress?

Admiral Griffin: He got himself in a position with the Joint Atomic Energy Commission. He got himself in just absolutely tight as a drum

Mr. Mason: Through Louis Strauss?

Admiral Griffin: Louis Strauss was one, but there were many others, people in Congress - Chet Holifield for example - very strongly.

He would give people support, he would give that Committee information that the Committee could not get from any other source. And they appreciated it. He treated the Committee damn well, and he got himself ingratiated into that Committee in such a way that he could do no wrong. He had tremendous power with them. And they, in turn, had an awful lot of power in the House and Senate.

Mr. Mason: Simultaneously he didn't seem to do the same thing in the Navy?

Admiral Griffin: No, he didn't at all. It had resulted in him never being invited to come over to the CNO's office at any time. Before Anderson he was ignored. This made him mad and so he took the other way out, and very successfully too. He got into all kinds of fields such as education and everything else. He took McNamara over the jumps a few times too, which tickled the devil out of me. I thought that was wonderful.

Mr. Mason: He had his period of service extended a number of times.

Admiral Griffin: Oh yes, he'll stay there as long as he lives. He has to have it extended by Congress. Up to age sixty-four of course the President can extend it. After that the Congress has to extend it. He is seventy-one or seventy-two now. He's been on it a long time.

Interview #11

Admiral Charles D. Griffin, USN, Ret.
Washington, D. C.

by John T. Mason, Jr
November 19, 1970

Mr. Mason: The last time you concluded your remarks with more or less an introduction to your new job as the Deputy CNO. Do you want to continue at this point?

Admiral Griffin: Yes. As I indicated before one of my important jobs as Deputy Chief of Naval Operations for Fleet Operations and Readiness, Op-03, was to prepare and defend the Navy ship construction budget. This, of course, included new construction ships and those that were scheduled for major change or conversion. By this I mean they would be out of commission for up to several years while these extensive alterations were being made.

The first part of this job involved selling our program within the Navy, then within the Defense Department, and then to the Bureau of the Budget. After these hurdles were cleared and the program was submitted to the Congress, I had to make four appearances before Congressional Committees.

Q: Sir, perhaps it would be a good idea at this point to take them step by step. You say that you had a problem of selling the new program, the new ships, within the Navy itself. What selling was necessary? What obstacles did you run into there?

Griffin: Each year, although the authorities would most assuredly never admit that there was any ceiling to the budget, there still was known to be a certain ceiling. There would be a figure for the Navy budget, which would be within certain parameters. Therefore each of us who was responsible for a part of the budget prepared our own case for the things that we had to defend.

In my case, it was shipbuilding and conversion. In the case of Op-05, it would be aircraft. In the case of Chief of Naval Personnel, it would be personnel matters. And each of us would put in our own recommendations for our own part of that budget.

You can readily see when you added all of these up, at least our first submissions, it undoubtedly would be greatly in excess of what the Navy expected to get for it's total budget.

There were certain items that could not be reduced - for instance, the cost of personnel, the pay and allowances for personnel. This was, so far as our budget was concerned, an irreducible sum. Therefore that stood. If we had a certain number of people, they were going to cost us a certain amount of money.

So the procurement items were the items that had to give in any budget. In effect it came to a question of the CNO and SecNav balancing the requirements of ships, the requirements for aircraft, the requirements for new materiel and

Research and Development, (I'll speak more later on this point) and then coming up with a rounded program which they calculated would be best for the Navy of the future. This program had to be submitted to the Department of Defense, because the Department of Defense also was operating under an understanding as to the type ceiling that they would have, and also to permit reduction of duplication between the various departments.

And the same principle applied to the Department of Defense as applied in the Department of the Navy. In other words the Army, the Navy, the Air Force, the Marine Corps would all come in with their proposals. You added them all up together and they would undoubtedly be much higher than we could reasonably expect to get. Therefore trimming had to take place.

Q: I thought that you had inferred perhaps that there was some opposition or some selling necessary for different types of ships, new ships.

Griffin: No question about that. Within Op-03 itself, we had people who favored building many more amphibious ships. We had those who favored building many more new submarines. We had those who favored building many more destroyer types and many more cruiser types and many more carriers - all of these right in Op-03 alone.

Q: And then within the Navy Department as a whole.

Griffin: Yes. For instance the people who were responsible for the overhaul and maintenance would want to have ships overhauled more frequently than some people thought necessary.

This is the type of thing that went on, and all the way up the line until you got to the Congress.

In the Congress, we appeared before four Committees - the House Appropriations and Armed Services Committees and the Senate Appropriations and Armed Services Committees. You appeared before these Committees each one of them two times, one for authorization legislation and then the second time for the actual budgeting of money, obtaining of money from the Congress, which of course had to start in the House.

This was a very interesting experience on the part of all of us who went over there on the Hill, because you ran into all kinds of questions. Many of the questions, of course, were loaded politically. And you had to be knowledgeable in the field of politics or else you were liable to get yourself in a little bit of difficulty.

I will never forget one particular experience I had. I had been asked a question by a member of the House Appropriations Committee, a Congressman from the state of Ohio. The questioning had proceeded very nicely and I was asked a question that required me to answer in point of time. In other words, "At what time did you do certain things?" I answered that question by saying, "This was just about the time of the so-called missle gap."

This particular Congressman, who had asked the question, had had about four or five of his very close friends defeated in the past election because of this so-called missile gap, which President Kennedy had used very effectively in his campaign and which after the campaign was all over proved to be a complete hoax. There was no truth in it at all.

Q: I take it this Congressman was a Republican?

Griffin: He was a Republican. And when I used that term 'missile gap,' he just hit the overhead and just gave me one of the worst lacings I'd ever gotten in my life. As a matter of fact, it was so bad that several of his friends took it upon themselves to defend me right there in the presence of the whole Committee. "Now the Admiral was not saying this. He was not saying that there was a missile gap, he was just trying to identify the time of this particular thing."

It turned out all right, because several days later I had a call from him. He asked me to come over to his office and he apologized in person for his flare-up at that time.

This can show you how one little thing can set something off, and you can really have yourself a very interesting experience.

Q: Did you get any help from JAG in these appearances before the Committees?

Griffin: Oh yes. Their help is available all the time.

What we usually did was - those of us that were going to appear before Committees of Congress on important budgetary matters would have dry runs. We would have people from OpNav, and if there were legal aspects involved, we would have people from JAG. All the people that might be interested in the program would come in, listen to it, ask questions as though they were members of the Committees of Congress.

As a consequence of these re-hashes which we had beforehand, the individuals who were appearing before Congressional Committees were much better equipped to handle questions than would have otherwise been the case. Also, factors such as legal factors would be usually brought out in the preliminaries before we actually went over.

One thing about the Congress, in most cases, they will permit you to make reasonable alterations in the record or they will allow you to insert something. If they ask you a question and you don't have the entire answer available in the many data books you have in addition to the knowledge that's in your head, then you are permitted to insert the answer at a later date. You also have assistants with you for back-up, that is usually.

Q: What sort of staff do you have with you when you go?

Griffin: Usually two or three assistants will be there who are highly qualified in specific areas. But most of the time you can handle the questions yourself.

Some times they'll recognize the fact that a question will be so complicated that you'll not be able to give it right off the top of your head. They'll want a resume of the trends in shipbuilding over the past ten years giving detailed figures and so forth. And they'll say, "Please insert that for the record." So you go back in with that question, after you finish your testimony, get all the answers together, send it over to them, and they stick it in as the answer to that question.

Q: In effect then you have an opportunity to edit your testimony.

Griffin: You have an opportunity to edit your testimony, and some times this can be interpreted rather liberally.

Q: It is in terms of the Congressional record I know.

Griffin: That's right.

In fact I had occasion under this authorization, one time when I was sort of riding herd on Navy witnesses before the Symington Sub-committee, to take the answer given (just for illustrative purposes) which would be 'yes' and under this editing authorization I would so change the wording by the time you finished reading it instead of "yes" the answer was "no." So this can be done sometimes. It depends a great deal on what Committee is involved.

It's really an art, the business of testifying before a Congressional Committee. People have to understand certain basic elements of the whole system. Don't ever argue with a Congressman or a Senator on the Committee. He undoubtedly has good reasons for asking certain questions. On many occasions the reason is simply to get himself in the Congressional record, so he can take excerpts from that and send it out to all his constituents and say, "Look how busy I am."

Q: This basic awareness is necessary really.

Griffin: This is very necessary. And in some cases, they want to say, "Look how I took this big shot brass over the coals on this particular thing."

Q: Yes. The higher your rank the more likely you are -

Griffin: The more likely you are to be subjected to that.

Don't argue with them is one basic rule of the business. And don't talk down to them, don't pontificate. And if you don't know the answer to a question, don't try to bumble it through. Say, "I'm sorry but I don't have the answer to that, but I will get in and fill it in for the record."

A lot of these Congressmen are very conscientious hard-working people who really know what they're talking about. Some of them have been in the business for 25, 30, 35, 40 years and they're really experts.

Q": The knowledge is cumulative.

Griffin: The knowledge is cumulative and they really know what they're talking about.

Of course you try to get some friends in court before the hearings even start, by going around and making calls on the various Chairmen of the various Committees. Drop in and say 'hello' so that they'll know your face and what program you're going to be identified with, and hopefully with a view to having a friend in court when you get over there.

Q: Is it helpful to meet some of these men on the cocktail-dinner circuits in Washington?

Griffin: It's better to see them in their office first, and then you can see them on other circuits, but there isn't a great deal that's done on the circuits. More is done on those circuits in the attache field. You have to be very careful too because when you go to cocktail parties if the individuals you want to contact are having a few drinks, something may be said which can be misinterpreted. It's something to be very, very careful about.

Q: But I would think the value would be in having a social contact with them. Then you don't go into the Committee cold and as a stranger.

Griffin: The social contact is fine, that's right, that's correct. But many of the social contacts are most beneficially made on the golf course rather than at cocktail parties.

#11 - Griffin - 515

My point really is - Make the social contact after you have made the call in his office. And then you can work that into something that's useful and desirable. It's very difficult to do it without having known him beforehand. At least that's not the best way to do it, in my opinion.

But this is a very interesting part of the job. It also is one which certainly can give you a much better understanding of the total workings of the Congress and our government than you would otherwise have.

Q: Would you comment briefly on the two fold procedure - first the authorization, and then ultimately the appropriation for your program? Why the need for a two fold operation? Does not the authorization imply implementation?

Griffin: Yes it does imply implementation, but the Congress in its wisdom decided that it would be best to have both. This would permit them to get additional testimony. It would permit them also to have all the facts available early in the session so they could go over them and get the sense of the whole Congress before taking the final action which will be on the passage of the actual Appropriations Bills.

Of course, this has had a concomitant effect of delaying Appropriation Bills, which has not been good. For example right now, we're in a lame duck session right now. There are a number of Appropriation Bills and here we're half way through the fiscal year. A number of very important Appropriation

Bills have not yet been passed by the Congress.

Q: This is becoming more and more noticable in the last few years.

Griffin: That's right. And it makes it very difficult for the operating agencies of government to handle their affairs in any reasonably efficient way at all. It makes it very difficult for the operating agency to function, because it's quite possible to go completely through the first half of the year without knowing definitely how much in the way of appropriations you're going to get.

You can see how this would affect an operating agency, if at the last minute twenty percent is cut out of their budget because of unusual conditions that have come up. If twenty percent is cut out of their budget, and they had been proceeding for a half year on the basis of getting a hundred percent of the budget, then they have only a half year to absorb the twenty percent reduction. Which means that they'll have to stop doing a lot of things, more things than they would have had to stop doing if they had been able to level it off through the entire year.

Q: Does it also mean that now, with this time lag becoming more and more apparent every year, in your planning stage you have to make allowance for this time lag of six months or so?

Griffin: Oh yes. If you are a very, very conservative type

administrator, the probability is that you would underspend and then you can actually get into a situation where in order to use money that has been appropriated you have to overspend and as a consequence perhaps spend very inefficiently during the latter months of the fiscal year. So it has bad effects generally speaking all around.

Q: I would think that ultimately it would force, say, the Navy to change a bit it's system of rotation. I mean, a man like you as Deputy CNO involved in these operations would be more valuable if he could serve for a longer period of time because these things can't be acquired over night, a knowledge of this sort of thing.

Griffin: That's correct.

Q: Is there any tendency here to keep a man in a billet like that for a longer period now?

Griffin: There is a tendency to do that, yes there is. But I don't think it will ever get to the point where they are kept in long enough to realize the maximum benefit from the individual.

After all the people that are in these various jobs are Vice Admirals. And most of them aspire to getting a fourth star, and the best way you can get that is to move on to another and more responsible job. So if you establish as your goal to get three stars, then you could stay there for a long time. But very few people want to do that.

Of course under the McNamara regime, the total effects of some of the testimonies that were given were somewhat decreased over what had been given in earlier years. Because McNamara took it upon himself to give the Department of Defense testimony for each and every item of everybody's budget. Incidentally the Congress took a very dim view of this.

This brought another aspect of the questioning to a head. Because we would be asked, "Now Admiral I understand that you asked for so many ships, but Mr. McNamara cut you down to so many ships. Is this true?" At first it caused a little bit of confusion.

One time Carl Vinson made a comment when I was appearing, this was some time before I was Op-03, that, "Now Admiral, I understand that this thing has happened over in the Pentagon. I'm not going to ask you whether this is true or not, but I tell you now I have it on very good authority." And they usually did, they had extremely good authority as to exactly what was happening.

Finally the Defense Department had to put out a notice to the effect that if you were asked questions like this, you could answer them truthfully. And you could also answer your reasoning why you asked for that, provided you also included the Defense Department's reason for its action. These were the guide lines that we used in Congressional testimony.

Q: This was McNamara's attempt to really coordinate everything within the services --

Griffin: As I said before I think, practically every Secretary of Defense I knew about, except Forrestal and he left under very unusual conditions, and except George Marshall, said in effect when he left the job, "If I'd only had more authority I could have done a better job."

They had plenty of authority, and this authority was added to over the years because of these letters and reports that the outgoing Secretaries would make.

When McNamara came in he knew he had the authority and the best way to exercise that, in his opinion, to do the things that he wanted to do was to get control of the budgets of the Services in detail. And this he did. He had control of the budgets of the Services in complete detail and this was the way he ran the Pentagon.

I think that history has shown that this was a sure way to get control of the Pentagon, but it was not a good way to run the railroad.

I think we can leave the subject of relations with Congress at this time. I'll only add one other thing -

The Congress was really getting an earful from McNamara during this period. They were completely flabbergasted when he came over on his first budget, because he delivered to them about a 450 page statement which included the details of all the budgets of all the Services. This was something that the Congress had never seen before.

They were very curious and they started to ask him a lot of questions. And strangely enough in their view, I think, he knew most of the detail answers that he was being asked for. This was something that the Congress had never seen before. So they were rather amazed.

This caused considerable amount of comment. And I would say that the early comment was, much of it, very favorable.

But after time went on, it became quite apparent if the Congress would go along with this type of operation that it could no longer adequately carry out it's own responsibilities under the Constitution. Because what the Congress needs, in order to carry out it's obligations under the Constitution, is information. And if you only get one answer and one statement and one opinion from the entire Defense Department, they don't have much option. They can either take it or reject it. If they reject it, what are their reasons for rejecting it?

So the smart ones saw very quickly that this was not for them, and they weren't about to let McNamara get away with telling them that, "This is the Department of Defense testimony." They said, "No. We want to get the boys from the various Services to come over here and testify just as they'd done in the past."

Q: Did he appreciate their point of view?

Griffin: He knew what they were talking about, sure.

At first blush, relations with Congress were very good. Then they dropped very rapidly after awhile. Most Secretaries of Defense get smartened up real fast on this business of relations with the Congress.

It took McNamara somewhat longer because one of his essential characteristics is that he can do nothing wrong. When he's figured the thing out, and studied it, and analyzed it, he comes up with a solution and that's it. No one else can be right. He was completely arrogant in this respect.

Q: The present Secretary of Defense must have come in with a built in knowledge.

Griffin: He did. And he was a very good Congressman, extremely fine. He was on the Appropriations Committee and on the Defense Sub-committee. He was one of the people, as a matter of fact, whom I called on before we went over to testify.

He knew it. He knew the Department of Defense budget inside and out. And he no longer does what McNamara did, submit this all inclusive document. But rather he goes over and makes broad statements of policy and so forth with the details appended to his formal statement, rather than going through the details in his statement.

McNamara would spend three of four days before each Committee, just delivering the statement, not reading the statement, but including questions. It would be two or three days before they'd even get to the point where they could ask him any questions.

This was a very unusual period. And I must say it was unusual for me. Because I had had several tours of duty in Washington, and to come back after having been away for a couple of years into this system, it was quite a shock. I hope that one day the Department of Defense will be able to recover from the effects of McNamara.

Among other things that were involved in the job of Op-03 was coming up with the best equipment for our ships, and the best types of ships and ship's platforms to put these on.

The war in Indo-China was accelerating, at a reasonable pace you might say at that time. And it became apparent rather quickly that in order for the Navy to become more closely involved in that war, that we had to have the ability to operate in the river areas of Indo-China.

We of course, were providing assistance to the Vietnamese in their efforts in this respect. We were providing a staff assistance ashore. We were providing considerable amount of, at times over a half of all and initially most, the air protection that was there.

But the net result of all of our studies was to come up with the formation of what we now call SEAL teams. These were put, I think very appropriately, under the amphibious forces. We had, of course, in the amphibious forces the frogmen and their groups.

This generated a requirement for more high speed fast boats. We had built very few of these since the war. About the only ones we had left were the old World War II PT-boats, and not very many of those were in commission. Most of them were a little cumbersome, they were not too good a platform for mounting guns.

So our first effort was to buy some from abroad. We bought many of the boats from the Norwegians.

Q: Why had they been building these speedy small boats?

Griffin: Their whole philosophy was entirely offshore, close in offshore work, the fjords, entirely defensive. So we got some of the boats from them.

Much of this developmental work, in connection with this particular subject, was worked out in coordination with a Committee that had been set up by President Kennedy. It included Deputy Secretary of Defense Gilpatrick, the President's brother, Robert Kennedy, and General Maxwell Taylor.

This Committee investigated the requirements for guerilla type operations throughout the world, one of it's principal efforts. These SEAL teams were developed as the Navy part of our total contribution in this effort.

Q: You sat on that Committee then, did you?

Griffin: No, I didn't sit on that Committee.

This was the DepSecDef Gilpatrick, Robert Kennedy, Maxwell Taylor, the Director of CIA, and two or three others.

It was a very active Committee. They generated the requirements and levied these on the Services for execution. SEAL teams were one of our answers to these requirements generated by that Committee.

We also were trying to move as rapidly as we could at this time in the field of ASW. And in connection with that, the development of Sonars that would have a remarkably increased range.

We developed the SQ-26 sonar, which had these characteristics and was a great advance. The basic difficulty with it, when you put in on the bow of a ship it increased the draft of that ship 12 - 14 feet. Which meant that in the case of some cruisers, if you put one of these on one of the cruisers, there were many ports that the cruiser couldn't get into.

Q: Did it also impede it's speed?

Griffin: No, it had very little effect on speed because it was a bulbous type bow.

If you will recall the underwater construction of many ships - of the old days actually, some of the early ships had these underwater rams. And only after they had been developed for the purpose of ramming another ship, did some engineers find out that this actually gave the ship a little more speed. Because the effect of this ram going forward and penetrating the water, the water flow was much less disturbed rather than being pushed by the blunt bow of a ship.

We developed at this time also the roll-on roll-off ships which are still being developed and are now being used commercially. The impetus for developing this type was to be found in the turn around times in port. It was not unusual in these days, when you had something to go to a busy port and you shipped it in a merchant ship, to have that merchant ship lie there in the harbor or on the roads outside of the harbor as much as 30 days before it was unloaded. This was a very inefficient method of handling things. The roll-on roll-off with the packaged containers helped decrease the turn-around time appreciably.

Q: Had containers come into vogue --

Griffin: They were just beginning to, we were thinking of them. As roll-on roll-off was actually to load units that could be rolled on and off, and the logical extension to that were containers.

Another thing that we developed, of course we were working on radars on a continuing basis and several break throughs occurred in this field. We developed the SPS-48 radar, which is an extremely good one. It's almost automatic. When you combine these new radars that reach way out, high power, with the computer systems that go with them, it meant that the capability of the field of air defense was increased by many, many factors.

Q: Admiral, in the work on radar I should imagine it wasn't all confined to the Defense Department. Were industries involved? Was Union Carbide, for instance?

Griffin: Oh yes. Industries were very much involved in this. We had General Motors and General Electric, to take just two outstanding examples, that were very much involved in a lot of these things.

The APL of Johns Hopkins at Silver Spring was one of the leading government laboratories in the field of development. This is the outfit that developed the proximity fuze, for example. And they continued work in the field of radars and also did some sonar work too.

Government laboratories were very much mixed up with this. And industry very much mixed up with it. Raytheon and many of our big companies had tremendous stakes in this.

Q: Did your job put you in actual touch with these industries?

Griffin: No, because we didn't actually do the developing in our shop. We were sort of the administrators of this whole thing in the field of requirements. We established the requirements and then the technical bureaus were the ones that actually were dealing with them. The technical bureaus not only had the money to spend, but they also had the people who were qualified technically to discuss these things and to let the contracts and to ride herd on the contractors to develop them.

In this connection, one of the problems that we were having at this time was with our missile systems. We had missile systems that were the most highly advanced systems in the world, and many of them wouldn't work. They would work when you had experts there with them all the time, factory representatives there all the time. But you got rid of all these experts, and we had very much difficulty in making these work.

One of the basic troubles in this connection was, this was what I was referring to just a few seconds ago, the lack of detail plans. These systems would be designed and then when they were installed in the ship, it would be obvious that certain changes had to be made. These changes would be made on the spot, and the documentation of this was so slow getting back into the system that quite often you'd have 50 changes and no documentation for this change.

Navy personnel many times did not know what changes had been made and what hadn't been made, and they had the old documentation. We had the devil of a time. We finally had to set up a special office to handle just this thing. And it took years and very much money to get the situation under control.

Q: And how was this done?

Griffin: By riding herd on the contractors to get their documentation. That was essentially it. Get the documentation out to the Fleet. We had quite a time with this one.

At this same time we were furnishing some missiles to the Italians, for example. They had crews on these missile ships of theirs that were there, you might say, for the duration. They were the experts they had in the Italian navy. And they took these missiles of ours that we were having difficulty with and made them work.

Q: What does this say about our system, the rotation again?

Griffin: It says that our system of rotation has very serious disadvantages. As we get more highly sophisticated, particularly in electronics but in any field, the less change the better. This is completely at the opposite end of the spectrum to the business of giving a guy the opportunity to get well-rounded and demonstrate his ability in many fields so as to go on up.

Q: It means that ultimately then something will have to be done about the promotional system.

Griffin: That's right, that's correct.

It would indicate, for example, one thing that has been suggested from time to time has been a 'wet and dry' list so-called. Something that the British had during the war. The 'dry' list never went to sea. They were the technical guys, the administrators and so forth, and they stayed ashore all the time. And the operators went to sea. There are obvious disadvantages to this, of course.

Another system has been tried, particularly in the Army, is that you have a certain percentage of promotions within each group.

Even though you are a line officer, if you're a technical specialist, sub-specialist, you'll not be penalized for not having the number of Commands at sea, for example, as somebody else has had.

Q: What are other navies of the world doing in this technical area, in terms of their personnel? Do you know?

Griffin: In the first place, there aren't very many navies of the world that have the sophisticated equipment that we have.

The Russians have very little problem in this, because of their dictatorial type of society and their expertize in the broad subject of missiles.

Q: Do they keep a man on the job --

Griffin: They'll keep people on the job for an indeterminate period of time.

The British have come down so much, in other words their navy has shrunk so greatly in recent years, that they have enough people available to do this. And they subscribe almost completely to the system of even though an individual hadn't had a series of commands, we'll promote him if he's good technically. So they had a system in Britain which is quite different in many respect from ours.

For example, I saw Lord Louis Mountbatten not too long ago.

And he had a chap with him who was a Vice Admiral, who was on active duty, who had been with him since he was a Lieutenant Commander. That was the only duty he ever had from Lieutenant Commander to Vice Admiral, as Aide and Senior Assistant to Admiral Mountbatten. Something like that would not be possible in the United States Navy. I don't think that particular example is one to be recommended, but it just indicates a difference in philosophy.

Q: Since you were talking about missiles and so forth, this was the time when the POLARIS was being turned out in larger numbers, wasn't it?

Griffin: That's correct.

In this we come back again to the question of budgets. The POLARIS program was a program that was subscribed to completely by most everyone in the Navy. We had to find the money in the Navy for much of that which was spent for the program.

For example, the buy of aircraft was reduced by about fifty percent to find money for the POLARIS program. I remember one figure that sticks in my mind. We went from about four billion dollars a year to about two billions a year, so as to find two billion dollars for POLARIS. Otherwise it would have been years later before we would have gotten the number of ships which we actually needed for this program.

Q: Was the Congress in 1962 receptive to the idea of the development of the POLARIS program? Or was this a sell business too?

Griffin: They were receptive, but it required a great deal of selling. And they weren't about to put out tremendously large sums unless proven because you had many competing requirements.

Don't forget - you had SAC for example, that was in the strategic field. And the amount of money that was devoted to the strategic field was very large, but still in relation to the general purpose forces it was smaller. The basic philosophy was that we needed an umbrella of protected strategic forces.

These forces could be calculated fairly finitely. When you got the number of forces you needed in the strategic field, that was it. Then the general purpose forces -- the budget for them was much larger than for the strategic forces. They would operate under the umbrella of the strategic forces which were designed to be a deterrent. This being the case it was difficult to shall we say "break into the strategic field." Land-based missiles and SAC were essentially it until the Sea-based missiles were built and demonstrated. The Navy had to find the money to do this.

Q: This was possible in 1962, because there was no challenge on the part of the Russians at that point, was there?

Griffin: Yes. They had very significant strategic forces at that time, but not anywhere near parity.

Ever since then, of course, we have been going down hill on the percentage basis. They've closed the gap until now it's pretty much parity between the two so-called nuclear giants.

Included in these new ships that we built were the CVANs. Once you get into the field of carriers you automatically are going to have a lot of argument about how many you need and so forth.

The Air Force is intensely interested in this, because obviously if you have a large number of attack carriers, their requirements for Air Force tactical forces will be decreased. So they are very touchy on the subject of carriers.

In this era another element entered into this. And that was the subject of nuclear power for the carriers. We had proposals for nuclear powered carriers to be built every year, and McNamara would have these studied.

I don't know of any subject in the Defense Department that has been studied more than the attack carrier. Approaching it from any direction at all, this has been studied. You ask the question and there's a study to cover it, there's no question about it.

Q: Largely at the instigation of the Air Force?

Griffin: Originally the Air Force. And then of course studies were prepared early in the game to establish the number of carriers that would be required for the total forces of the United States. The arguments there would take place in the Joint Chiefs of Staff organization. Then these studies would be presented to the Congress for authorization and appropriations for the monies necessary to build them.

The attack carrier is a system really. As these systems

got more sophisticated they got more expensive. The studies grew in quantity as a consequence of this.

The Navy wanted very much to get nuclear power in it's major surface ships, but nuclear power costs an awful lot. If you're operating on a limited budget, despite what McNamara would say all the time --

He said, "The President has given me no ceiling under which I have to operate." He would say all the time, "The President told me that we can afford anything we need. It's your job to determine what we need and make sure that your determination is based upon the minimum amount that we need, no surplus in any direction." He said, "And that's what I'm doing."

He had many ways of trying to prove to someone else that his determination was the correct one. In the final analysis, one of the things that he always did was he just arbitrarily reduced the threat. In case he felt he had to cut forces, he would reduce the threat, his estimate of the external threat, despite what the intelligence services said.

Q: That's what you call Russian roulette, isn't it?

Griffin: That's absolutely correct, he'd do it.

The advantages of the nuclear powered task force over the conventional fossil fuel task force were so large that we felt that we should preceed in this direction. It would have other effects too, because the more of this type ship we built the less expensive they would become per unit. And this has certainly proved to be the case in the case of nuclear power.

For example the ENTERPRISE, our first nuclear powered carrier, had eight reactors. And these were very expensive. They powered that ship for about four years, before they had to be re-corded, and it was an expensive job to re-core them.

This same job can now be done by two reactors. And these two reactors would have a long enough life so that the ship would only have to be re-cored once in it's lifetime because these two reactors would last about fifteen years. You have one set for fifteen years, and another set for the next fifteen years. Presumably at the end of that time, the ship's over thirty years old, it would be scraped.

Q: Is this the result of research?

Griffin: This is the result of research and of experience in the actual operations of these systems. So you move very rapidly in this field.

You have a task force that's a nuclear powered task force that can move anywhere in the waters of the world at thirty knots or better, and it's immediately ready to operate when it arrives. You don't have to have tankers around.

There is a requirement to have ammunition ships and units such as that available because there's a limited capacity in fossil fueled ships. But the capacity for ammunition and for food stuffs (beans and bullets, so to speak) is greatly increased in nuclear ships because of the lack of requirement for using these large spaces for storages of fossil fuels.

I won't attempt to go into all the details of the advantages of nuclear powered task forces over conventional powered task forces, but they are very, very significant. So we decided we would try to move in this direction.

Of course McNamara, who had the job of making a certain amount of money go around despite what he said his orders were, would have it studied. So it would be studied and studied until it was -- CVAN-67, I think, was delayed over two and a half years, just by the simple expedient of having it studied.

Q: Admiral so many of these developments you mention depend largely for their conception and inception in R and D. What was the status of this during the McNamara regime?

Griffin: All these things that I have been mentioning so far, of course, were the result of R and D that took place before McNamara ever got there.

He cut down, on a percentage basis, on Research and Development. And I have seen very little that's come out of the Defense Department as a consequence of any development that he sponsored.

There were many things that were accomplished during this period, and I would not be one qualified to speak in detail on this. But a number of the things that he wanted and forced through the services proved to be very bad.

The outstanding example of that was the F-111. This was something that ultimately really hit the fan.

#11 Griffin - 536

He was completely convinced, his cost analysis boys backed him up, that if you had an airplane with a high degree of commonality, as he called it, for the Air Force and the Navy then we would really save a lot of money. He projected these savings in savings of billions of dollars.

The Air Force, with their Board, studied this whole thing and came up very solidly with the opinion that it should not be done.

The Navy did exactly the same thing, and they recommended very strongly that it not be done. Both said that the operating requirements for the Air Force and for the Navy were so different that it simply could not be done and still get the type of aircraft that each of the services wanted.

However he ruled, and both Navy and Air Force said, "We'll do our best." And they went ahead with it.

It went through the normal cycle and the award was finally made to General Dynamics to build this aircraft. This award was made not in accord with the recommendations of either the Air Force or the Navy.

They had source selection boards in both the Air Force and the Navy which were comprised of people who had been in the selection business for aircraft for many, many years.

There was highly qualified civilians on this, in addition to the Officer personnel who had been in this business for the Navy for many years.

They went over everything and the Navy recommendation and

the Air Force recommendation, arrived at completely separately, was to award the contract to Boeing. However, it was awarded to General Dynamics.

Then there was an investigation on this. The McClellan Committee got in on this one. The testimony was expected to be very interesting.

What Mr. McNamara wanted to know was what Admiral Anderson's testimony was going to be. McNamara had a battery of lawyers in his office working furiously on this whole thing. The answer he always got from Admiral Anderson's office was that he hadn't written his statement yet, he hadn't finished it yet. That continued right up until the day before he actually went over and appeared before the McClellan Committee.

This didn't endear him to Mr. McNamara at all, and caused a great deal of coolness between the two individuals. Their relationships had never been too cordial anyway, since the Cuban crisis.

I haven't mentioned the Cuban crisis yet.

Q: No, but I'm very cognizant of that.

Griffin: Admiral Anderson went over and delivered his statement before the McClellan Committee, and it just infuriated McNamara.

I'll comment a little bit later about other relationships with McNamara.

Admiral Anderson was not on good terms with McNamara.

He was at first. But then McNamara appreciated the fact that he had an individual there who was damn smart, and who knew what the score was.

Admiral Anderson was an individual who was very politically minded and he was on extremely fine terms with President Kennedy. He received the Leatare Medal from the University of Notre Dame, the year after this was presented to President Kennedy, Laetare Medal being awarded to an outstanding Catholic layman in the country.

Q: Anderson's name we can't forget, his middle name is Whelan.

Griffin: That's right, exactly, George Whelan Anderson, Jr.

This was a very peculiar relationship. Since I've gotten this far on this thing, I might as well go ahead and finish this up.

It was a very, very unusual relationship there. Here you had the Chief of Naval Operations, a very brilliant individual, very politically minded, not really trusting the Secretary of Defense. And the Secretary of Defense in turn knew he didn't trust him.

Andy didn't agree with many of the things the Secretary of Defense was trying to do, and yet he was on extremely fine terms with the President. The President would invite him to be his guest, for example, at his box at the Orange Bowl game or things like that.

I had been very close to Anderson, (we were classmates)

ever since we were Midshipmen. He and Herb Riley and I were very close friends.

Andy and I, in many respects, had parallel careers. We moved along in the aviation field. He had the Sixth Fleet when I had the Seventh Fleet. And he moved on as CNO and I came back as his Deputy, which I was very happy to do.

I felt that I could talk very frankly with Andy about any subject. One point that I made with him, after I could see what was happening was, "Andy please don't put yourself in a position where the President has to make a decision between you and McNamara, because if you do in my humble opinion he is going to make that in McNamara's favor. The President is an individual who is a cold blooded politician. And there's no question in my mind about what he'll do. It doesn't make any difference whether he does invite you down to a bowl game. You can see him at any time in the White House. You and Mrs. Merriweather Post are on very close terms, and all this that and the other. When the decision time comes, and McNamara puts it up to him and it's either him or you, there's no question in my mind who it's going to be."

Q: That was a very shrewd estimate of the situation.

Griffin: It proved to be correct, I think. Because he was fired, there wasn't any question about that.

Q: He was sent off to Spain, wasn't he?

Griffin: He was made the U. S. Ambassador to Portugal. There was some feeling at that time that he should not have accepted that appointment. That in doing so, it decreased his ability to speak out strongly about many things that he felt were most important. This decreased his influence in this field.

So the only thing that he ever said publicly after that was his talk at the National Press Club, before he was formally appointed the Ambassador, before he was sworn in as Ambassador. And this talk, because of the impending appointment had to be carefully and obliqily phrased. So much effect was lost.

His not being reappointed came as quite a shock to him and to Mrs. Anderson.

Q: This might have been a very well planned appointment too, to Spain.

Griffin: No, to Portugal. No question about that at all.

Of course before he accepted this, he called the White House and went over and he had a fifty minute talk with the President, only the two of them were present. So only Admiral Anderson knows precisely everything that was said there.

There have been many rumors about this. That they promised him, "When McNamara leaves, I'll bring you back and make you the Chairman of the Joint Chiefs." and all kinds of things like that. But these are all rumors, and I don't think anybody outside of Admiral Anderson really knows the full effect of all of the conversation he had with the President.

But I keep coming back to the thing of great significance to me, and that is this Laetare Medal. He received that Laetare Medal and Kennedy received it the year before. One may draw his own conclusions.

Q: This is designated for efforts toward peace, or what?

Griffin: No. The Board at Notre Dame selects the individual. It's awarded to an outstanding Catholic layman, with no restrictions as to field of specialty. In some years they do not award it to anyone. But to show you the caliber of it, it was President Kennedy the year before. You don't get it for just building a better mouse trap. Its a very prestigious award.

I cannot help but feel there's something in connection with this that would have an important bearing on why he accepted the appointment to Portugal.

Q: There was a strong religious bond between them. This is significant in itself.

You were talking about McNamara and Research and Development in his regime. I wanted to ask this question - Since he indicated on occasion that he could reduce the estimate of the threat from abroad, did he basically not think there was any great threat from a potential enemy? Is this perhaps at the root of his willingness to cut down on Research and Development and a future program as a result?

Griffin: I think that he wanted to make a great reputation as a Secretary of Defense who saved money. He harped on money all the time.

He would never admit that he had any budget ceiling, although it was certainly well recognized that ball park figures were bandied around throughout the Administration every year. And you had a pretty darn good idea, and he would have a very good idea, as to precisely what the President had in mind to be spent for overall defense. So there were figures that were around. He wanted to equal or better any of these figures.

He embarked on many of these so-called cost reduction campaigns. Some of the reports that were sent in from the field as being savings and were accomplished under his direction were just absolutely cockeyed. And were not true.

This guy had a terrific mania, damn close to that, of being right. He was arrogant to the point that he had to be right all the time.

A good example of that is when Hanson Baldwin made a trip out to Southeast Asia and said there was a bomb shortage. He was writing for the NEW YORK TIMES, he came back and said there was a bomb shortage. McNamara hit the ceiling and he barred Hanson Baldwin from the Pentagon and a few things like that.

Well there was a shortage of bombs in Vietnam at that time. Aircraft were going out only half loaded with the bombs that they needed. There were some occasions when some Navy Aircraft were dropping depth charges on land, to get some device that would explode.

Now he was technically correct in this respect - If you took all the bombs that the services had all over the world, they had what they needed.

Now all he would have to have said, without lying about it, and he lied in this case, was to have said, "I read this article with the great deal of interest. It is true that there has been a temporary shortage of certain types of bombs and weapons in Southeast Asia. However, we've got them around the world. They're being moved right now to Southeast Asia. In a very short period of time we will have there all that we need. I'm sure that you would not have wanted me to do the alternative.

"The alternative would have been to have stockpiled all over the world tremendous quantities of these, and it would have cost you ten billion dollars more per year to have them.

"I'm sure you wouldn't want me to do that. So rather then doing that, we've got to have these stockpiles in one particular place. They are being moved from other stockpiles where they are not being needed now, to where they are needed."

If he had gotten up and said something like that, that would have been the end of it. But in my opinion, he did not have it within him to admit to anything that, in his opinion, would be derogatory, such as that.

Q: Admiral in the year 1962, there were several references turned up on developments in Antarctica, the Byrd Station and various other things, Operation DEEP FREEZE. What was your role, what was your philosophy in regard to these scientific efforts sponsored by the Navy?

Griffin: We very much were in favor of continuing reasonable efforts in the Antarctica. The results and earlier efforts there had been very profitable from the scientific and geophysical point of view. From a strategic point of view, of course we were always interested in learning more about areas as vast as the Antarctica because of it's possible use for military operations, particularly in the missile age.

Our DEEP FREEZE Forces were under the operational control of the Commander in Chief U. S. Atlantic Fleet. And he was charged with the responsibility of operating them and providing for their support.

However we, in the Fleet Operations Sections, that Division of my shop, had a group who monitored this very carefully, and cranked in the requirements in our overall budget, and kept in touch with the Staff of the DEEP FREEZE group when they were up in the Washington area.

When they were not actually down in Antarctica, they were provided office space in the Washington area. They did all the planning in Washington and maintained constant liaison with people in my group.

Q: It was in a sense an inter-departmental thing, was it?

Griffin: It was. The Coast Guard was very much interested in this. Interior was interested in it.

When it was decided to put a Nuclear Power Plant down there that brought in other agencies. This was an ideal place for a Nuclear Power Plant, because it would be relatively small, it had a long life, and could generate the power that was needed.

Q: Nobody could object except the emperor penguins.

Griffin: That's right.

This also is one area where there was probably more cooperation on the spot between representatives of various countries than any other single place I can think of on the face of the earth. The scientific endeavors of the Soviet Union down there, that is the personnel who were involved in this down there, got along extremely well any time they met with any of the personnel from other countries.

Q: Why is cooperation in the scientific field much more possible with the nations of the earth, than cooperation in a political sense or a military sense?

Griffin: I think probably the simplest answer to that would be that scientists deal in concrete fact. And there's very little argument about the fact that two and two equals four.

In the political field, some times two and two does not equal four. That's very much of an oversimplification.

Scientists, generally speaking also tend to feel that their endeavors transcend any basic national considerations.

They, therefore, feel they have a right to exchange information with other people in other countries. They feel that their total effort is for the betterment of all mankind, and generally speaking they want to exchange information with other scientists. They recognize that others are proceeding along paths that they might not be proceeding on, and this will give them in their work a much broader coverage of the total spectrum.

For example, our aeronautical engineers, and professors who were involved in this type work, had very close liaison with German scientists before World War II, right up until the very end.

Q: And I suppose the best possible illustration is seen in the International Geophysical Year, 1957.

Griffin: Now of course in some countries it's not possible for scientists to have the freedom that they would like to have. The Soviet Union, I think, is a particularly good example of that. They do not have the freedom that they would undoubtedly like to have. They are inhibited in what they can say in any field, but they recognize the fact that their own system does exist there and within these limitations they try to be reasonable.

I think that the only reason the Soviet Union can get away with their system is that they have elevated these scientists to a position in the total community much higher than that which is occupied by a scientist in our own community. And they have done this deliberately in order to retain those scientists within

#11 Griffin 547

their governmental system. I think this is the only way they have been able to keep their able scientists, and let no one be mistaken about that, they've got some very, very good scientists.

Q: But their liberty is somewhat limited.

Griffin: Their liberty is somewhat limited. I think the scientists are willing to accept this, certainly for a temporary basis anyway, in exchange for the privileges and position which they occupy in their society.

Q: Admiral, Fred Korth came in as the new Secretary of the Navy just about the time you came in to take over Op-03. What kind of Secretary did he prove to be? How much cooperation did you have with him?

Griffin: My first meeting with Mr. Korth was a very pleasant one. I met his wife and two of the children. His wife was very active in the Episcopal Church, which shall we say sort of endeared me to her or her to me, because I had been active in Episcopal Church work.

After I had been there some time, it seemd to me that Mr. Korth was not in the right position. I don't think that he had enough of a technical background, which could equip him to do a good job in an atmosphere of the type we had in the Services with McNamara as Secretary of Defense.

Let me explain that a little bit - Mr. Korth would be

asked to come down to the Secretary of Defense's office because McNamara liked to deal with the Service Secretaries rather than with the Service Chiefs. On many occasions Mr. McNamara would raise points with Mr. Korth that Mr. Korth could have answered had he had some one there with him who knew these answers such as the CNO, but he was not prone or perhaps he wasn't permitted to take anyone in uniform with him. As a consequence, on some occasions he apparantly would get the devil bawled out of him by McNamara and then he'd have a tendency to come back and take that out on the people in uniform. This was not a very good setup, in my opinion.

I must admit that I had one run in with Mr. Korth that was not very pleasant. We were attending a program planning meeting, this was a meeting of about 45 or 50 people, for the purpose of presenting a paper which had been prepared to substantiate the development of certain badly needed items.

One was being presented which I had cognizance of. In the middle of it, some phraseology was used which prompted Mr. Korth to remark that we wouldn't have things like this happen any more as in the past, and it was just as well that he and Mr. McNamara were now in charge because they would straighten everything out.

Q: New directions?

Griffin: Yes. And I must admit that I got a little hot under the collar, at this type of comment, which went on for several minutes. Apparently Mr. Korth thought that we should all feel very happy that "the great saviour" had arrived and now had us under his benevolent protection.

I, in effect, said, "Mr. Secretary, I think even you will probably recognize and admit that we have probably the greatest Navy that the world has ever seen. And I can assure you that we do not get this Navy by having a bunch of stupid individuals in uniform sitting around on their duffs doing nothing these past years." When I made that comment, there was rather shocked silence in the room.

Finally the Secretary said, "Well I hardly think that this conversation need proceed any further. We're not getting very far." I said, "Mr. Secretary, I agree completely."

From then on our relationship was very cool. He did not have very much to say to me on any occasion. I think it was probably for a month or two he didn't even speak to me. But at least he knew how I felt about it.

I had several people who came to me later on. One of them surprised me. An old friend came to me and said, "Gee you just cut your own throat with that comment, didn't you? I'm surprised that you would make a comment like that."

Well, I remarked that it needed to be said, and I didn't know anybody better qualified in that room to say it, so I said it.

Most of the people came to me and said, "Thank God you had the guts to stand up and tell him where to head in."

That was not a very pleasant thing though. I hate to see things like that. It's the only occasion that I ever had, to have a run in with any of the civilian Secretaries.

I don't have any information at all about the events which led up to his ultimate dismissal, so I can't comment on that at all.

I can only say that the relationships between him and me were rather strained.

Q: Obviously it didn't put a damper on your career.

Griffin: Well I don't know. There were people who thought it would have.

Let me comment briefly on one other aspect that was one of the highlights of the time I was there. And that was the Cuban crisis.

Q: You can be as expansive as you want to be on that, sir. It's quite all right.

Griffin: I won't go into too much of it, because an awful lot of it has already been said, and I cannot add too much to it.

We were concerned about the buildup in Cuba.

Q: How far back did your concern make itself apparent?

Griffin: It had gone back several months before October.

The Navy keeps a fairly good count of shipping on the high seas. There seemed to be an extraordinary amount, an increasing amount, that was going from the Soviet Union to Cuba. We had no definite reason to suspect any particular thing, but it was enough to alert us to the fact that something was going on there. And we had asked the powers that be to increase aerial surveillance of the Island. This went on for a couple of months.

I had a commitment down at the Naval Air Station, Pensacola at the Basic Training Command, to make a speech and to attend the graduation down there. This was in October.

The Cuban situation was getting a little bit warm at that time because by this time our aerial intelligence had indicated what appeared to be the nature of the buildup. So I went to CNO and told him I had this engagement down there and did he want me to keep it. He said, "Go ahead and take the A3D."

We had an A3D Jet that was equipped to carry about six people. The inside of it had been configured to carry about six people. I went down in that aircraft. The reason was to have it available so that I could get back to Washington within an hour and a half.

I went on down and made the speech and then got a call from Washington saying, "Get back here in a hurry." So I hopped in the airplane and back came. By the time I got back to Washington, in that short period of time, again the fan was hit.

The highest people in the Administration, by that time, knew precisely what was going on. The President had made his determination as to what action he was going to take.

I got back in the afternoon, and the President's speech was made that night. That was the 22nd, I believe, of October.

#11 Griffin - 552

Q: He announced the naval quarantine of Cuba on the 22nd.

Griffin: He announced the naval quarantine and designated Admiral Anderson to run this.

We augmented our plotting room in the Pentagon, the Navy plotting room in the Pentagon. We had special intelligence people put in. The Chiefs were in almost continuous session. And we set up a 'around the clock' watch at the Pentagon.

During the day when Admiral Anderson would be down in the tank with the Chiefs, practically the entire day, I sat at his desk in the Pentagon. I was either there, where we had a special White House phone, or in Flag Plot.

A Committee over in the White House was meeting almost constantly. And I would be called from time to time by the Committee, usually by Gilpatrick. I would be in touch with the White House, and of course in touch with units of the Fleet and in touch with Dennison in Norfolk.

Then we set up a watch at night. We had a Vice Admiral at the desk all night long. This continued during the entire crisis.

We also had a direct personal representative of the boss of CIA there in our office. This was sort of a clearing house for a lot of things, messages that had to be passed back and forth.

Also I was in a position on private lines to give Dennison some of the background of thinking and give him advance notice of operational requirements that might come up and so forth.

It was a very interesting period. For the first few days, Mr. McNamara had very little to say about the details of it because he was obviously in a business about which he had no knowledge at all. He was smart enough not to make an oaf out of himself in this business, but after a little while he started asking a lot of questions. Many of them took place when I was not there. Some of his run ins that he had with Admiral Anderson, only one of them took place while I was there.

He was very unhappy that Admiral Anderson indicated to him that he, Admiral Anderson, knew how to run a blockade and he would have no difficulty in doing it.

In the meantime the White House was in touch with the U. S. Ambassador to the United Nations in New York. Mr. Cleveland, who was over in the State Department, who had the UN desk in the State Department, was mixed up in this very considerably.

Messages were going back and forth apparently over the hot line and so forth. And there were many exchanges between our government and the Soviet government that we in the Pentagon knew little or nothing about. We had our job to do and we were doing it, keeping track of all the ships that were going there.

In this connection the thing that really invited our attention to something of strategic nature was the size of the hatches on these ships. Practically all the big hatch ships that the Soviet Union had were put in this trade to Cuba. You've got to have a big hatch ship in order to get the missiles down in the hold or else you put them on deck. Some of them were on deck. But all the big hatch ships that they had were put

#11 Griffin - 554

into the Cuban trade at that time.

Then of course later we saw the pictures of the build up. We saw the pictures of 28s being put together and turned up on the fields.

All I can say is that it was a very interesting period.

Q: At one point the Secretary had a telecast I remember and used these photographs.

Griffin: That's right.

In an earlier one we were ready to go in there, in the Bay of Pigs. We had brought Amphibious Forces from a landing group all the way from the West Coast and we were ready to go in.

But this was the missile crisis.

Q: What role did Senator Keating play in the bringing of this thing to the fore - his several pronouncements in the Senate and so forth? And what were the sources for his information?

Griffin: Really I don't know what the sources of his information were. But it certainly alerted everyone to the fact that something was going on there.

This was something that we had known, so far as I was concerned. When Senator Keating made these comments, it was something that all I could say was, "Yes I agree."

Now he, I think, used imagination a little bit ahead of time and was pretty right in a lot of the comments that he made. We knew the Senator wanted to talk, and we wanted to get more information from the air.

One of the difficulties in going into a great amount of detail about some of these things is the secrecy with which the White House held them. Even the Chiefs would be uninformed about certain things. I don't think that the Chiefs were being really kept up to date on the negotiations that were going on in New York, and from the White House to Moscow.

Kennedy had had a sour experience in the Bay of Pigs. You could see this, in the way he handled the uniformed people in the Pentagon in practically all of his dealings. This was a sour experience which, to a great degree, was his own fault, in the Bay of Pigs. And he paid dearly for it later on.

We established this blockade. We put Russian speaking people on various ships down there. We had them available to the Commanders on the spot so if any ships was apt to be the one to intercept a given ship, we made sure that we had a Russian speaking individual on the ship. We just ran it as a blockade would be run in the traditional sense, except this time it was very heavily augmented by air.

Now at this time we had anti-submarine warfare forces very actively involved, because the Russians had submarines down in that area. We sat on top of many of them. As a matter of fact, this gave us a very good workout and a very good test of just how good our anti-submarine system was. I must say it was very gratifying to see the ability of some of our ships to sit on top of a Russian submarine until he had to come up for air. They'd keep with him, stay with him. Some of our longer range detection devices proved to be very helpful in this respect.

I don't want to paint a picture that we were perfect by any stretch of the imagination, but I will say that we had that particular submarine threat under control.

Q: These were war games for real, weren't they?

Griffin: They were war games for real, absolutely. And we'd sit on top of these guys, as I say, until they had to come up for air.

This certainly taught the Russians a lesson, no question about it in my mind, not at all. It taught them a very, very significant lesson. The basic lesson was that if they're going to get involved in adventurisms far removed from their own home country, they're going to have control of the sea.

As a consequence, ever since that time, they have been developing their total naval power. They have exercised it, largely in the Mediterranean, but well removed from their shores. They have had forces operating in the Indian Ocean, in the Arabian Sea, in the Western Atlantic, in addition to the other parts of the Atlantic and Pacific Oceans.

I think that the experience there in Cuba taught them a lesson and gave them an impetus toward development of this total naval capability. I say total naval capability - By that I mean also their merchant marine, building that up. It taught them a lesson which they converted into a program.

Q: What was their actual purpose in this escapade? And was there a certain degree of naivete involved in it on their part?

Griffin: I think there probably was some naivete. My feeling pretty much at the time, and I see that this has been collaborated recently by accounts that have been written, was that Krushchev in his meeting with Kennedy had assessed him as being an individual that he, Krushchev, could control rather easily. And he didn't have to worry about him, and could bluff him right out of his shoes.

He figured with the Bay of Pigs thing Kennedy was so indecisive, didn't move militarily when he was fully prepared to move militarily, Krushchev knew all this. Then the talk he had with him over in Europe, in Vienna, left him with the impression that here was a guy that he could push around a bit. And what better way to increase, at very small relative cost, the strategic position of the Soviet Union vis-a-vis the United States. And by putting missiles right there in Cuba, ninety miles away from the United States, the USSR could cover an awful lot of targets.

If he got away with that one, he was really headed for the high timber, but he didn't. The guy (Kennedy) was tougher than he thought he would be.

But they learned this lesson, and it has had a very definite continuing effect ever since.

Q: Speaking of learning lessons - did Secretary McNamara learn from this that threat from without was a real one? Did he show any signs of reform in his attitude?

Griffin: Not appreciably, not at all.

I'll only have one more comment really to make on this Op-03 business. The question of where I would go after Op-03 was a very active one. We knew that the chances were that one job would open up in Europe, also the CincPac job would be available. The feeling was, I think, in much of the Navy that I had been prepped for the CinCPac job for many, many years with all the jobs I'd had.

Then I had this run in with Secretary Korth. I had also had a conversation with Nitze at one time, who was ISA at that time. I think the word had gotten around that I was not one to be pushed around too much. Note - maybe I was just undiplomatic.

Q: This was the gist of your conversation with Paul Nitze too?

Griffin: I had a conversation with Paul, as part of a briefing which we gave him on ASW. He had a couple of his cost analysis guys there. During the course of the conversation, something was said to the effect that in order to understand this problem it was not necessary to have any practical experience in operating some of these ASW systems. And I took exception to that.

I think this contributed to the word getting around. Later, I was playing golf at Burning Tree in a member guest tournament at Burning Tree. I received a phone call, when we finished the first nine, from Admiral Anderson.

He said, "You're going to Europe. You're going to London with four stars." That was the first word I had.

So I went to London, rather than going out to the Pacific and probably getting fired as CincPac.

Q: Were you keenly disappointed at the moment?

Griffin: I was disappointed at the moment, because I had been trained for that job. Really much of my life had been spent studying the Pacific. I knew the Pacific quite well, in all modesty. I knew so many of the leaders out there - Diem, Chiang-kai-chek, the works.

Q: And who went there instead?

Griffin: Sharp went there. He went there about four or five months later, because that job was opening up later on.

Interview # 12

Admiral C. D. Griffin
Washington, D. C.

By John T. Mason
November 18, 1971

Mr. Mason: Admiral, it seems like old times to see you, being back here in the same chair, and prepared for another chapter in your most interesting career.

Last time, it was a year ago when we broke off, you had learned at the Burning Tree Golf Club that you were going to London to become CINCNELM and Commander-in-Chief of the U. S. Naval Forces in Europe. And you actually went there in June of 1963. So, you want to resume your story –

Admiral Griffin: Yes, indeed.

As I recall I did mention that there was a little bit of disappointment in this for me, because in fact my whole record had been one which really prepped me to go to the top job out in the Pacific. However, it was also apparent to me, from my experience in Op-03, that I would have a most difficult job getting along with the McNamara group in Washington, and that on second thought going to the job in Europe was not so bad after all.

Mr. Mason: And, in retrospect, I think you can thank your lucky star that you didn't go.

Admiral Griffin: In retrospect, I certainly do, very, very much –

There is one important event which I have not mentioned and which took place shortly before I received the news that I would go to London. And that had to do with Admiral Anderson, the CNO.

One Sunday afternoon, I'm afraid I can't recall the exact date, he was called on by theDeputy SecDef, Roswell Gilpatrick, who informed him that the President would not reappoint him as the Chief of Naval Operations at the end of his two year term. This came as very much of a surprise and I'm sure a very deep shock to Admiral Anderson. It was also a very grave shock to Mrs. Anderson.

Mr. Mason: Was this the usual kind of channel in which to be informed?

Admiral Griffin: No, this varies. The channel by which you are informed can vary all over the lot.

I recall Admiral Denfeld, when he found out that he was to be fired, received the news from the Naval Aide in the White House who called him and read to him a news item from the news ticker in the White House. And that was the first time he knew about it. The Secretary didn't even have the courtesy to call him and tell him. So it can happen most anyway.

Anyway this came as quite a shock to the Andersons, and I am quite sure was completely unexpected. Later on that evening the Vice Chief of Naval Operations, Admiral Claude Ricketts had a meeting of the Deputies in his quarters to inform the Deputies and discuss the stand that we might take, which to be quite brief was that this was something that was being handled at the highest level and we had no option but to accept it. And even though we were not in agreement with this action, at the same time it was something that had been decided and we had no other course open to us except to do our best for continuity in the running of the naval establishment.

I did find out some time later on, by what I consider to be a fairly good source, that at one time the administration in the Pentagon was seriously considering firing Anderson, Ricketts, and me - the three top people in the uniform branch of the Pentagon in the Navy. It was apparently invited to their attention that if McNamara would fire these three top uniformed people in the Navy, all of whom had very considerable following within the Navy, that the repercussions of it would be tremendous. And therefore, the decision was made to keep Claude Ricketts in the job as VCNO, and send me to Europe, and fire Anderson. This apparently is what happened. That is what I understand to be factual, although an abbreviated statement of what was happening at that time. This was before Anderson got the news that he was to be fired.

Q: Was he given any reason for this action?

Griffin: No, he was given no reason. Although I don't think he really needed a reason, because it was perfectly obvious to everyone who was close to the situation that he did not see eye to eye with Mr. McNamara on many many items, and McNamara preferred to have someone else in there. That, of course, put the President in quite a spot as he personally was very fond of George Anderson.

Both the President and George Anderson were very prominent Catholic laymen. The President received the Laetare Medal from Notre Dame that year; Anderson had received the Laetare Medal from Notre Dame the year before.

The President took Andy with him on several occasions, for example to the Orange Bowl game in Florida and places that had an affair such as that.

The Andersons were very popular socially in Washington. So he enjoyed a very fine rapport with the President.

However the President was, in the final analysis, certainly a hard-boiled hard-nosed politician. And he had a Secretary of Defense in the Pentagon whom he trusted and to whom he delegated considerable authority, and that that individual in the Pentagon said he couldn't get along with the Chief of Naval Operations and recommended that he not be reappointed - that put the President in a very difficult position.

Some people have said that the out for the President was to offer George Anderson the job as U. S. Ambassador to Portugal. There were very few of us who knew that he had been offered that job, and quite frankly some felt that he should not accept it. Because if he didn't accept it this would give him much more in the way of options to speak out in regard to what he considered to be the bad features of the McNamara regime in the

Pentagon. On the other hand if he did accept it he was in a position then where he couldn't very well talk too much.

Q: He was a part of the administration.

Griffin: He did, however, after accepting it make a speech at the National Press Club, in which he rather skillfully got across some of his oppositions to the McNamara regime in the Pentagon.

I have never forgotten an article written by George Dixon, which covered the retirement ceremony of George Anderson. It was, as I recall, entitled THE ROSE GARDEN, because this ceremony took place in the Rose Garden. McNamara spoke, the Secretary of the Navy, Mr. Korth spoke, and the President spoke. Dixon said that all were talking about this paragon of virtue and the greatest naval man since John Paul Jones, and it sort of got him so that he was emotionally hardly able to walk as he got up. Then suddenly it dawned on him - this is the guy they just fired. It was a very well written article.

Andy went on to be the U. S. Ambassador to Portugal for several years, which he performed with great merit. He did a splendid job there, and is recognized by everyone, including some of the old State Department diehards who didn't particularly like to see a military officer usurping one of their fine posts.

He did a splendid job, and was very much liked by the Portuguese, and represented the U. S. extremely well there.

Let me get on now to follow up on getting the news that I was going to go to London. There wasn't too much time after I got the news to get ready to get packed up. We had all the usual farewell parties. We had to separate all of our household possessions, because we had to leave most of those in storage since the accomodations in London were fully furnished

I also persuaded Mort Neely, who had just completed a tour of duty as executive officer of a destroyer, and who had earlier been my aide when I had command of the Seventh Fleet, to come with me as my senior aide to London. He accepted this, and as usual did a splendid job.

We flew over to London on the 23rd of June, 1963. There we were met by Dave MacDonald, who was the CNO designate. MacDonald had only been in the job about a month, and in fact was on one of his early inspection trips when he was turned around by a phone call in Turkey to come back and proceed rather rapidly to Washington - that he had been selected to take over the CNO job.

Q: Did he welcome this change?

Griffin: Mac - all of us who knew the MacDonalds for many years called him Mac. Newer friends call him Dave.

Mac, I would say, received this news very much with mixed feelings. Both he and Tommy loved to play golf, and this was an ideal place for that. Mac never was one who went out of his way to seek a lot of unnecessary work. If there were four ways of doing a job to get the same results, and one required the least amount of effort - he would always take that one. I don't blame him. He had some idea of what the job of CNO was all about, but I don't believe ever in his life had he ever faced a job which would require so much of his time as this one would. As a consequence, having just gotten the news and having not had immediately previous duty in the Pentagon, he was extremely interested in all aspects of it. So I spent the better part of the next few days actually briefing him on the CNO job, in particular his relationships with the Joint Chiefs of Staff, McNamara, and so forth.

In between times, while he and Tommy were packing I would get briefed on various elements of the two main jobs that I was inheriting. The two jobs in London - one was Commander-in-Chief U. S. Naval Forces Europe, in which I reported as the component commander of the European Command directly to Lemnitzer, who was the U. S. CincEur (Commander-in-Chief Europe), the unified commander. Then I had a second job which was CincNELM (Commander-in-Chief Eastern Atlantic and Mediterranean). This was a specified command under the Joint Chiefs of Staff, and involved responsibility in the Mediterranean and the Near East and going all the way through to India.

For example - we had a small group of U. S. Air Force people in Saudi Arabia on a training mission. They reported directly to me.

This was a specified command and I reported directly to the Joint Chiefs of Staff for this.

Q: This meant you had two different staffs then.

Griffin: I had two different staffs. I had my CincNELM staff, - the Chief of Staff was a Major General in the U. S. Air Force. I had a Brigadier General in the U. S. Army, and a Brigadier General in the U. S. Marine Corps on that staff. There were two different staffs in the same headquarters building.

I think I might just as well deal with the CincNELM thing right at this time, in order to shall we say get rid of it.

There was under way at this time a study in the Joint Chiefs of Staff which had been prompted by Secretary McNamara to set up, a U. S. Strike Command. This was finally accepted by McNamara, over the objections and dissent of the Navy and the Marine Corps. The Strike Command would be headed by an Army officer, with an Air Force Deputy, and a unified staff. It would consist of forces which would be assigned to it by the Services, and would operate out of a headquarters in the vicinity of Tampa, Florida, actually at McDill Air Force Base. Forces would be assigned by the Joint Chiefs of Staff and the Services to the Strike Command for training exercises. The forces assigned would be designed to be airlifted to any spot in the world and to put out brush fires. That was the principal purpose for this command.

As I said the Navy and Marine Corps were very much opposed to it, because quite frankly the Navy and Marine Corps felt that this was one early step in the dissolution of the Marine Corps.

Q: That being their specific function.

Griffin: That is their function. It would also have a very definite impact upon the amphibious forces of the U. S. Navy.

Anyway despite the objections, this was what McNamara wanted to do and he did it.

He had looked to the Air Force to provide the very large transport aircraft, and the Army to train the troops to move. The question of heavy equipment and other items which would be required for a very considerable stay in the place didn't seem to bear too heavily on Mr. McNamara at this time. It was one of the elements, however, that the Navy and Marine Corps brought out very strongly. After all the amphibious forces of the Navy were equipped, while they could not move as fast as the Air Force aircraft could move, at the same time when they moved they were fully equipped to go some place and to stay there for a considerable period of time together with all of the necessary support that they required.

The decision was made to set up the Strike Command, and the responsibilities that CincNELM had going all throughout the Middle East were taken from him and assigned to the Strike Command. This left ConcNELM with no responsibility, and therefore that post was eliminated as a specified command under the Joint Chiefs of Staff.

Q: No responsibility within the Mediterranean itself?

Griffin: No. The Strike Command was given the responsibility for that, which Lemnitzer didn't like very much.

Q: What happened to the Sixth Fleet then as an entity?

Griffin: The idea was that if the Strike Command has use for the Sixth Fleet he would ask for the Joint Chiefs of Staff to order the Sixth Fleet to report to him for operational control.

So CincNELM, as a command, was disestablished in 1964, I think it was June of 1964.

At the seme time CincLANT, who had responsibility for a considerable portion of Africa, lost all of that and that responsibility was given to CincSTRIKE. The Pacific Command had responsibility in Asia, and that was taken away and given to CincSTRIKE. So all of the old commanders lost something from setting up this new command.

I'm moving ahead in order to get rid of this particular topic. The transition and transfer of authority went off very smoothly. I instructed my staff, I said, "We don't like this, of course, but the decision has been made so let's get on with the business of doing it as orderly as we possibly can and be of all the assistance that we can possibly be to the Strike Command." This attitude was appreciated very much. We received several very fine letters and messages expressing their gratitude for our help in turning over the responsibilities.

I note, paranthetically, that orders have gone out right now to disestablish the Strike Command. This was proved not to be the panacea that Mr. McNamara thought it would be.

Q: And with the idea of reestablishing the similar set up to what we had?

Griffin: I don't know whether CincNELM will be reestablished, but certainly the responsibility of CincLANT, for example, and CincPAC, and others will. CincUSAFE for example, U. S. Air Forces Europe, had responsibilities in Africa too - that was all taken. So those responsibilities will certainly be returned.

I doubt whether CincNELM will be reestablished - that was too much of an oddity, I think, at the time. At the time it was established it was very necessary and it proved to be a very workable thing. But in modern times it would be, I think, a little bit too awkward.

Q: Was there any reaction in Congress to the establishment of CincSTRIKE?

Griffin: There were many questions that were asked, yes. And I might say rather obviously, a lot of them were planted. But at the same time there wasn't enough feeling in the Congress to take any blocking action, because clearly the Secretary of Defense was operating within his own authority on this. In this particular case you didn't have the internal U. S. political pressures that might be applied to block something like that, becau-e it was essentially outside of the U. S. where most of the responsibility laid.

Q: What, sir, was the McNamara rationale for this?

Griffin: He felt that there was a great future for large

aircraft airlift, and rather than taking thirty days to lift a division from the East Coast to Europe you could do it in a matter of hours.

Some times many of these cost effectiveness people tended to forget that you've got to have the gas there, you've got to have the landing areas protected so that in fact the field will be there when the planes arrive, you've got to have instrument landing provisions at all of these fields, you've got to have the equipment at the fields to marry up with the personnel after you get them there, and you've got to have enough gas there to fill the aircraft up again to get them back home. These are just a few of the very primary things that are required. In other words it's not a panacea.

For example - one division was withdrawn one time from Europe, and a regiment was kept in Europe on a rotating basis. The division's heavy equipment - tanks, personnel carriers, all kinds of stuff like that - was left over there. The decision was made to have a big exercise flying this division over. The European Command had to use fifteen hundred men five months ahead of time to get all of the equipment in working order to marry up with the personnel when they came over there.

It doesn't solve all the problems.

Q: And that sort of advance preparation and notice doesn't come with brush fires.

Griffin: It doesn't come at all, absolutely.

I wanted to get the CincNELM thing out of the way with those few comments so that we could just spend the rest of the time on CincUSNAVEUR.

Q: May I ask this question - during the brief time that CincNELM existed under your command did you function in any way, did you make any trips, did you do anything as CincNELM?

Griffin: The trips that I made were made in the dual capacity, and I would discuss both things. However, I did not get over into the Middle East, I did not get a chance to do that. I had those trips set up, but then the word came that this action was in the mill so I cancelled them and stuck to the business of getting everything ready for turnover to CincSTRIKE.

After relieving MacDonald and he shoved off for Washington, I of course made my initial calls in the London area on the British and American dignitaries.

The American Ambassador there was David Bruce, who was just one of the greatest gentlemen I think I have ever seen. He was a terrific representative, a real pro in the business of being Ambassador. He had earlier been U. S. Ambassador in Germany, and U. S. Ambassador in France. He was getting along in years, but the succeeding Presidents wanted him to stay there and do the job. He was doing it extremely well, he was very well liked by the British, and as I say just a complete pro in the business of being an American Ambassador. I got along with him extremely well. We met regularly and discussed affairs. I kept him completely up to date and briefed on everything that was happening in the field of my responsibility. I cherish the relationship that I had with David Bruce.

I don't mean by not mentioning Evangeline Bruce that she wasn't charming also. This was in a slightly different field. This was David's second wife, she was much younger than he. They had two children that were at that time in their middle teens.

While we were there in London, incidentally, his daughter by his first wife and her husband were lost down in the Caribbean. This very much broke David up, he aged ten years overnight.

On the British side there was also a very colorful individual. Admiral of the Fleet Lord Louis Mountbatten was the Chairman of the British Joint Chiefs, and of course as we all know a very famous figure. I got along quite well with Dickie Mountbatten as I got to know him. He, at that time, was making preparations to move the British Chiefs out of their old separate quarters that they had been in for centuries into a new building on the Thames, which was automatically called the London Pentagon. He had in there a war room set up which was fashioned somewhat after the war room that the U. S. Chiefs had in Washington. He invited me over to go through it with him, and it was an extremely fine office to permit the proper functioning of the Chiefs and got them all together in the same building.

Q: Was that done simultaneously with the setting up of the

Ministry of Defense and used by the Ministry in London?

Griffin: Yes, that's right. It was actually part of that.

Q: How did the Admiralty feel about being incorporated into a Ministry of Defense?

Griffin: They didn't like it.

Q: They had such a long tradition.

Griffin: As the senior service.

Q: They ceased to exist from this point as a separate department, didn't they?

Griffin: Pretty much so.

At this time the First Sea Lord was David Luce, who had coincindentally been the Commander-in-Chief Far East Station with headquarters in Singapore when I had command of the Seventh Fleet. I'd gotten to know David and Mary Luce quite well there so it was with great pleasure that I found out that he was there, and I enjoyed our relationships.

Q: That should have proved to be pretty helpful to you.

Griffin: It was very helpful. And incidentally, some time later he was fired, or rather he resigned because of action which the British government took.

It takes some time to get all the various calls made in the London area. Incidentally I mentioned David Bruce as the

Ambassador, Louis Jones was the Minister there at the time. I saw in the paper where he died just a few days ago here in Washington.

Our relations there with the State Department were very good, and also with the British. David Luce was the First Sea Lord, and Lord Carrington was the First Lord of the Admiralty - a very sharp guy.

My next series of calls was to establish my relationship with my boss, who was the U. S. Commander-in-Chief Europe, General Lemnitzer. He had two hats - he was the Supreme Allied Commander of Europe, NATO job, and the U. S. CincEUR. I reported to him in his U. S. CincEUR hat, since I had no NATO responsibilities there, it was entirely U. S.

The headquarters building was at 20 Grosvenor Square, and had been there for practically the entire time that the command had existed. This was a building in which General Eisenhower did some of his preliminary planning for the Overlord operation across the channel. It's a fine building, and right adjacent to the American Embassy. It had ample office space in it, and also it had enough space so that the Commander-in-Chief could have a flat in that office building. So I had a flat in the office building which consisted of three bedrooms and two baths, a big living room, a dining room, and servants quarters. It made it very handy.

My official residence, however, was out in Surrey, about twenty-five miles southwest of London at a place called Romany in the Wentworth Estate at Virginia Water in Surrey. This was an absolutely magnificent building. It was on about three and a half acres of land, the grounds were beautifully manicured with lovely flowers, and just a perfectly wonderful place for entertaining, which I had to do a lot of. There was considerable entertaining to be done, and this provided a wonderful place to do it. It was fully staffed with Filipino stewards.

I normally would go out to Romany on Friday afternoon and come back on Monday morning, and generally speaking stayed at the flat during the week right at the headquarters building. I had special phones, however, out at Romany so that I could carry on classified conversations with my headquarters in London and with Washington. So I was not out of communication at any time.

This Wentworth Estate is a beautiful part of England. Romany was right between two magnificent golf courses in the Wentworth Estate, the east course and the west course. Having residence there also gave me honorary membership in the Wentworth Golf Club, and I took full advantage of this while I was there. It was really a perfect set up.

This residence was leased by the U. S. government until right after the war in 1947 when Admiral Connoly, who was the CincUSNAVEUR at that time, persuaded the State Department to purchase it as the official residence for the individual occupying the job that I had. So after considerable discussion, and from reading the correspondence it was apparent to me that the

American Ambassador at that time finally made the decision to go ahead and purchase it for the U. S. government in order to get Admiral Connoly out of his hair. He was just making a nuisance of himself about it. But it certainly proved to be an extremely fine investment. If the U. S. government has to get rid of it at any time they can probably get about ten times as much as they paid for it. It's an absolutely beautiful place.

Q: Is it a manor house?

Griffin: Yes, it's a large house. It has a master bedroom suite, four other bedrooms and three baths, plus a whole servants wing, a large living room, a library, a porch, a dining room, lavatories, and magnificent grounds. Of course the rainfall over there is such and the temperature is so moderate that one gardener took care of all of these grounds. Whereas, for example, in the Washington area it would be impossible for him to do it - with the weeds growing and dry spells and things like that he just couldn't do it. But over there one gardener did it, full time. Incidentally he had a flat in the building adjacent to the main building. The Commander-in-Chief's chauffeur, who was a British citizen, had a flat in that building too. So they were both right there.

It was a very, very wonderful set up, and no wonder Admiral MacDonald and Mrs. MacDonald didn't want to leave it.

I then started my visits to my boss and my contemporaries. My first visit being to call on General Lemnitzer, the U. S.

CincEUR who was in his headquarters outside of Paris. Then I called on CincUSAEUR, Commander-in-Chief U. S. Army Forces Europe. His headquarters were in Heidelberg. And then on CincUSAFE, Commander-in-Chief U. S. Air Forces Europe, whose headquarters was in Stuttgart, Germany.

Following this I made a trip up to Scotland for the principal purpose of inspecting our facilities at Holy Loch, our Polaris submarine base where we had a tender which maintained the submarines between their deployments.

After this trip to Holy Loch I returned to London, and had scheduled a trip to the Sixth Fleet. I wanted very much at an early time to get a trip to the Sixth Fleet because the Sixth Fleet was under my immediate operational control.

We were packing for that trip and about three o'clock in the afternoon I went up to check on the progress that we were making. I went up to the flat which was on the fourth floor, my office was on the second floor, and about ten minutes after I got up there my wife who had been packing went out of the bedroom. She was all packed, she went in to write a check at her desk in the living room, and didn't come back for some time. I went in and she was slumped over the desk. She had had a very sudden heart attack and died. I didn't realize it at the time, but I got the doctors right away. I was trying to massage her. I had a female aide there, Lieutenant Paula Fish. It was something that was completely out of the blue.

Of course that immediately cancelled the trip at that time.

That was on August the 9th. We had only been there about six weeks.

I called Admiral MacDonald right away and told him about it. Ike Kidd was his senior aide at that time. Dear Old Ike was one of my wonderful friends who had worked with me on several occasions. He took charge of everything on the Washington end. We flew back and stayed at Herb Riley's house down at the Washington Navy Yard. He was the Director of the Joint Staff at that time. My daughter was in Florida, and she came up. My son was on a destroyer out in the Pacific - he had graduated from the Academy the year before - he was given emergency leave and came on back there. The funeral was held at St. Albans with interment at ARlington Cemetery. After that we flew back to London.

As a result of my visits to the component commanders, the commanders of Heidelberg, Stuttgart, and General Lemnitzer outside of Paris, and with consideration for what we had in our headquarters building in London, and also the emergency headquarters which was at an RAF base outside of London, it became apparent to me that we didn't have in this command the proper type of communications. This was one of the first things that I set myself on after arriving at this conclusion.

I went through the war plans which were in existance at that time, and I noted that CincUSNAVEUR was not listed as one of those in the chain of command. In other words, if higher headquarters were destroyed you passed the command down. It was apparent to me why CincUSNAVEUR was not. He was incapable with the communications he had of providing effective direction to the U. S. forces we had in Europe. So CincUSNAVEUR was not even in the chain of command.

This to me was a very serious matter, so I got in touch with our friends in Washington. At that time we had in Washington a group which was becoming rapidly quite expert at converting commands through the use of data processing equipment - not the "whiz kids," the name of this group was NavCASSACI.

One of the first places where we needed to modernize was in the headquarters in London. We were completely incapable with any rapidity of receiving, collating, analyzing the intelligence information that we got. It wasn't a prehistoric set up, but it was close to it. We just simply didn't have the means of doing any of these things rapidly. The tremendous logistic problem that we had - we were handling them the same way we did back in the 1920s and 30s.

So I asked the experts in the field to come on over - the data handling computer programing group. They did and were extremely helpful. Then I took one captain off the staff and gave him full time duty to work on this problem - to develop a physical headquarters with necessary equipment that would give us the capability of exercising effective command. We worked hard on this but I had left before it was finished. However, shortly after Admiral Thach, who relieved me, took over they opened the new headquarters system up, and it proved to be extremely successful.

Q: May I ask why the set up there was primitive, why you found it in the primitive state when this command was only established as a result of World War II, was it not?

Griffin: Yes, that's right, Admiral Stark was the first one there.

Q: So why wasn't it more up to date in its ability to absorb all these things and function?

Griffin: I hate to throw any brickbats at anybody, but I think generally speaking once you got over there where one could enjoy the wonderful set up at Romany and the flat, these short comings sort of faded in the background.

The Unified Command system, of course, was not set up for some time after the war. And for a long time the people there considered that - "All I have to do is be able to talk to the Sixth Fleet," which was the main operating unit that belonged to CincUSNAVEUR, "if I can talk to him and tell him what I want done okay."

However, it was a rapidly moving scheme of events that were developing in the Sixth Fleet area, where Russian strength was being built up in the Mediterranean at an ever increasing rate, and the Unified Command system had been strengthened very much. The Chiefs of the services no longer really commanded anything; the forces were trained and then turned over the Unified Commanders as forces to be used under this changing system. I considered that I had to have much more ability than that - than just to talk to the Sixth Fleet. I had to talk to USCincEUR, and I felt that we should be in the chain of command. If the headquarters on the continent were blown up, I should have a headquarters in UK that would make it possible for me to command the U. S. forces in Europe. That was the objective.

Now they have the equipment there that makes that possible. They handle intelligence activities very nicely, logistic activities very nicely, and they have accurate and fast communications. So it's a much better system, much better now than it was.

Q: Did the Secretary of Defense nod in approval at the changes you made?

Griffin: I don't think it probably ever came to his attention.

Q: He was concerned, I believe, with the Air Force Command in Europe at that time. It had something to do with atomic weapons and the use of atomic weapons. He interfered there. I was wondering if he was concerned about the naval --

Griffin: I really don't know whether he knew very much about this. I doubt very much that he knew the situation was as bad as it was.

He was, of course, interested perhaps more with the Air Force because of his past association with the Air Force, and with the fact that they were sitting right there on the continent and not too far away from Russian penetration.

There were a couple of other things that I determined to do as a consequence of my early experience in London. One was to get to know the many European CNOs better. That would involve a considerable amount of traveling. I felt that this was worthwhile because in my opinion the military input to the political process in most nations on the continent was essentially Army and Air Force. Most of the armed forces on the continent - the armies were the important military force, followed by the Air Force, and lastly the Navy. (Only in the case of Britain is the Navy predominent.) That being the case it seemed to me that in order to get naval voices heard we had to establish a rapport where we could exchange information, get to know each other, and possibly be of some assistance in connection with shipbuilding programs, modern communications for ships, and so forth.

So I started on a program to get to know all of the CNOs in Europe. As I said, this called for a lot of traveling but that was okay with me. I would just as soon at that time get in a lot of traveling, having just gone through the traumatic experience of losing my wife of some thirty years.

Another thing that I found out was that very few people in the Sixth Fleet knew anything about CincUSNAVEUR. People would come up to London on leave from the Sixth Fleet and I had a chance to talk with some of them - they were a little fuzzy on where this guy up in London stood, who he belonged to, and who belonged to him.

So I went down to the Sixth Fleet and spent some time with them and gave a talk on who this guy in London was and what his position was. This had a very salutary effect.

Before I forget it I also want to mention that in getting people interested in the Sixth Fleet, I did a little spade work in General Lemnitzer's own headquarters and found out that very few of his general officers knew much about it. So I set up a series of programs which involved a rather steady flow of high ranking staff officers, mostly Army and Air Force people, from headquarters down to the Sixth Fleet - this was very beneficial because some of these people had little knowledge as to what navies were all about. (Incidentally in that respect General Eisenhower was very much up to date on navies. He had had occasion to use the Navy.)

Also I got to know a large number of American business men in the U. K. area. I would say that, generally speaking, they were almost uniformly a very high caliber group of people and they represented their companies well. But they also represented the U.S. well. They got along extremely well with the British people. They didn't make themselves obnoxious as so many tourists do. The American tourist is probably one of the most arrogant guys in the world without having very much reason to be so. I've seen too much of that. But the American military people overseas, generally speaking, are a great credit to the United States. The American business men overseas are a great credit to the U. S.

Q: This was really at the beginning of the great upsurge of locating plants abroad, was it not?

Griffin: That's correct, and so American business had some very sharp people over there.

I found that most of them played golf. So I ended up with a group of perhaps fifteen to twenty people who played golf every week-end. Although I was sitting there in Romany right in between two beautiful golf courses, I actually ended up playing more at Sunningdale which was only about ten minutes away by car because most of my friends played over there. Occasionally we would play at Wentworth at the Burma Road - called this because it was such a tough course. (That's where several of the big pro tournaments have taken place.) But we played usually on Saturdays and Sundays and holidays, and we played at nine o'clock. We had an eight o'clock service at church on Sunday morning in Virginia Water. I'd go to the eight o'clock service, and then make the nine o'clock time on the first tee. We didn't have any set games, we'd just appear as a group. If there were eight people we'd have two foursomes, if there were twelve we'd have three foursomes. If there were nine, we'd have three threesomes. We'd split up that way. We had small bets, none of this was large wagering, within a foursome and between foursomes. So it usually took about an hour to figure out who owed who what after we came back from playing golf. But it was a very wonderful experience for me with a fine group of people. Many of them are very dear friends of mine right to this date.

When I left there to go to Naples they presented me with a painting which I have upstairs here of one of the holes in Sunningdale. It's signed down below, presented to me, "With the great affection of his many friends at Sunningdale who have spent much pleasurable time playing with him, although he takes all the money,' or words to that effect. That's one of my treasured possessions.

As you are certainly aware London was sort of a crossroads, and so we had visitors that were coming through there almost all the time. Some times I would have them stay at the flat. It depended upon the status that they were in. If they were representing an American business on an expense account, I felt it was proper that they stay at a hotel. On the other hand, if they were on a personal trip I'd have them stay at the flat, provided that my one bedroom that I had for guests was available.

Among those who came over was Red Fay, he was the Under Secretary of the Navy at that time, and a great friend of President Kennedy's.

I mention him because he told me that his father was coming over on a round the world trip, and he would appreciate it very much if I would take care of him. He would not stay at the flat; he would stay at a hotel. If I would give him a ring and check in with him, he'd appreciate it very much.

It was a couple of months later that his father came. I got this call, and offered to set up various things for Mr. Fay, and found out that he wasn't feeling too well. I said, "Let me send a doctor over." He had been on the trip for a couple of months. I sent a doctor over there and found out that Mr. Fay had bruised his leg two weeks before that and it wouldn't heal, and he was having a real tough time. The doctor found out that he was taking strong medicine which had been prescribed by a doctor in Los Angeles to thin out his blood and apparently he misunderstood his instructions and he didn't stop, he just kept taking it. So when the doctor got Mr. Fay, he put him in the Air Force hospital right away, just outside of London and took him off of this medicine, and undoubtedly saved his live.

It was a very curious thing - this is a type of medicine that you only take for a short time to thin out the blood for a particular purpose - maybe you've got a small clot or something that you want to let dissolve. But he had been taking this for a long time, and as I say the bruise wouldn't even heal, nothing would heal. The doctors got him in the hospital in time and kept him under other medication for about a week.

Then we sent him down to Southhampton, after checking with the representative of the U. S. Line in London, and in turn with the doctor who was going to be on the UNITED STATES who assured us that he had equipment and everything to handle a case such as this on board. Then we sent him down to the UNITED STATES at Southhampton in an ambulance and put him on board to go back home. If he hadn't checked in with us I believe that he would have died, or certainly come very close to it.

Q: Admiral, you mentioned some time back that you had a trip to Holy Loch where we had atomic submarines stationed. Did you have jurdisdiction and cognizance also of Rota and the Spanish bases?

Griffin: Yes, but only for logistic support, and of course the relationships with the U. S. and the local people - in that case the Spaniards, in the other case the British. The actual operational control of the submarines remained with ComSubLant. They did not come under my operational control, he controlled them entirely. But we were responsible for their logistic support and for the necessary arrangements at Holy Loch and Rota.

Q: And just an incidental question - how did the British and the Spaniards as well react to the idea that we had atomic submarines based on their land?

Griffin: It was perfectly all right. The British, for example, only a very few fringe radicals would protest from time to time, but the great majority of the people accepted this. Of course the British authorities themselves were fully cognizant of it and had their own atomic power installation not far away.

At that time we had a special arrangement with the British on exchange of atomic information which we did not have with any other country in Europe. Therefore, this provided another element in the chain of relationships between Britain and the United States so far as atomic submarines were concerned.

The requirements that we had on our ships for inspection of the water and so forth, safety precautions that we had in effect, were fully acceptable by the British. In turn we urged them to go ahead and make their own tests with their own equipment to make sure that there was no effluent that would be harmful at all. It was a very carefully controlled thing.

As I say except for a few leftist radicals from time to time everything was fine. After all, the naval force there provided considerable support to the economy of the area. We had this special arrangement with Britain of exchange of atomic information, we provided them with the know how to build their own atomic submarines. It was a very close relationship.

The Spanish - while we didn't have an arrangement with them on exchange of atomic information, the Spanish were very understanding in this field. Having a base there helped their enonomy too. It also provided them with a lever, if you will, to get certain concessions from the United States. And believe me, these were all very much worthwhile because the Spanish were providing us with extremely fine facilities there that you couldn't get any other place. Having Rota available was the equivalent of having several additional Polaris submarines.

If we had to take all the submarines that were operating from Rota and shift them back to operating from the East Coast of the United States the transit time alone would be a serious factor. The amount of time that they'd be out of range of their missile targets would be a factor. When you add all these factors up you see that having the base at Rota was the equivalent of having x-number of additional Polaris submarines, because the name of the game was to keep the same number of missiles on target.

Q: When you made the grand tour of Europe visiting the CNOs, did you visit the Spanish CNO and the Portuguese CNO?

Griffin: Yes indeed, and enjoyed that very much.

As a matter of fact I still correspond from time to time with the Spanish Minister of Marine. Actually the CNO has died who was there when I was there. The one I was closest to there was the number two man, General Munoz Grandes. He was the number two to Franco - a very fine gentleman. He spoke no English, fortunately my Spanish was good enough so that I could carry on a fair conversation.

Q: Did you have anything to do with IberLant?

Griffin: No. I, of course, got a briefing on it when I was in Portugal.

This program had been underway for ten years, and it hadn't gotten off the drawing board. It took an awful long time to set that up. It got to be almost a joke with those of us who had been in the planning business for a long time.

Q: But it had something to do with Churchill, didn't it? The reason why it was so long delayed.

Griffin: That's one of them. But we many times thought it would never come to fruition.

It was a question of Command relationships over there, British and American. The relationship of the Sixth Fleet with the British forces in the Mediterranean was all mixed up in this too. I'll get into that later on -

Another thing that I'll mention - as a consequence of my

good friendship with these American business men and others in London I arranged for some of them to go down and visit the Sixth Fleet as guests. I had gotten authority from the Navy Department to fly them down there and go aboard units of the Sixth Fleet, and they went aboard at this particular time the carrier ENTERPRISE. The ENTERPRISE was in the Sixth Fleet.

They got a big kick out of going aboard a nuclear powered carrier and seeing flight operations day and night and seeing the other ships. They came back, and shortly thereafter I suggested to them that maybe they might like to start a London chapter of the Navy League of the U. S.

This is fact actually was done. The national President of the Navy League, Bob Barnum, was in the class of 1933 at the Naval Academy, a reserve Rear Admiral, and was special assistant to the President of U. S. Steel at the time - came over and set up the London chapter of the Navy League which is still functioning, and I hope is doing a good job.

One of the calls that I will always remember was the call on Pope Paul VI. The arrangements had been made for a private audience with him. I found this extremely interesting.

I had been part of a small party back just after the war with Admiral Mitscher - Mitscher, Burke, Anderson, and I together called on Pope Pius XII.

I had seen pictures of Pope Paul. He had of course followed John XXIII, who was probably the most liberal Pope that they had in modern time. I wondered just how this Pope would be, because from his pictures he looked more like Pius XII than he did like John XXIII. But in our discussions and in his actions he actually was nearer John XXIII than he was Pius XII.

We had a very, very interesting conversation. He understands some English. (I had some Spanish and a little French, but no Italian, and my Latin certainly never got me any place.) I spoke very slowly in English and he understood pretty much what I was saying. He had an interpreter, of course.

I had two aides of mine, plus the priest who had made the arrangements in London in Rome for this call. It was extremely interesting. Just at the tail end of it he signalled and a photographer came in and we lined up and two pictures were taken.

The interview started at eleven o'clock in the morning. About six o'clock that evening in the hotel we got a package of seventeen color pictures. According to my aide Mort Neely I said, "He shouldn't have done that. This is too much, this is too much." Mort said at the time, "Admiral, you just wait, don't go overboard here."

The next morning when we were leaving and Mort paid all of my bills he said, "Admiral, you know what was on your bill?" I said, "No." He said, "Eighteen color prints." I think it was about seventy-five bucks or something like that. He said, "Not only was it eighteen color prints you had to pay for, but you only got seventeen." He got the biggest kick out of that. I'll never forget it.

But it was a very, very interesting experience. Pope Paul is a very sharp man, tending to be liberal in some aspects, but from what I could see rigidly conservative in others. And that since has proved to be the case in several synods that they've had. His liberalism couldn't compare with John XXIII, and actually he's moving more and more in line with Pius XII from what I've been able to see.

One Friday afternoon I left the office to go out to Romany, I left about five o'clock, and on the way out I looked up and here was this Britisher driving a car alongside of us waving. So I rolled down the window. I'll never forget what he said. He said, "The President has been assassinated." And that was the day that Kennedy was shot in Dallas. He didn't say - your President. He saw my car (which was an American cadillac) with diplomatic plates on it and he knew that it was an American official in the car. He said, "The President has been assassinated," not "yours," but "the."

It was quite apparent that that was the way the British people felt about John Kennedy. He occupied a very warm spot in their hearts, which has been erased I'm sure a little bit now with the actions of his younger brother Teddy. He's been telling the British to withdraw their forces from Northern Ireland.

They set up immediately a book in the Embassy for signatures. The crowd got so tremendous they finally ended up with four books in the Embassy, each one of them with a long line of people coming in to sign their names.

I flew back for the funeral. I'll never forget that period. You couldn't turn on T.V. and hear anything else but for about three days - that's the only thing you could hear.

Q: This was in London?

Griffin: Yes, in London. The effect of the Kennedy assassination in Lodon was, from what I could see of all the British people, tremendous. He had come over there on a visit. Of course he was remembered when his father was the Ambassador there at the Court of St. James, as a young man who was very attractive with a wonderful personality.

His older brother (Joseph) was remembered annually at a place down on the coast of Britain from which he took off on the mission in which he was killed. They have a plaque in a little church down there. I sent a representative from my headquarters down there on the anniversary of Joe's death, John's older brother, and reported to Bobby Kennedy what I had done. I thought it would be of interest to him and the family - a report of the actual ceremony that took place there every year.

Stemming from all of these things and then Kennedy's own visit over there, which made a tremendous impression on the people, he was well received, his death was a terrific shock. He was a young man in the eyes of the British who was a harbinger of better things in the future, a young man with a bit in his teeth and President of the great United States, all ready to solve a lot of the ills of the world and so forth. Somewhat optimistic I might say, but nevertheless that's the way they felt.

As I say they ended up with four books in the American Embassy with lines running twenty-four hours around the clock.

I flew back to Washington for the services, then back to London the following Tuesday. We cancelled all the activities that we had for the remainder of the year, including our Christmas parties and so forth.

The traumatic effect of Kennedy's assassination continued for a considerable period of time in Britain.

Q: Did you have any relationships with the French? It was in 1964 that De Gaulle withdrew French officers from the NATO commands and the English Channel and so forth. Even though you weren't NATO yourself, did you have anything to do with the French?

Griffin: Yes, not too much, but the answer is yes.

In two things - the twentieth anniversary of the Normandy landings took place while I was there, and I was designated as the U. S. Navy representative for that. I went over and they had a series of ceremonies at various places, and I took all of those in. (Incidentally I have a little plaque which was given to the participants in this.) One thing that was noticable at all the ceremonies was the absence of De Gaulle, he didn't show up. He didn't show up at any of them. This was in 1964.

Incidentally, here is the little medallion that was given to me by Pope Paul. It was struck to commemorate his visit to the Holy Land.

Another thing of interest in the way of mementoes - this is the first round the world cruise of the nuclear powered task force - the ENTERPRISE, the LONG BEACH, and the BAINBRIDGE. This started in the Mediterranean - Commander Carrier Division Two. Rear Admiral Strean at that time was in command of that group.

This is from the deck planking of MIKASA, which was Tojo's flag ship at the Battle of Tsushima given to me by a group over there in '61 when I had the Seventh Fleet. Tojo just beat the devil out of the Russians.

Q: You said that De Gaulle didn't show up at any of the services

Griffin: De Gaulle did not show up at any of these services. He was still, I think, a little mad at the Americans and the British. There was only one service, and that was almost a private service, that he had in a ceremony on the outskirts of Paris where he made an appearance. But none of the affairs down on the coast were attended by him, which was very unusual.

He was quite an individual, but quite frankly the actions which he took did not come as any great surprise to me. As a matter of fact I discussed this with David Bruce on several ovvasions - principally his withdrawal of French forces from NATO and other actions which he took.

I had given this some thought and I finally ended up by writing a long dispatch back to the CNO analyzing De Gaulle and the actions that he might take. I thought this was timely because from the best I could see I didn't see any evidence of any study being made of this in the Joint Chiefs or in the Navy Department, and I thought that they should that they should be prepared.

I drafted this dispatch and took it over and showed it to David Bruce, and he read it very carefully and said he thought it was a fine dispatch.

In essence what I was driving at was - don't take De Gaulle lightly, that he really means what he says. He will never in his entire life forget what he considers to be the insulting manner in which Roosevelt and Churchill handled him during the war. That was true on one side. He was so intensely devoted to his own country that he felt the only way to let his country resume what he considered to be its normal and natural and proper place in history - in other words to increase the prestige on the mainland - was to decrease the American prestige on the mainland. As a consequence he would take actions which were calculated to produce these results.

One of the blind spots that he had, in my opinion, was that if by actions such as he was advocating the American influence in the continent was decreased he failed completely to appreciate the fact that the final result of that might well be that the German influence would increase rather than the French influence increasing. He missed that, I thought, entirely.

I said in essence - don't ever think that this guy is kidding around, because he's not. He's serious and he means business and anything can happen. And I think we ought to have contingency plans for complete withdrawal of all of his forces and for kicking all of the American headquarters out of France and other actions such as this.

It was six months later I guess when he actually did lower the boom and say, "You get your headquarters out of France."

To me it was clear as a bell that that's the way he was heading.

The big blind spot that I could see was his inability to see that the Germans would be the ones who would reap the great benefits of any diminution of American prestige on the continent of Europe.

Q: His intense nationalism, I suppose, prevented him from seeing that.

Griffin: That's right, he was intensely nationistic. And he did an awful lot for his country, no question about that. As I reported before earlier in these interviews, I was in Marseilles when he took over, and you could see the difference in the faces of the people. It was absolutely fantastic.

Q: You said there were two relationships with the French --

Griffin: I did want to comment just on De Gaulle.

The other was the French Navy. I called on the French CNO. Over there most of them are called Chiefs of Naval Staff same as CNO, but I use the term CNO for descriptive purposes. They were very nice, all the French that I talked to were very nice. They tended to be relatively incommunicado because for the most part I had the feeling they didn't want to take any action or say anything that could possibly get back to De Gaulle and cause him to think that they were being disloyal to him. So they were very, very careful.

The French in the Mediterranean were continuing to operate with the American forces in joint exercises, and things were going on fine. Many of these things De Gaulle did not know were going on. If you could do something without him finding out about it, fine. The French naval officers all wanted to do that very much, because they knew that they were getting a great deal of benefit out of the training exercises that were being conducted with the American forces. They wanted to continue it, but please don't put it in the newspapers, so to speak.

Some time later on, as a matter of fact, the flag ship of the Sixth Fleet had to shift its home port from southern France to Italy. I understand, I can't back this up completely, that De Gaulle did not know that the flag ship of the Sixth Fleet was home ported in Villefranche. When finally he found that out he immediately hit the overhead, and it wasn't too long before the flag ship of the Sixth Fleet was not home ported in Villefranche, they'd moved down to Italy.

Admiral Charles D. Griffin by John T. Mason
Washington, D. C. December 2, 1971

Q: As usual it's a pleasure to see you, Admiral. It's always stimulating to be with you.

Last time you had been talking about your tour of duty in London, and I think you want to continue today with that same tour.

Griffin: Yes indeed. It's good to be with you again.

The last time I believe I ended by talking about our relationships with the French. I think that this probably leads naturally into a brief discussion on some of the visits that I made while I was CincUSNAVEUR.

First let me comment on a visit which I made to Holland. It so happened that this visit was made in early May, of 1964, when the tulips were in full bloom. I've seen many pictures of tulips blooming in Holland, but it was the first time that I'd ever had a chance to see them personally. I must say that it's simply a gorgeous sight.

During the course of that visit I also visited Scheveningen. This is a seaport town, a resprt area, and it brought back memories of the visit which I had made there as a Midshipman. That was in 1924. At that time the people who ran the beach resort area had rules about going swimming. It would cost you so much to be permitted to put on a suit and go on the beach, it would cost you so much to put on a suit and go in the water, and it would cost you more to put on a suit and be able to stay on the beach or go in the water at your own discression. The latter also was a different kind of a suit. Some of the suits were horizontal stripes, others were vertical stripes, and the latter which allowed you to do everything had no stripes at all. Of course we knew nothing about it and didn't understand the Dutch language to begin with, so we all had the wrong type of suits on. Furthermore we never had seen anything like that before, so the whole visit that day to the beach area was a shambles because we were constantly in touch with the police for doing the wrong thing.

This latter visit here reminded me of that earlier one. It is a very lovely beach area. During the summer time these Dutch beaches are just packed with people.

I found the authorities in Holland very pleasant to deal with. All accept the fact that their country is no longer the great maritime power that it was, and I think accept it gracefully. It was a very pleasant visit.

Let me comment on the visit to Morocco. The principal bases that we had there, at the time of my visit in 1964, were all associated with our communications facilities. As you will recall, at one time we had several Strategic Air Command bases there.

We spent hundreds and hundreds of millions of dollars there, and I remember at one time a very senior Navy Admiral commented that at the rate we were going we were going to pave North Africa.

By the time of my visit the political situation had gotten to the point where it was no longer tenable for us to hold those bases. The pressures from the Arab world and other pressures were such that the Moroccans felt that they had to take over the Strategic Air Command bases, and such had been done at the time of my visit.

This left Kenitra, which was formerly known as Port Lyautey, in a rather peculiar position. It was rather tenuous. But in the discussions with the Moroccans it was pointed out that these Navy facilities were not being used for any offensive purposes, but merely to support our communication facilities in that part of the world. This view was accepted.

I might comment that at this time it was difficult to get answers out of the Moroccan government. The French, when they withdrew, took with them of course most of the know how in running governments and administrating governments. What we call 'civil servants' who were in important positions in the various departments of government and really made those departments function were almost entirely French. When they withdrew it left a very big vacuum there. The French had by no means taught the Moroccans how to run a government.

I can't help but contrast this with the way the British handled some of their possessions. For example, when the

British withdrew from South Asia they left India. However Indians in government had been trained by the British, and they were quite capable of running a soverign government themselves. This was not the case in Morocco at all.

When you consider the external influences played on the Moroccans, particularly on the King, Hussan, it was rather remarkable that the country was able to function at all. The pressure from the Algerians was very heavy. The border between Morocco and Algeria, particularly in the southern section, the exact location of this border has been very much in doubt for many years. As a consequence there were always a series of border incidents taking place, and that sort of kept the tribes stirred up in the area and little wars going on all the time.

Then when the French withdrew and left a rather unstable government in Morocco the countries knew this and began to apply pressure.

Morocco is a very interesting country to me, because with a good strong stable government it had everything really to make it pretty much of a paradise. It has a wonderful sea coast, and plenty of water. There are very large deposits of water underground down the south part of Morocco. They have the Atlas Mountains, which are beautiful. They have all kinds of minerals in those mountains. The country could grow agricultural products with the greatest of ease. And so it had everything going for it really to make it an extremely fine investment, you might say.

With regard to the difficulties in handling the governmental departments, in particular the relationship between the various departments of governments --

For example, in our country if a request comes in from a foreign country which involves two departments of government it's a very simple, easy matter for the two departments to get together and settle affairs in very short order. But it seemed to be almost impossible for this to happen in Morocco.

The people knew so little about the administration of departments of government that when any question came in, no matter how minor, it would be sent to one department, and there it had to go all the way to the top in that department, and then go from that department head over to the next department head, and then down to the action officer. So this could take an awful long time.

Q: What did the Moroccans do with the bases they took over?

Griffin: They used them ostensibly for housing. They wanted to provide better housing for their people. Many of the people who were lined up to go into these houses were accustomed to living in tents most of their lives. This was another thing that the Moroccans had a big problem on. They would move families into what we would call very nice low-income row houses, and they might stay one night under the roof and the next morning pitch a tent in the front yard. So they had difficulties.

Q: When was it you were in Morocco?

Griffin: That was in the summer of '64.

A comment now on the visit to Ankara - that was for the purpose of paying a call on Admiral Uran, who was the Chief of the Turkish Naval Staff. At that time General Sunay was the Chief of the Turkish General Staff, a very very fine old gentleman who had fought side by side with Inonu, who was the Prime Minister. The Prime Minister was over eighty at the time. Inonu and Sunay were people who worked very closely with Ataturk.

Inonu at this time was the prime Minister, he was over eighty and in not too good health, and he was the last stronghold in government of the Ataturk regime.

The position of the Chief of General Staff in Turkey has always been interesting to me. No matter what kind of government they had in Turkey the Chief of the General Staff occupies a very strong position, and if in the opinion of the armed forces the politicians who are running the government at the time are not doing it properly they don't hesitate to move in and take over.

Sunay was the Chief of General Staff, and he was one of the more, shall we say, enlightened and less militant individuals. This does not mean that he was not strong, because he was, a very strong individual.

I will comment later on in these talks more in detail when I get to discussions with the Turks at the time when I was CincSOUTH.

I did want to comment on who were there at this time, because Sunay is at the present time the President of Turkey.

My visit to Athens was a very pleasant one, and I must point out that all these visits were for the purpose of seeing the Chief of the Naval Staff and establishing a rapport with all of these naval chiefs in various countries. As I indicated earlier I felt that one of the things that I could do which would be beneficial to all the naval establishments of Europe would be to establish a good rapport with all of the Chiefs of the Naval Staffs. That was the purpose of these visits.

At the time of my visit to Athens Mr. Garafolius was the Defense Minister. He was a very brilliant lawyer who had a law degree from England. He was a very wealthy business man also, and proved to be a very fine Defense Minister. I'll have more to comment on about him later on when I also get to the CincSOUTH part of this talk.

At this time Mr. Papandreou, George Papandreou, was the Prime Minister. His son, Andreas Papandreou, was not very active at least on the surface at that time. Vice Admiral Angarus was the Chief of the Naval Staff, and Lieutenant General Pipilis was the Chief of the General Staff.

These visits were all very very pleasant. I found the Greeks very easy to get along with. They seemed to speak the same language as we. Of course they have a long history of maritime work and employment, and it was rather easy to talk to them.

I had a visit also to Norway. This was a very interesting one. This was to attend a ship launching. The Norwegians were building several what they called frigates. It's smaller than what the Americans call a frigate. It was more of a DE, rather than a frigate. One of them was being launched at a yard outside of Oslo, and I attended as the U. S. representative because the U. S. was providing about fifty percent of the cost of this ship.

Q: Why?

Griffin: Because they promised to make these ships available to NATO for common defense. This was also part of our commitment to many countries in the way of Foreign Aid. It was a combination of these two things.

Princess Astrid was the sponsor of this ship. They had something that I had never seen before. Instead of having the sponsor take a champagne bottle and physically break it on the bow of the ship, which has caused the United States some very humorous incidents including several women who have missed the ship entirely with the bottle which is always considered to be a sign of poor luck for that ship, the Norwegians had pretty much of a fool proof affair. They had a ribbon which was on a little platform, when the sponsor cut that ribbon it released the bottle which was on the end of about a ten foot rope and had a fulcrum about half way between the platform and the ship - the ribbon was cut, the bottle was released and it swung down, and there wasn't any question about the fact that the bottle was going to hit the ship. And the lady never got splashed. This worked quite well.

The King was the principal speaker at the luncheon which followed this launching. And very much to my surprise at the end of his talk he introduced me for remarks - this was the first time that I understood that I was expected to make any remarks.

Q: Had you known him in Washington during the war?

Griffin: No, I had not known him in Washington.

He was a very fine gent, he was very athletic, he was a member of the Norwegian Olympic Ski Team. He did a fine job.

I recall that during his speech, which he made half in Norwegian and half in English, the wife of the Norwegian CNO sitting next to me leaned over and whispered, "He speaks better English than he does Norwegian."

I made some impromptu remarks which seemed to go all right. It was a very pleasant visit to Norway.

Let me comment on just a few other visits - a visit to Rome, the highlight of which really was a private audience with the Pope. I had been interested in seeing the Pope, because I had been a member of a party which had private audience with Pius XII. In the meantime John XXIII had been the Pope for awhile, and now Paul VI was the Pope. From pictures that I had seen of Paul I was sort of under the impression that he was more like Pius XII than John XXIII, but some of his actions which he was taking seemed to be quite liberal as compared to Pius XII.

Our meeting was a very cordial one. I was warned that he could understand some English if I spoke very, very slowly, which I did. My principal trust of my arguments was to get across to him the real meaning of the Sixth Fleet's motto, which was "Power for Peace." I also extended an invitation to him to visit the Sixth Fleet some time if he could do so.

The Pope at the end presented me with a silver medalion which had been struck to commemorate his visit to the Holy Land, which I have here on the table on which I have several memorabilia.

One very humorous thing happened. This interview took place at eleven o'clock in the morning. Just before we left the Vatican photographer came in and took pictures of our group. I had two of my personal aides, the Monsignor who had arranged the visit, and the U. S. Naval Attache in Rome were in the party. We had our picture taken with the Pope.

Later on that afternoon about six o'clock this package arrived at the hotel. I opened it up and there were seventeen color pictures of this group. I commented very, very strenuously, "This was too nice, it was too much, and the Pope shouldn't have done this," and on and on. My aide said, "Admiral, don't go overboard too much on this."

The next morning my aide said, "Admiral you remember talking last night about how good the Pope was and all."

I said, "Yes." He said, "Well if you recall I said don't go overboard on it." I said, "What do you mean?" He said, "There's an item on your bill at the hotel for eighty bucks for eighteen pictures, and you only got seventeen."

Q: These visits you made were almost in the NATO category weren't they?

Griffin: They really were, except this was entirely on the U. S. Navy side. The visit to the Pope was a little bit out of that character. But nevertheless the essential purpose of all these visits was to establish a rapport, as I said before, with the Chief of the Naval Staffs so that we could be in a position of exchanging information, writing letters back and forth to each other and so forth, and we'd understand each other much better.

The visit to Madrid also was most interesting. Admiral Nieto was the Minister of Marine there at that time, and he in fact ran the navy. The Spanish had, of course, an admiral who was their CNO, Chief of the Navy Staff, but he occupied a much weaker position, shall we say, in the organization than would be normal in these circumstances. This was because of the way Franco wanted to run it, and p ticularly that his number two wanted to run it - at that time Captain General Munoz-Grandes was the individual who ran Spain under the direction of course of the Premier.

Munoz-Grandes had been a very close friend of Franco for

many, many years, and he in fact ran most of the details. Franco made the policy decisions, but Munoz-Grandes carried them out. He was Captain General, he was the Chief of the High General Staff, and he was the Vice President to the Cabinet. He ran Spain.

I had pleasure talking to him. My Spanish wasn't too good and he had very little English at all, but I found that I could carry on a conversation with him. We covered the waterfront whenever I was there on a visit, and I enjoyed talking to him.

He was a very positive individual - there wasn't any question about where Spain stood in the world and of their relationships with the communists and so forth. He was always interested in making sure that the United States understood the dangers of many things, particularly that of the ultra-liberals and the communists.

Admiral Nieto as Minister of Marine was really in that job because he was a very close friend of Franco's, and he was one of his constant companions whenever Franco wanted to go on a hunting trip or a fishing trip or something like that - Nieto was always with him. That's why he occupied that position.

The Spanish were very strong for the United States. They were distressed at some of the actions that the United States would take from time to time, but at the same time, so far as I was concerned, they could be counted on to back us up in case of any difficulty. And certainly their feelings were very much proved by the actions which they took in making bases available to us, some times under very considerable pressure to do otherwise.

Q: Did they seem to understand our political system?

Griffin: They understood our political system, but they'd keep coming back and say, "Why don't you take a stronger position?" They could get in some nice little digs, there was no question about that.

They, generally speaking, would prefer to talk to a military man. It was for that reason really that Forrest Sherman was sent over there to conduct the negotiations for the Spanish bases. That was about 1953, '54.

Q: Was that before John Lodge was there?

Griffin: That was before John Lodge was there.

These were all military people. A foreign military man could get across points much better with them than our Ambassador could.

This of course created a situation in Madrid that had to be handled very much with kid gloves, because if the American Ambassador happened to be one who was a little bit thin-skinned and liked to stand on his own normal prerogatives he would certainly have a tough time with the senior American military man there, who for many years was Lieutenant General Donovan of the U. S. Air Force. He, Donovan, had two tours of duty there. On many occasions he conducted directly negotiations for the American government, and then would inform the American Ambassador afterwards as to what the decision was. This is not a very good way of doing business, but it just recognized the facts of life in Madrid at that time.

The Ambassador who accepted this got along extremely well. I know that Ambassador Woodward, who is really a wonderful gentleman, didn't like it, but he recognized the facts of life there and accepted. As a consequence he was tremendously effective. Simply as a result of being willing to accept something that was quite unusual.

Now let me comment on one other thing - during this period of time I was a bachelor Commander-in-Chief. As you recall, my wife had died very suddenly when I arrived in London. This was something that I must admit I was not prepared to take very gracefully. There were all kinds of things that happened. I got many suggestions that, "Don't you think that since you no longer have a wife, don't you think you ought to retire," and all kinds of things like that. Hostesses would try to pair me up. I'm sure they were merely trying to be kind.

I never thought about it before, but for the first time in my life I found that I could be very lonely in a crowd. I had never really heard that expression before, or else if I had I didn't pay any attention to it. But for the first time, after some thirty years of marriage, I found that it is quite true - one could be quite lonely in a crowd.

I was sent back in May of that year, '64, (this was after the Holland visit) to be President of the Flag Selection Board.

There were many things that happened during that visit in Washington. My mother and father were still living in their house in Silver Spring. I determined it was just a matter of a relatively short time before they simply would not be able to handle their house, so I made arrangements for them to move into an apartment during that trip. This made the trip very busy, because I was working from about eight o'clock in the morning until seven or eight o'clock at night on the Selection Board every day. However, I did make the plans for my mother and father to move. They are still, incidentally, in that apartment that I moved them into at that time.

It so happened that two of my closest friends here in Washington with whom I had gone to school, Helen and Channing Walker had a dinner party for me one of the nights. At that dinner party I was introduced to a Mrs. Shaefer who was a widow living in Washington. It turned out that we had many, probably thirty of forty, mutual friends, but we had never met. It came out in the conversation that evening that she was scheduled to make a North Cape cruise that summer. So to make a long story short - the conversation that evening and in correspondence to follow up on this, I suggested that she cut her North Cape cruise short and spend a little time in London. This she did at the end of the cruise. It was during that time that we became engaged. We were married on the 21st of November in Washington.

Q: That was a very happy development.

13 Griffin - 615

Griffin: It certainly was.

Let me now get to a very interesting incident that happened during my stay in London.

Mr. Churchill had been ill for some time, was failing and finally died. Among the important people who came to the funeral was General Eisenhower. He came over for the funeral, not as a part of the official delegation but as a personal friend of the Churchill family. He was invited in that category.

He arrived in London and stayed at the Dorchester. I called on him and extended to him an invitation to come over and see his old headquarters building. Part of the planning for the OVERLORD operation had taken place in 20 Grosvenor Square, which was my headquarters building, and had been his headquarters building before the OVERLORD operation. There's a plaque outside the building which invites everyone's attention to that fact.

He said that he would like very much to come over to see the building later on, but at that time he was waiting for a call and two or three other items to come to fruition. However, extended an invitation to me to come over and chat with him while he was waiting for these telephone calls. So I went over and talked to him for about an hour and a half. It was an extremely interesting conversation, much of it was just in a form of reminiscing on his part, but it covered a number of interesting points.

I'll tell you one very humorous thing that he mentioned. He said, "You know, because of my general heart condition, my doctors will not permit me to watch the Army-Navy game in person, on T.V., or listen to it on radio. They have ordered me to go out and play golf, and when the game is over to come on in and have some one then tell me what the final score is. Then I can watch replays of it. This has come about because the doctors know that I feel so strongly about this game that they are quite concerned that if I don't know the final score I will have a fatal heart attack. And therefore, they have taken this precautionary measure."

I thought that this was extremely interesting. And there's no question about it - he just felt mighty strongly about the Army-Navy football game.

It's perfectly obvious that he was a very smart politician, he was to begin with. It took a smart politician to take all of those people over in Europe and get them to pull together as a team.

I talked to people who knew him, who were on his staff at the time he was the Supreme Commander in Europe, who have pointed out how he could handle difficult assignments, personel wise, with the greatest of ease, and have these people who would be normally fighting with each other working together in the greatest of harmony.

Recently I had occasion to talk with George Reedy, who was Johndon's press secretary at one time and who had been a long time member of the Democratic National Committee hierarchy. He asked me did I know Eisenhower. I said, "Well I didn't know him all that well, but I felt I knew him fairly well." He said,

"I have been giving an awful lot of thought to President Eisenhower, particularly since I wrote the book about President Johnson and the presidency (Twilight of the Presidency). I'd like to try this reaction on you for size. I am now getting the feeling that Eisenhower was much smarter than most people gave him credit for."

I said, "George, I couldn't agree with you more. All the polls and everything say that he's way down the bottom quarter of presidents, but I don't agree with that. I don't agree with it at all. He took a war situation (Korea) and calmed it down in a devil of a hurry. He kept the country in good shape economically and so forth. And he did it with a great deal of difficulty because he was in the hospital so much of the time. He was a great man."

"My feeling is that he was smart enough to achieve things like this - for example the Democratic National Committee would have set up a course of action which they were convinced would be embarrassing for the President and this would be put into effect. It wouldn't be until perhaps six or eight months or a year later that they'd find out that they were actually largely conned into this position by Eisenhower himself."

George Reedy said that he had arrived at precisely the same feeling about many things that they had done, and this was the purpose of his conversation with me.

The net result of this whole thing, of course, really is that I am convinced that Eisenhower on good mature analysis, rather than being one of our poor presidents, will turn out to be in history one of our greater presidents. This is with the perspective of time.

That's one major point that I'd like to make about him.

He possessed great understanding of the place in history and the value of naval forces, and I might say in particular that of attack carriers which in the minds of many Army or Air Force people had been a very controversial subject. I want to emphasize carriers because carriers played almost a neglibile role in his OVERLORD operation going across the channel. They were not employed in that; there was no place for them there.

So it's a great credit to his understanding, the broadness of his vision, that he understood so well the place of naval forces, and in particular carriers. He was a strong advocate of having effective naval forces, and particularly carriers, even at the expense some times of cutting down on Army and Air Force forces. He could see that quite clearly. Also he was quite willing to discuss the personalities of some U. S. Navy people that he knew - some he liked, some he didn't.

Q: Some of this took place during your conversation with him?

Griffin: All of this took place during the conversation with him at the Dorchester.

He thought that the two finest Navy people that he had known were Radford and Anderson. He probably thought as much of George Anderson as of any Naval individual he ever saw.

You will recall that after the war when Ike first was made the Supreme Commander in Europe - he went over there with a very small staff. However, there was no one on it from the U. S. Navy.

At that time George Anderson was on the Sixth Fleet Staff. He was moved from the Sixth Fleet Staff up to Paris to be on Ike's Staff as the senior U. S. Navy individual. Anderson was a Captain at that time.

During the months that followed, there occurred the development of the SacEUR Staff, the writing of many position papers, the setting up of NATO in Europe - Anderson was right in there with him. His comments, his staff work, and such - Ike said that he could not have had a better job done by anyone, and it extended not only in just purely naval subjects but in all broad subjects in the military-political spectrum as effecting Europe.

He, of course, thought very highly of Radford. Raddy was CincPac, and I was his Plans Officer, when the President-designate came out headed for his trip to Korea. It was then that he selected Raddy to be Chairman of the Joint Chiefs of Staff.

He was very lukewarm on Admiral Denfeld, and simply did not like Carney at all and made no bones about saying so.

I just want to say that this was a conversation which I will always treasure. It was largely in the form of reminiscences, and I've hit the highlights of these things as I remembered them.

Q: Did he reminisce about his period in London?

13 Griffin - 620

Griffin: Yes, to a degree, but not too much. I think so much had been written on that that he felt that this was common knowledge and he wanted to hit on some things that had not been written about. His own book, <u>Crusade In Europe</u>, had covered so much of the details of the planning and the relationships with the countries concerned and representatives of these countries.

Relationships with the Joint Chiefs of Staff and with the Combined Chiefs of Staff - he didn't, except casually, refer to them from time to time. I didn't get into any of the details like that. This was really more on a personal basis.

He recalled with great pleasure my treatment of him and his son and daughter-in-law when he made his visit out to the Philippines and to the Far East. We chatted about that for quite some time. I never will forget that day - that was a terrific day for him. Here he was not too young, and had had a very serious illness. The temperature that day was ninety-five degrees and the humidity about the same. He was going from eight o'clock in the morning until late that night, and in the middle of the day got the word that he can't go to Japan. This was all calculated to be not too easy on his heart.

He reminisced about that for some time, and expressed again his pleasure at being able to just be on board ship and relax for a couple of days. It gave him the breathing spell that he needed.

The day of the Churchill funeral was also the day of another event in London. I mentioned before that I had a WAVE aide on my staff whose name was Paula Fish. She had been with me in the Seventh Fleet, and back in Washington, and now was one of my staff as assistant aide in London. She had met another officer on my staff, a Lieutenant Commander named Pat Ragan, and they decided to be married. Their marriage was set up a couple months ahead of time, and it ended up being on the same day as the Churchill funeral. Just getting around London that day really was quite difficult. So rather than having a big reception at the hotel where it had been planned and which was down at the west end and close to alot of the activities around St. Paul's, they had the reception at our flat in the headquarters building. The marriage took place at a church only about three blocks away, so we could do it all by foot. And I had the pleasure of giving her away in marriage.

I might say that, parenthetically, they were here in Washington last Friday and Saturday with a young baby. The little girl was christened at St. Albans Church last Friday, the day after Thanksgiving. Mrs. Griffin and I are Godparents.

I have a note on one thing that happened the latter part of '64. I must admit that I had been in the habit of keeping the heat on my communicators all the time. Whenever we had a breakdown of communications or something would happen or a message was delayed or missed or what have you, I would tend to have a habit of saying, "Well, I guess we'll have to go back to the days of the carrier pigeons. I guess I'd better get some here, because that's the only way we seem to be able to communicate." I'd also point out that back in the days of the Roman Empire they could get a message from Rome to Constantinople in twenty-four hours using the towers that the Romans had built. I said, "Some times we can't do as well as that."

An officer who was on my staff, the Assistant Chief of Staff of Communications, a Captain in the Navy was being detached. He arrived at my office to make his farewell call and brought a box. The box was about a foot on each side. I noticed that there were some holes in the box. He presented the box to me, and I held the box up and looked in these holes and there I was eye to eye with a pigeon. That tickled the devil out of me.

I must admit that all of this had some effect. We did improve in communications, and with many of the changes that had been made as a consequence of my early moves in this direction it was gradually improving our communications ability. And we were working to getting afully automated system there in the headquarters building. That work was preceeding very, very nicely.

Q: What is the background to your special interest in this area?

Griffin: The principal reason is that any operator depends on communication to a very, very severe extent. I had been in plans and operations for most of my career. Usually when something broke down, or something went wrong, it was because of faulty communications. And therefore, I made an effort to improve this field as much as I possibly could.

As I indicated before I went back to Washington on a very pleasurable trip in the latter part of November. Mrs. Griffin, Marion, and I were married on the 21st of November.

I arrived there the morning of the 20th and Mrs. Griffin met me at the Washington National Airport. I had a Navy aircraft. She met me at the airport and then dropped me at the Pentagon, where I had business. Our plans were that we were to meet in the afternoon about three o'clock and have a talk with the minister who was going to perform the ceremony the next day. Then we were going to get together that night with my parents and her mother and other friends.

We landed at eight o'clock in the morning. She met me at the airplane and drove me to the Pentagon, and then started back towards her house driving north in Rock Creek Park. As you undoubtedly know at that time of the morning Rock Creek Park is one way coming south. This was all so exciting to her that she forgot all about that; she went around the corner and was in a collision with another car around that corner. She later called and told me about that. She said, "He wasn't nice at all. In fact he wasn't a gentleman, he was so mad. I told him that I was being married the next day, and it didn't make any difference to him at all." I said, "Who was this?" She said, "Well, the Chief Justice," (the Chief Justice of the United States, Mr. Warren).

13 Griffin - 624

The Park policeman that came there looked around and said, "You know this is the first time I've seen two cadillacs come together in the Park for a long time."

It seems as though the Chief Justice was late for a very urgent meeting of the Supreme Court, and he ended up by getting in a little Volkswagon with a chap who came by and took him to the Supreme Court Building. His chauffeur said that the Chief Justice was very upset and very nervous because a month before that he had been in a rather serious accident. He himself didn't get hurt badly, but he got shaken up, so he had been sort of jumpy about automobile accidents.

Some of the ultra-conservative friends of ours I'm afraid chose to comment that "maybe you didn't hit him hard enough."

An interesting follow-up on that - after we were married we went to the Homestead for our honeymoon, and came back in time to ride up with the Chief of Naval Operations to the Army-Navy game in Philadelphia in his train. The CNO was Admiral McDonald One of the other guests of the CNO was Justice Potter Stewart. During the trip up to Philadelphia, he regaled everybody with the story of the Chief Justice arriving very disheveled, mad, talking about some crazy woman who tried to run him down in the Park, and all this that and the other. Bunny let him go on for quite some time and finally she turned to him and said, "That was me." So we had a great time discussing that.

After the Army-Navy game we came back to London. Later we went over to Berchtesgaden, Germany. We spent Christmas over there with my good friends of a long time, General and Mrs. Paul Freeman, who was at that time Commander-in-Chief of U. S. Army Forces Europe.

Just after getting back to London I was alerted by the CNO that I was probably going to go to Naples to relieve Admiral Russell as CincSOUTH. His tour of duty there would normally have ended at the end of March of '65. However, Mrs. Russell, his wife, was very critically ill of cancer and had been sent back to Washington. The prognosis in the late fall was that it would be a miracle if she would live much beyond Christmas. So I had been alerted for an early move down there in the event Admiral Russell chose to retire early because of these circumstances.

However he decided not to, and he stayed on until his normal time of retirement. In the meantime, much to everyone's surprise Mrs. Russell continued to live in Washington at the hospital at Bethesda, and actually lived until a week after he returned in April. It was absolutely amazing, and the doctors could find no reason for her being able to live that long in all their medical experience. It was just a question that she was determined that she was going to do it, and she did until Russell was relieved and came back there.

Finally, In received orders to go down to Naples as Cinc SOUTH and all preparations were made to leave the latter part of March to go right on down. I saw no purpose to be served at that time for taking any leave, and so I didn't request any.

Admiral Jimmy Thach, a classmate of mine, who was Op-05,

the Deputy Chief of Naval Operations for Air, was designated as my relief and he came over. I turned over to him the latter part of March and immediately flew down to Naples.

Q: Before you turn your attention in that direction, to the Mediterranean, I wonder if you would comment on several points that I'd like to raise.

In July of 1964 the British announced the withdrawal to the home waters of their Mediterranean-based submarines, and this also was true I understand of the surface units. This reflects a changed policy on the part of the Royal Navy. The Mediterranean had always been a mare nostrum for them for many generations. Do you want to talk about that change in policy because it occurred during your regime in London?

Griffin: Yes. It was not really so much a change in policy as it was a reflection of the economic facts of life that were facing the British government. They were not doing too well economically.

The balance of payments was a major problem for the British at that time. The United States was having difficulty also in this respect. However, the United States problem was not nearly as great as was the British. This was something many Americans did not seem to appreciate. The British were having real trouble. Their economy was in bad shape; they just had to retrench.

For years they had been covering the world, so to speak, with their forces. They had relatively strong forces stationed in the Far East Station with headquarters in Singapore. They provided naval forces for the U. N. action in the Korean affair. They stood by always to react to emergency situations in the Persian Gulf area, in the Indian Ocean in general, and of course, the life line to India - the Mediterranean. This certainly had been a mare nostrum so far as the British are concerned.

However, they arrived at a point where they simply had to retrench. The three big areas for consideration were the Far East Station with headquarters at Singapore, their total investment shall we say in the Arabian Peninsula area, and in the Mediterranean.

The difficulties associated with cutting things loose in Singapore were very obvious. They had been having tremendous difficulty in Malaya, and it had finally gotten to the point where for the first time communist guerrilla activities had been taken care of. The only way to continue that, and to continue the development of Malaya as an independent entity, and to help continue the progress that New Zealand and Australia were making was by keeping the U.K. naval presence in the Singapore area. So that was one of the last things that they wanted to relinquish.

Another thing that they hesitated to do at that time was to cut too rapidly their land-based holdings and activities in the Arabian Peninsula area; Aden was the headquarters.

This, therefore, left them with the Mediterranean. Since the Mediterranean was relatively close to the British Isles, they felt that they could in fact withdraw sizable units from the Mediterranean, put them in the home fleet, and then to do as much as the United States had done - rotate units from the home fleet to the Mediterranean.

Q: Except in our case we had a fleet in being in the Mediterranean.

Griffin: That's correct.

They had a Mediterranean fleet for many, many years, and it was headed up by a British Admiral in Malta. The size of the British Navy, however, had gradually been cut and cut and cut. So they simply didn't have enough left to spread all over the place.

The decision was made very reluctantly. And since the United States had the fleet which the British felt could take on much of the responsibility that had been formerly provided by the British fleet there, since that fleet included some submarines, they decided to go ahead and move their own forces out.

This caused a lot of difficulty in many places, particularly in Malta because the British Naval Forces that had been home-ported in the Mediterranean provided the work and the labor that was necessary to keep the naval shipyards in Malta going. Once that work load dropped people were being laid off from the shipyards there. It made a major difference in the economy of Malta, and actually precipitated the situation which we have at the present time there. It must be remembered that the principal element of the Maltese economy was the shipyards.

Q: Why was it not possible for the Sixth Fleet to use more frequently the facilities at Malta?

Griffin: This was one thing that was done, it was during my time when I was CincSOUTH. I worked very closely with the new CincUSNAVEUR on this and we sent U. S. ships down to Malta and put them in the dockyards and had a lot of work done on them just for the purpose of providing the income, revenues, that were needed to help the economy of Malta.

During this entire time, of course, the Maltese government was not a very strong one. One of the strongest individuals in Malta was Dom Mintoff, who was the labor leader and who now is the Prime Minister.

The situation there gradually got increasingly worse, precipitated of course largely by the withdrawal of the British Navy and other Army and Air units. The British air, land, and naval units were all there in Malta. With so many of those withdrawn it affected the economy very adversely.

The first thing that the government of Malta did, and this was before Mintoff came in, this was with the old government, was they recognized the Soviet Union. They did this by permitting the Russian Ambassador to London to also represent the Russian government in Malta. This was done very much over the objection of the United States, not officially but they were informed that the United States government was not looking favorably on this because we were very conscious of the effect of having good shipyards opened up to Russian ships in the Mediterranean.

To get back to the number one question here - the withdrawal of the British forces. This was simply something that had to be done because of the overwhelming financial pressures on the U.K. government. They just didn't have the funds to keep them going.

Q: Do you recall any conversations with Royal Navy officers at the time?

Griffin: Yes. The Royal Navy was very unhappy about this.

And it was along about this time that the decision was also made to cut from their building program a couple of carriers that had been previously planned and rather to go ahead with the development of land-based aircraft. This was a decision which was of course accepted by the Royal Navy, but not very graciously and precipitated the resignation of Sir David Luce the First Sea Lord. He resigned in protest. And the First Lord of the Admiralty resigned in protest over this decision.

I guess from the practical point of view the British government felt that they had to do this, although it hit the Royal Navy very hard.

The story that they told about the land-based aircraft being able to do the job that the Navy had been doing fell on deaf ears, because it was quite apparent to anyone who knew anything about that sort of thing that they simply couldn't do it. They couldn't do the job in the Indian Ocean, for example, with long-range aircraft which you could do with naval forces. You just simply couldn't do it.

On the practical side, British aviation had been taking quite a beating, and it was about ready to go down the drain. The Australian government had decided to buy some United States aircraft rather than British aircraft, which of course cost millions of millions of pounds to develop. This was pretty much the last straw for the British aviation industry. If on top of that they had wiped out the long-range bomber program for the RAF this would have left the RAF with nothing but some fighters, intercepters, helicopters, and so forth. It would have just completely ruined the RAF, and also would have removed one of the few possible markets for British aviation industry.

So with all of these things being fed in the hopper the decision was made to go ahead with the bomber program. It was, I think, quite obvious to many people at that time that even the bomber program was not going to help British aviation very much. They were really in the doldrums.

I talked to quite a number of people over there about this, including some civilians who were mixed up in the business of government contracts, and I recall using this argument - "Unless the British aviation industry is successful in selling its products outside of the Commonwealth, it's simply not going to be able to function." I pointed out that, "In the Commonwealth you don't have enough buying power to provide the funds necessary to stoke this tremendous industry. This is how the United States does it. The United States companies are selling their aircraft all over the world."

And as a consequence of that later on the British government in fact did take this chap to whom I was talking, Sir Ray Brown - he was Ray Brown at that time - (He was the President of Rayco Electric Company there. He had been very successful in selling a lot of his products to countries all over the world, including the United States.) and put him in the job of selling British products worldwide. He did so well on this that they knighted him. He has been a good friend of mine all these years, and I still correspond with him from time to time.

Q: This was another area where the British had to break out of their previous concept of the Empire, wasn't it, and become a worldwide Commonwealth.

Griffin: Right, and the only way they could do it would be to get markets for their products worldwide. They had to do it. They just simply couldn't afford to put out the money for large military forces to stand guard around the world. They had just gotten out of that, and they recognized it. It was a shame to see a country that had been so great for so long just fall very, very gradually but surely into a second class status.

Q: Simultaneously, Navy wise they began to develop Polaris-type submarines and nuclear-powered submarines, the DREADNAUGHT.

Griffin: They felt the one way they could continue to be a world power of first magnitude, and to keep a seat at the table so to speak, was to be able to pariticipate in the strategic deterrent role. It was quite obvious that sitting there on that island, having land-based bombers, would not satisfy that condition. They had to have it in something that was protected, and that was the nuclear submarines.

The United States, as I mentioned before, had a special agreement with the United Kingdom which permitted us to give them certain nuclear information. This was by no means all inclusive, but we could give the British certain information withou violating the terms of the Atomic Energy Act of 1954, to permit them, with equipment developed in the United States, to build Polaris submarines and other nuclear attack submarines, but principally Polaris submarines. So they went ahead with that as being their least expensive way of keeping a seat at the strategic deterrent table.

Q: They had to sacrifice to do it.

Griffin: And they had to sacrifice to do that, no question about it. They had to sacrifice tremendously to do it. It was really a shame to see this great power just crumbling away on all sides as a consequence of a perfectly horrible economic situation. I can't believe that they even realized the importance of productivity.

Q: I'm sure this was a NATO matter, but perhaps you had something to do with in - in 1964 Secretary McNamara announced that the BIDDLE, which was a missile destroyer, would have an international crew. This was an experimental thing, and European navies contributed to this conglomerate crew.

Griffin: This was an idea which had been actually developed by Walt Rostow. People in the Pentagon, principally the Navy Department, were briefed on this when I was the Deputy Chief for Fleet Operations and Readiness.

I must say that we didn't think very much of it. The idea was to have each one of these crews an international crew. But when you get people from different backgrounds, with different dietary habits, in the habit of serving under different discipline, and so forth, and put them into very close cramped quarters on ship, and particularly submarines (the idea was also that if it worked well with the BIDDLE it would be expanded all the way to submarines), we just didn't think that this would work. We didn't think it would work at all.

But the decision was made to go ahead with it, to try it out. As a matter of fact when I was in London, Admiral Ricketts, who was then Vice Chief of Naval Operations, came over there on a couple of occasions to make talks on the subject. He was the U. S. Navy's expert in this field. And as a matter of fact when he died the name of the BIDDLE, with the approval of the Biddle family, was changed to the CLAUD V. RICKETTS.

There was considerable lack of enthusiasm for this project

on the part of the countries to whom I talked. So I don't really think the thing ever really got off the ground.

Q: How did they handle the language barrier?

Griffin: The individuals were assigned to the crew and given instructions in English. All the crew members had to be bilingual.

This is not too unknown really. International aviation uses English for the towers, so the tower operators and pilots of aircraft have to know some English.

The people were highly selected, no question about it. They were the cream of the crop. But there were just too many obstacles in the way of having something like that work.

This is sort of like Wendell Wilkie's 'one world' idea. The world wasn't ready for something like that.

Q: And who'd have thought in a military sense we could become one world.

There was an operation, a very interesting one, called STEEL PIKE in southern Spain which occurred in October of '64 and involved a number of our naval vessels and at least 60,000 of our Marines and Navy personnel. Did you have anything to do with that?

Griffin: Yes, largely however, in the support role.

This exercise was done under the overall command of Cinc LANT Fleet in coordination with the Spanish. The forces that were employed in the Mediterranean remained under the command of Commander Sixth Fleet, and therefore, under my command. In the Atlantic they were under CincLANT Fleet, then Commander Second Fleet and ComPhibLant.

However, the Sixth Fleet provided some forces for Steel Pike. When they operated in the Mediterranean, they remained under the command of the Sixth Fleet, but they had orders to report to Second Fleet for additional duty. They carried out their operations from the Mediterranean, actually largely under the control of the Atlantic Command rather than the European Command.

The idea was, of course, to have this in Spain principally to reassure the Spanish as to the willingness of the United States, to support them even though several NATO countries opposed firmly any overtures to Spain about joining NATO.

NATO, particularly the northern socialistic end of NATO - the Scandanavians and the British - very much opposed any thoughts of Spain getting associated with NATO. We were all aware of the difficulties between Spain and the United Kingdom over Gibraltar.

So the idea here was to bolster up the courage, so to speak, of the Spanish and to restore, if this was necessary, any failing confidence in the American-Spanish relationship field.

There were some in Spain who felt that - the Americans are giving us a run around. They make all these promises and so forth, but when the chips are actually down they won't be in here to help us.

In this type of exercise it put some meat on the bones,

so to speak. It was largely political, and very successful, in that sense.

The exercise was done very expertly, people were put ashore, and it attracted a lot of attention. Any time you put a large number of people ashore though you're going to risk having a lot of damage done. So the United States very promptly compensated the locals for all the damage that was done there, which helped also.

The political results of the exercise were very good, and I think it was very much worthwhile. We were all involved in this - I was, CincLant Fleet was, and the CNO was.

The major plans for the exercise were written by the Amphibious Command of the Atlantic Fleet. This was one of the longest amphibious operations that had taken place since World War II. It started all the way from the East Coast of the United States and came over to Spain.

Politically it was a very good exercise. Militarily it was a good exercise in testing the capabilities of the Atlantic Fleet units, both in transit because there were opposing forces to their transit, and also they had opposition forces in the actual landing. Militarily it was very good, and politically it was very good. It worked quite well.

Q: Tell me a little bit about the required social activities which you engaged in in London while serving as CincUSNAVEUR.

Griffin: London is certainly one of the major crossroads of

the world, and you find it major in all the social activities that are involved.

The CINC there, of course, was on the embassy social circuit, on the attache social circuit, besides all the personal relationships that one develops in a job such as that. Generally speaking I would say that that job and also the one in Naples is comparable to a major embassy in the field of social relationships.

In London I had a flat in the headquarters building, which I described before. I entertained there during the week. If I had any entertaining to do over the week-ends I did it at Romany out in the country. Every time either the Secretary of the Navy or the Under Secretary of the Navy or an Assistant Secretary of the Navy or the Chief of Naval Operations or some other high ranking individual paid us a visit I would entertain for them by having a reception, a dinner party, or what have you. These got to be pretty constant.

The guest list is very carefully generated, and is something that you pay a lot of attention to.

One of the things that I found in the Seventh Fleet and over in Europe, one of the more difficult things, was to try to keep up with this 'presento business.' Every time you make an official visit to a city, as when I made an official visit to Rome, I had something to present to everyone of the individuals on whom I made an official call, a gift. Usually if it was the first time around I would have a command plaque with a little plate on it, which would be quite appropriate.

I had some silver cigarette boxes that I would have appropriately engraved, also autographed photographs, and things like that. After you'd been in the job for awhile and started going around the second time it tends to become more difficult.

I think I commented on the Far East. It's particularly touchy there, because they are very conscious of it. And if they think that you've given them something a little better than they gave you it will be a quantum of jump the next time, until you're exchanging cadillacs.

You try to keep this within bounds. I used all kinds of things. For example, the NATIONAL GEOGRAPHIC has some very nice books on the United States that I used. The Naval Institute has some books which I bought, and things like that. But it is something which requires quite a bit of time and attention.

Q: It means that you can't be quite as flexible with your schedule as you might want to be.

Griffin: No indeed. Usually these things are set up two or three months ahead of time. Your personal life is entirely secondary to all of these things that you have to do.

If the Secretary of the Navy is coming over you have to change plans you may have had to make sure that you are there to introduce him properly to the people that he must see there, and so he can learn the things that he wants to learn, and do the things that he wants to do. The presumption is he can go back to Washington and do the job much better there as a consequence of what he learns on the inspection trip.

Interview # 14

Admiral Charles D. Griffin
Washington, D. C.

by John T. Mason
December 16, 1971

Q: As we begin chapter fourteen, I think you have several items that you want to add to the story of the London tour of duty, CincUSNAVEUR.

Griffin: Yes, I do. I'd like to comment briefly on one thing which I don't believe I covered in my earlier conversation.

The Mediterranean was the initial point of a rather historic naval cruise. This was the first round-the-world cruise of a nuclear-powered task force. The task force included the carrier ENTERPRISE, the cruiser LONG BEACH, and the frigate BAINBRIDGE. I went down to the Mediterranean and visited the Task Force before it sailed.

One of the elements which was being considered very carefully at that time was the amount of life which was left in the ENTERPRISE reactors. This had been very carefully calculated so as to make sure the ship could get back to the United States East Coast round-the-world with enough of a factor of safety in event of any unusual circumstances coming up.

Q: Yes, it would have nullified the whole effect of the cruise.

Griffin: To say the least, it would have been rather embarrassing to have the ship the size of the ENTERPRISE floating around in a large ocean without any power.

However, there was very little doubt regarding that. All the various people who had been engaged in these calculations, and having them all checked by Rickover on many, many occasions, there was very little doubt in my mind that the figure was accurate.

This was a rather historic occasion, and I thought it was fitting to fly down to the Mediterranean and visit the three ships. So I did that shortly before they left.

The tactical command for this cruise was under the command of Carrier Division Two, who was Rear Admiral Strean.

They had a marble plaque made to commemorate this, and they were kind to give me the first one of these plaques, which I have on my mememto table.

Q: What is the cruising endurance of the ENTERPRISE?

Griffin: This depends on the speed, and also what kind of reactors it has. With the reactors that they had in the ENTERPRISE at that time (you must recognize that these were very early type reactors) the life was approximately five years at fairly high speed. There were eight reactors in the ship.

Development in this field has been so rapid that right now two reactors could be put in the ENTERPRISE which would have a life of between fifteen and twenty years without recording. So you can see the tremendous strides that have taken place in the technology in connection with reactors and nuclear power.

Q: Would you say then that this makes it worthwhile, the difference between the conventionally powered carrier and the nuclear powered carrier?

Griffin: No question about it. Not only the difference in cost, but the ability to proceed at sustained high speed throughout the oceans of the world is a tremendous advantage. You don't have to stop the ship or slow down the ship for refueling. It's not necessary to have oilers go along. And you can proceed to any place in the world that is reachable from the high seas at sustained high speed, and will be ready for complete action on arrival. This is a tremendous strategic and tactical advantage which accrues to the country which has this type of weapons system.

As a matter of fact from the newspaper reports it's apparent that the ENTERPRISE is being used for this purpose now. They are apparently headed for the Bay of Bengal, and I suppose they are very close to being there now, or perhaps already in the Bay of Bengal.

Q: This point of view which you've expressed about the effectiveness wasn't fully appreciated I take it then when Secretary McNamara ordered that the carrier building after the ENTERPRISE would be a conventional type.

Griffin: No indeed, he didn't appreciate it at all. One of

the methods that he and his 'whiz kinds' used was to order additional study.

Perhaps no weapon system in the world has been studied as much as the attack carrier. Although studies had been made ad infinitum on the carrier, he ordered additional studies and under that guise delayed construction of the ship.

The Navy strongly recommending that the ship be a nuclear powered ship. However, he determined that the carrier coming up would be a conventionally powered carrier in order to give time for these additional studies to be made.

The advantages of nuclear power over conventional power of course are absolute. They are very, very great. Admitedly the cost of nuclear power is considerably higher than that of conventional power, fossil fuel power, but because of the great advantages in mobility which would contribute to strategic surprise and tactical advantages which would accrue we strongly supported all efforts to have these ships nuclear powered. However, we were unable to get Mr. McNamara to agree to that at that time, and as I say he ordered additional studies, although the whole subject had been studied to death. It's just a shame he was so pig-headed on this point.

Q: Did he come around to that point of view later on?

Griffin: Later on he came around to that point of view. He was forced to acknowledge that there were very few elements of studies which had really not been made about the carrier, and he could no longer use the guise of having one more study made.

He was forced, largely by figures which were presented to him and which he could not refute, to agree to having the next attack carrier nuclear powered. That carrier will be the EISENHOWER.

Let me comment on one other item on my tour in London, and that is my relationship with a very well known man in the world, Mr. J. Paul Getty. I don't think that I have commented on this before.

I got to know Paul Getty quite well. As we all know he's one of the world's richest men and the head of the tremendously large Getty oil interest. He is in residence about twenty-five miles outside of London; his residence is called Sutton Place, near Guilford, England. It's an old castle built in the fifteenth century, and at one time was one of the famous castles of Henry VIII. He has it filled with all kinds of art objects. He proved to me to be a most interesting man to talk to.

It's rather difficult for the average individual to get to know Paul Getty. He's almost a recluse, because I think a man in his circumstances perhaps ultimately has to be that way because practically everyone who comes to see him or asks to see him has an ax to grind - they want to get something from him. This tends to make an individual like that shy away and draw back in his shell.

Our relationship was a very wonderful thing to me. I think it was to him too. Because he sensed, and he knew later, that there wasn't anything that he had that I wanted. On the other hand he admitted to me that when he was a young man one of the things he wanted to be most was an admiral in the U. S. Navy, and he was sorely tempted at one time to go in the Navy and make the Navy his career. So an individual who happened to be an admiral in the Navy was an individual who he instinctively tended to admire. With the combination of these two factors we became very good friends.

Q: How did you meet him?

Griffin: He was on the guest list for the reception after I assumed command. He came there and I had a short talk with him at that time, but later on went down to visit him at Sutton Place and our relationship developed from there. We got together on a great number of occasions.

As I say I found him to be an extremely interesting man. Of course, he had proved himself in the field of industry, and was as everyone knows one of the most wealthy men in the world. As a matter of curiosity one time I asked one of his senior staff members just how much he was worth and he said, "We estimate that he is worth perhaps three and three-quarter billion dollars, but Mr. Getty feels that that may be somewhat underestimated."

Of course when you get up into figures like that I imagine it's most difficult to figure out just what his total worth is, because not everyone is in agreement on the value of the art objects.

Paul Getty also was a man who had proved himself in the field of art. He picked up a painting, for example, at one time paying just a few hundred dollars for it and it turned out eighteen years later to be a Raphael which was worth almost a million dollars. Not only in the field of painting but in the field of tapestry - he's one of the experts on tapestry in the world. His house out there was filled with objects d'art and with his tremendous holdings in the state of California, in his museum in California he obviously is one of the world leaders in this field. He's still very active in this field, and has agents who are picking up pieces all over the world for him.

He speaks about five or six languages, many of them fluently, including a passable Arabic, which very few Americans, unless they devote a tremendous amount of time to it, will have any capability in.

Q: I suppose his oil interest led him there.

Griffin: The oil interest led him to the Middle East, and he found that it was a very profitable thing to be able to understand some of that language. Actually it got him into very profitable leasing arrangements early in the game before many of the big companies actually got into the Middle East.

All in all I found him an extremely interesting man. To tie this all together - after I had left London and gone to Naples, Paul Getty came down to Italy and was looking for an old place that he could buy and renovate. One of the places where he visited was Naples. He told me that he was coming, and called after he got there. We had him out to the Villa for lunch on one occasion and dinner on another occasion. It happened to be near Thanksgiving, and we had some mince pie and ice cream which we had made in the Villa. Among my trips back to the States I had bought a hand-cranked freezer, and we made our own ice cream. This was the first time he'd had some real good American mince pie and ice cream in a long time and he had about three helpings of it.

A very interesting thing took place there too. While he was in Naples he had some tooth trouble. The filling came out of it and I sent him over to our dispensary and one of the dentists took care of him. He was most grateful for this because he didn't trust an Italian dentist at all - to have an American dentist take care of him there and do it very well was just what he needed. This was of course a great thrill for that young dentist to do the job for him.

Q: He's an ex-patriot, isn't he? He doesn't really live in this country at all.

Griffin: No, he lives mostly in England.

He did buy a very sizable villa on the coast just below Rome, but on the coast. I think by now that the restoration of that villa should be just about completed.

I did want to comment on my relationship with him, because he's a very fabulous man. As I say I found him most interesting, and we had some wonderful conversations. He's very much up on everything that's going on in the world, and he has very astute opinions on things that are taking place. Some governments could well use some of his advice from time to time I would have to say.

Another little story that I'd like to add to this collection is the story of a tablecloth. This story is in the 1951-'52 period when I was out in Pearl Harbor as Plans Officer for Admiral Radford.

After the election in November of 1951 and General Eisenhower was elected President, as you recall he made a trip out to Korea. He came through Pearl Harbor and was briefed there by Admiral Radford's staff. As the Plans Officer I was Admiral Radford's briefer, and so I briefed the President-elect, Mr. Wilson the Secretary of Defense designate, and Mr. Dulles the Secretary of State designate. Of course Admiral Radford talked to all of them privately in addition to these briefings and particularly so with General Eisenhower.

They went out to Korea and their visit out there was very successful. On the way back they just stayed at Hickam Field. Hoskins was the Commander of the Pacific Division of NATS (Military Air Transport Service.) He had a house at Hickam Field, and had extended an invitation to the President-elect and his party to have lunch with him on the way through so they could have an opportunity to stretch their legs while the airplane was being replenished.

Sue Hoskins, Johnny's wife, called my wife and asked if she could borrow a tablecloth she knew that we had. This was a beautiful tablecloth which I had bought in Hong Kong. Mrs. Radford had ordered a tablecloth to be made there, and the Chinese being very cautious in these affairs made two of them to make sure if there was any imperfection of one they would have a fall-back and not lose face by having an imperfect piece of material. It so happened that both of them turned out to be perfect, and so they had a spare one, and I bought this spare one at a very low price. This was the tablecloth that Sue Hoskins wanted to borrow because she had seen it and had admired it so much.

Q: How large is the tablecloth?

Griffin: It's a banquet cloth, it's about 140 inches long and some 40 inches wide.

My wife said, "Of course you can have it."

So during the course of the luncheon someone spilled a little wine on it. After the luncheon was over with Sue Hoskins sent it down to Honolulu - they had one good cleaner in Honolulu and that's about all - to be cleaned. Thenthe owner of the cleaning outfit called Sue up and said that they would not touch it. They felt that they could clean it all right and get that spot out, but they would not touch it unless she insured it for at least fifteen hundred dollars. So Sue had to take out an insurance policy to cover the fifteen hundred dollars. By the time she paid that and the cost of the cleaning and everything she returned the cloth to us and said, "The next time I borrow this cloth remind me to have my head examined."

I happened to think of that and thought it was a rather interesting little anecdote.

As a matter of fact as I recall I paid about seventy-five dollars for this cloth. I did later have it appraised, and it was appraised as being worth about twelve hundred dollars.

Q: That put you in the class of J. Paul Getty and his art works.

Griffin: Not quite.

I think that we can go on now and move down to Naples from London. I was succeeded in London by Admiral John Thach, who was a classmate of mine, a very good friend of mine, a fellow naval aviator, an individual who had made himself very famous by his splendid performance in World War II, and best known perhaps for the development of a fighter tactic called the 'Thach weave.' He was in on much of the heavy fighting in World War II, was a fighter ace, and a very brilliant naval aviator. I was delighted to see him come over, because I also know that he liked to play golf. It always seemed to me a shame to send somebody over in that beautiful set up in England who didn't play golf.

I had set his relief date at such time to permit me to just simply be relieved, fill the airplane up with our equipment, and fly down to Naples, arriving there about two days before I was to relieve Admiral Russell. We did this. I might say much to the amazement of our British friends who said, "My goodness, we would never think of going from one major command to another without at least three or four months leave." I said, "We don't always do it this way in the United States."

There was little point to having a lot of leave at this time anyway. I didn't feel any need for it, and I wanted to get on with the job of taking over in Napels. So we flew down to Naples and arrived there on the 29th of March. I relieved Admiral Russell as the Commander-in-Chief Allied Forces Southern Europe on 31 March.

Q: Which made you a part of NATO.

Griffin: That made me a part of NATO.

I think it would be interesting to explain briefly the command structure of Allied Forces Southern Europe. The Commander-in-Chief Allied Forces Southern Europe is one of the major subordinate commanders of the Supreme Allied Commander Europe. At that time, the time that I relieved, the headquarters Supreme Allied Commander Europe was just outside of Paris. It later was moved to Belguim. CincSOUTH at that time, was one of four major subordinate Commanders of SACEUR. The Commander Allied Forces Northern Europe was headquartered in Norway, and was a British Army General. The Commander Allied Forces Central Europe was a French General and was headquartered just outside of Fontainebleau in France. I was the Commander-in-Chief Allied Forces Southern Europe. Then Commander-in-Chief Allied Forces Mediterranean was a British Admiral with headquarters in Malta.

Later on, while I was CincSOUTH, the Command in Malta,

CincAFMED, was eliminated and the Command there was taken over, since it was entirely a naval command, by one of my subordinate commanders, Commander Naval Forces South. So instead of the Allied Forces Mediterranean we had Naval Forces South.

Q: It sounded a little redundant.

Griffin: It did. There were many political aspects to this whole command structure. First the British - so far as they were concerned the Mediterranean had been a British lake for many, many years. The position of the U. S. Sixth Fleet also was a rather touchy one, because the United States was not about to turn over full operation control of the Sixth Fleet to any foreign officer. Therefore, the Sixth Fleet, in its NATO capacity remained under CincSOUTH. All of these various elements that enter into the equation there forced the individual that set up the command structure to accept what was certainly much less than a natural command structure. You wouldn't have the problem if you didn't have so many nations involved in it.

Q: Does this also imply then that the cost of maintaining these various commands was increased because of the political considerations?

Griffin: Yes, no question about it.

In my own headquarters in Naples I found it most difficult to cut personnel there, although as a result of my first study shortly after I got there it seemed to me that we had entirely too many people in the headquarters to do the job that we had to do. But to say to the Italians, "I want you to cut your personnel here ten percent." or to the Greeks or the Turks or the British, "I want you to cut yours x percent," -- Almost inevitably they take this as an indication in the Commander-in-Chief's mind their role is diminishing. This is a very touchy thing. If you cut one by a certain percentage you've got to cut them all by a similar percentage.

The business of running a multi-national headquarters is a very interesting one, and of course this was the field in which General Eisenhower was really supreme. Because they all loved him, they worked for him, and he got them to do things that most people thought would be impossible.

AFSOUTH Command structure - the Commander-in-Chief was headquartered at Naples. His Chief of Staff was a Major General in the U. S. Army. Then there was a Major General in the Italian Army as an Assistant Chief of Staff, a Brigadier General in the Turkish Army as an Assistant Chief of Staff, a Brigadier General in the Greek Army as an Assistant Chief of Staff, a Rear Admiral in the U. S. Navy as an Assisthat Chief of Staff. These were the flag officers in the headquarters.

CincAFSOUTH, me, had several principal subordinate Commanders. Commander Air Forces South was headquartered in the same compound in Naples that I was, and was headed by a Lieutenant General in the U. S. Air Force. Under him were two Allied Tactical Air Forces. The Fifth ATAF, as we called them, was in Vicenza in Italy headed by a Lieutenant General in the Italian Air Force. The Sixth ATAF was headquartered in Ismir in Turkey and was headed by a Major General in the U. S. Air Force. We had a U. S. Air Force officer there in Ismir because he had under him Greeks and Turks. Neither Greece or Turkey would accept a Greek or Turk in command, so we had to use an American.

Q: With an overall commander of another nationality would they work together?

Griffin: Yes, they would. I'll get to this later on. That was the air part of it.

In the land part we had two principal land commanders. ComLanSouth with headquarters in Verona in Italy - this was headed by an Italian four star Army General. Then Commander Land Forces Southeast was at Ismir in Turkey - this was headquartered by an American Lieutenant General.

I tried for some time to get his rank raised to four-stars, but apparently some powers that be in the Pentagon would not go along with it as long as General Michaelis was there. Michaelis was a rather controversial Army General. He had an absolutely magnificent combat record, and as a matter of fact received two combat field promotions in Korea. He was a magnificent officer in all respects but had been promoted rather fast, and I think probably some of the inter-play in the Army General Staff system created a situation where there was some opposition to the job being made four-stars while he was in it. I might say that after he left, and after I left, the post was made four-stars and an American General was put in there. That's Commander Land Forces Southeast.

Under him, although he was only three-stars, there were the Greek and the Turkish Army Forces that were assigned to NATO headed by Generals who were on the Turkish side four-stars. So we had a rather peculiar situation there.

Then on the naval side we had Commander Striking Force South who was also Commander Sixth Fleet. He had assigned to him American forces in the Sixth Fleet, and also would have assigned to him other naval forces as determined by the individual countries concerned. This was a rather unusual type of set up, but it stemmed from the political considerations that had to do with the Mediterranean, and also the nuclear striking power of the U. S. Sixth Fleet. The American government was quite willing to let the U. S. Sixth Fleet be double-hatted as Commander Striking Force South because they reported directly to an American Admiral who was Commander-in-Chief Allied Forces Southern Europe.

Anyway we recognized the political considerations that governed so many of these command structures and accepted them and made them work. They worked all right.

As the Commander-in-Chief, I've pointed out my principal senior people, then I had actually three aides. I had a senior aide who was a Commander in the U. S. Navy. I had an Italian aide who was a Lieutenant Colonel in the Italian Air

Force. The other aide was in a billet which alternated between Greece and Turkey. At the time I arrived there the incumbent in that billet was a Major in the Greek Army who was named Kombokis.

I cite his name because his relationship with the King of Greece was a very close one. At the time the King of Greece, Constantine, when he was the Crown Prince he met a Danish Princess named Anna and they fell in love with each other. When King Paul died and Constantine came to the throne as the King of Greece Kombokis was his aide, and he used to spend quite a bit of time with the King traveling up to Denmark to visit Anna Maria during the courting days so to speak. Anna Maria had a Lady-in-waiting. Because of the relationship between the people whom they served this Lady-in-waiting and Kombokis were thrown together quite a bit. They fell in love and decided to marry. They married just after the King and Anna Maria did. I would also say as very dutiful subjects they had their first child just after the King and Anna Maria had theirs.

Major Kombokis and his wife were absolutely delightful, wonderful people to get along with. They were very knowledgeable of things in Europe. They obviously could travel in any circles with the greatest of ease, very smooth, and yet exremely nice - just genuinely nice people all around.

Another aspect which endeared them to us was that their wedding anniversary was the same as my wife and mine. So we on occasions used to have a small wedding anniversary celebration at Villa Niki - just the four of us.

14 Griffin 657

After taking over I must say that in my inspections around the area and around the headquarters, including my emergency command post which was in a mountain about forty kilometers from the main headquarters and was somewhat comparable to the present command post that our North American Defense Command has up in Cheyenne Mountain in Wyoming built of course at considerably less in cost than the one in the U. S. but a very good one, I noted that there was no golf course there except a little 'pitch and putt par three' course of only seven holes right in the headquarters compound which had been put in there most ingenuously. I mention this because it proved a source of lot of humorous comment and it became known throughout Italy that I was determined to get a golf course down in that area.

I inspected the area in the vicinity of the command post and my headquarters, and then set up a series of visits as an order of first business in my new command.

These took a natural order, and the first one was in April just a little over a week after I relieved. On April 8 and 9 I made a trip to Rome to visit the various officials there. I called on the President of the Republic Guiseppi Saragat, the Prime Minister who at that time was Aldo Moro, the American Ambassador who was Freddie Reinhardt, the Chief of the General Staff who was General Rossi, the Chief of the Army Staff who was General Aloia, the Chief of the Air Staff who was general Raymondin - a very interesting individual, and the Commanding General of the carabinieri Lieutenant General de Lorenzo.

14 Griffin 658

Q: Was that the Guardia Civil type of thing?

Griffin: Yes, except they occupied a very special place in the military hierarchy in Italy. The people in the carabinieri were very highly selected. Actually only one officer, and that's the Commanding General - a Lieutenant General who is provided by the Army and who is selected very carefully. The carabinieri pride themselves on being under no political influence, and are a very, very elite group.

I also called on the Foreign Minister at that time, Mr. Fanfani.

Q: Has he been elected President?

Griffin: No, the last report I saw of that in the paper just a day or so ago was the seventh ballot, or something like that, and they were still tied up. There are only two that are in it now, and it seems to be pretty well tied up.

I called on Rear Admiral Contu of the Italian Navy, who was Assistant Chief of Staff, because Admiral Giuriati was away and his number two, Admiral Sotgiu, was ill.

I forgot to include the Minister of Defense, Mr. Andreotti, a very interesting individual.

Q: Were you required to bring gifts to all these people?

Griffin: No, not on first calls.

I found these calls very, very interesting.

At that time the principal concern of the Italian Ministers and the Italian Chiefs was the amount of the budget that they would get. This of course is true not only of Italy, but in many other parts of the world too.

The Italian Armed Forces had been forced to take rather sharp reductions in budget for a period of several years. They did this and they accepted them with the understanding that they would come back to normalcy before too long. I use that in a rather vague term.

At the time of my calls for example, General Rossi had stated that he had obtained the government approval of an annual increase of six percent per year in the military budget. I asked him whether or not this was six percent over and above any inflationary tendencies and so forth, and he assured me that it was, and was guaranteed to be above any inflation. So that would actually represent in terms of purchasing power and equipment and so forth that much of an increase.

The effort here was to try to modernize the Italian Armed Forces. They were doing, I felt, quite well with what they had and from what I could see at that time. I was perhaps more familiar with the Italian Naval Forces than I was with the Army and Air Forces.

But as I will note later on I had already noted that, for example, the Italian Air Force was flying the 104 - an airplane which is a rather complicated advanced aircraft, which the Germans were having a terrific amount of difficulty with. They were having crashes all over the place. The Italians, however, were flying them and had a very good safety record with them. I might say that the Greeks and the Turks flew them and had very good safety records too.

Q: Why then were the Germans inadequate?

Griffin: The Germans were inadequate because they were putting pilots in these aircraft that were not experienced pilots. They were young pilots who didn't have the years of experience that the fliers that the air forces in the south required to put them into advanced aircraft.

Another thing that became perfectly clear - this happened about a year after this particular call when I was making an inspection trip to one of the Italian Air Force bases - a base which was used as one of the main logistic and overhaul bases for the Italian Air Force. At that time a division of four German 104s came through there and landed at the field for an overnight stay. The Italians looked at these aircraft and wouldn't let them take off the next day. They said they were in dangerous condition.

And this was the first time that I had had absolute proof that one of the things that must be happening in Germany was that they were receiving very poor maintenance, because the Italians said, "We will not permit these aircraft to take off from this field. They are unsafe in their present condition." They worked them over and got them in good enough shape so that the German pilots could take off and fly back to Germany in them.

Q: That really doesn't sound very compatible with the German character.

Griffin: It doesn't, but you have to remember that after World War II the German armed forces were disbanded completely and for about ten years they didn't have any. During that period of time they lost all of their non-coms and they are the guts of a service organization. And they lose all expertise. Now they are taking in young people. It wouldn't make much sense to enlist a guy who's forty years old and is already an expert technician. You've got to start right from scratch. It takes a long time to build up the expertise in a professional armed service. They lacked it all, and as a consequence in one year as I recall they had some eighty fatal crashes in the air force. I don't know why they didn't contract out their required maintenance.

Here in the South we were operating them (the 104s) perfectly all right, but we had proper maintenance in the South. The Italians and the Greeks and the Turks had good maintenance for their aricraft. What they lacked in the South was the money to really fly the aircraft very much. The average pilot would get only fifteen hours a month at the most, which wasn't very much, highly inadequate in fact.

My visit there was most interesting and I enjoyed seeing all the people. Prime Minister Moro left me with the impression that he was very much unsure of himself. He sort of seemed to be somewhat of a very quiet milktoast type of an individual. To me he looked tired and very nervous.

However I understood later that this was more a function of his own nature rather than a possible temporary situation due to overwork or anything like that. Because I noted that later on, I saw him many times and every time he always looked the same way. One of his difficulties, I think, was his inability to project himself strongly.

In contrast to him President Saragat was a very forthright, very positive, delightful man.

I won't go into details of all the conversations with the various people except to say that I do have in my records a resume of all these conversations and the highlights of them together with other information such as the number of people who were present at the various places, seating arrangements at tables for big functions and so forth, and they will be available.

I will comment on this first visit with Mr. Fanfani. I called on him about six o'clock and he was about a half hour late arriving there. He had just come back from Brussels and was on a very tight schedule. We had a very interesting talk, and when I left we were about twenty minutes in time from my anticipated take-off time at the airfield in Rome.

I had an honor guard of twelve carabinieri on motorcycles. This period of time, when I left the meeting with Mr. Fanfani, I had about twenty minutes to get over to the airport which was completely on the other side of town. It was at one of the busy times at night with high traffic density, and I have never had such a ride in my life.

We went through Rome at about sixty miles an hour with

the carabinieri up ahead sweeping automobiles out of the way. My Italian aide, who was an Italian Air Force officer and a jet pilot, finally took his hat off and started fanning his face with his hat and I felt very much the same way. How they accomplished it without any serious accident I will never know, except that it certainly attested to the marked ability of the carabinieri to handle themselves under these conditions. From time to time I would look up ahead and I could see nothing but a solid group of automobile lights all heading from us, but we threaded our way thrrough these things.

We made this trip back to Ciampiano which is the military airport in Rome, and returned to Capa di Chino which is our airport in Naples.

I might say at this time that one of the things which I determined right at the outset was to get as much knowledge as I possibly could of this whole command as early as possible, and to include not only going to the main headquarters in the principal cities but also to the outskirts. This included going to the border area between Italy and countries to the north, going to Greece and the border area between Greece and the countries to the north there, going to Turkey and all the way out to the eastern part of Turkey - Erzurum and their border with the Soviet Union out there. This was one of my projects.

General Bernabo was the ComLanSouth at that time. I went up and had a very interesting visit with him, and a briefing from him and his staff. We took in also the SETAF (Southern Eurpoe Task Force) which was the special American unit which had been set up in northern Italy in order to permit the United

States to provide atomic weapons to support the NATO forces. This was commanded by a Major General in the U. S. Army; at that time it was Major General Power. We visited General Bernabo's headquarters at Verona, and also General Power's headquarters. We also visited some of the SETAF installations in Vicenza. SETAF and installations in Verona and in Vicenza. Vicenza was also the headquarters of the Fifth Allied Tactical Air Force - at that time Lieutenant General De Porto. We received briefings at Five ATAF, and after a two day visit departed Villefranche airfield for Capa de Chino in Naples arriving there in the late afternoon of the 13th.

These early visits were principally for the purpose of meeting the commanders and receiving briefings on their activities which would give me an opportunity later on to be more understanding and to determine in my own mind how those commanders were doing, how efficient they were.

My next visit was a trip to Paris. This was on 21-23 April 1965 and came about at this particular time incident to a meeting of the major subordinate commanders which General Lemnitzer, who was SACERU at that time, had called. I stayed at Marshall of the Royal Air Force Pike's residence. Mrs. Griffin and I were their house guests. The other commanders were adequately taken care of by the other senior officers on SACEUR's staff.

This also gave me an opportunity, being a newcomer to the command, to call on the various Ambassadors to NATO - including a call on Secretary General Brasio who is a very interesting individual and a very talented man. Ambassador Brasio had been one of the better known Italian diplomats. He had been the Italian Ambassador to Moscow, he had been the Italian Ambassador to France, and he had been the Italian Ambassador to the United States in Washington. He was Secretary General of NATO at that time, and has in fact just been relieved within the last year. He is now acting as NATO's roving Ambassador toward bettering relationships between NATO and Warsaw Pact countries. He is a very, very interesting, very talented, brilliant man.

I called on U. S. Ambassador Finletter. As a matter of fact the United States at that time had two Ambassadors to NATO - Ambassador Finletter, and an old friend of mine Ambassador Durbrow.

I called on Ambassador Burgi of Turkey, and on Ambassador Allesandrini of Italy. Ambassador Palomis of Greece was away, so I called on his deputy Mr. Phrydas.

Each of the major subordinate commanders was given an opportunity to present the situation in his command which was followed by a series of questions and answers. Anyone of the senior people on the SHAPE staff, from General Lemnitzer on down - General Lemnitzer, General Parker his Chief of Staff, and the others - would have questions to ask, and the major subordinate commanders would answer these.

I have a series of notes on what the various NATO subordinate commanders talked about. This I can pin to the record just as is.

Q: As you talk about these visits and the visit to headquarters, it becomes very apparent of the elaborate nature of the NATO Command in all parts of Western Europe. What state of alert was maintained by the component parts of the NATO Command at this time?

Griffin: At this time we were in, shall we say, a stand down state of alert. This was a peacetime situation.

You're quite correct in thinking that this is a very complicated command structure. When you have as many countries involved as we had in NATO it inevitably is going to result in complicated command structure. The difference between the command structure for example in the Pacific, where the United Stat was in sole command, was quite clear cut and straightforward as compared with the command in the Atlantic-Mediterranean area. The only thing I can say is that you have a complicated structure when you have this many countries involved in it. Because as I pointed out earlier, if you try to streamline an organization you cut it to a point where somebody is going to feel hurt that they are not represented adequately. As a consequence you undertake to see that everyone is represented and almost inevitably will have more people doing the job than it actually requires. Both political and military conditions govern.

At this time we got together on at least an annual basis with the Supreme Allied Commander, General Lemnitzer. The principal purpose of this was to give him our personal views on the combat effectiveness of our command.

This will add to the answer to your question - in the South we maintained a state of alert which called for Army and

Air Force forces in the total amount of close to half a million people being ready to go within thirty days. The build up after that in about three months - the total commitment in the South was a million and a half people to be ready within minety days. This is the type of alert that we maintained.

Our headquarters was maintained twenty-four hours a day - we had people on watch for twenty-four hours around the clock. Each one of the major headquarters had an emergency command post. Mine, as I've indicated before, was out in the mountain about forty kilometers from Naples. We had that manned around the clock; the communications were manned around the clock. Our peacetime headquarters just outside of Naples had duty officers that were there around the clock. Communications, intelligence, and duty officers were there around the clock, and they could get in touch with us immediately by telephone. We maintained an alert which was adequate to the times.

Q: You characterize it as a stand down period. That being so, it must have been known generally within the command that this was the case, and since so much of it was land-based - how could you maintain high morale under those circumstances?

Griffin: Because so much of our work was involved in planning. One of the major things that we existed for was to plan for all the various contingencies that might take place. This called for not only having detailed knowledge of the capabilities of all the forces, but it called for many inspection trips around. Each time we would go to a different place inevitably the morale at that particular place would be raised by the attention of the Commander-in-Chief.

And the exercises that we'd put on at peridoic intervals throughout the year to test the current operational capabilities of the forces that were involved also contributed very heavily to this. We had a full series of peacetime exercises which were on top, of course, of the purely national exercises which were conducted by the forces in a given country. We were conducting these exercises at just about the maximum rate that we could conduct them consistent with the money, the budgets that these military forces had to spend on that particular type of thing.

I felt that the morale was high. We also stressed the great need of NATO, and would point out time and again to visitors that would come to the headquarters and be given briefings the fact that ever since NATO came into existance not a single square inch of territory had been taken by communist forces, which was certainly not true in other parts of the world. They were moving very rapidly in other parts. Our morale was okay.

Q: I suppose you had an assist from the Russians themselves occasionally when they got tough in Berlin or elsewhere.

Griffin: That's right. When they would get tough in Berlin as an example - we would alert our forces on the Eastern sector of Turkey, we would alert the Greeks in the northern part of their country to put their forces on the alert, and similarly in Italy

It didn't have to be in our back yard. If it affected NATO as a whole, we were very interested in it.

Q: Yesterday I read an article on NATO command in northern Europe, in Norway and Denmark especially. It was rather discouraging in that they were letting down the barriers and becoming sort of laisse-faire about the whole thing. Did you have any evidence of that in your time?

Griffin: Not in our part. We noted this tendency in the North, and it didn't help NATO as a whole. The feeling up North was one tending toward socialism. The feeling down South was away from that very considerably.

As a consequence - such things as our relationship with Centro-General Lemnitzer delegated to me the responsibility for maintaining liaison with then Cento organization, because quite frankly the NATO countries up North were not interested in having any relationship at all with Centro. And therefore we didn't feed any of the knowledge of our relationships, our joint plans that we had, and so forth to any of those countries up there. It went directly to SACEUR.

Q: Why then do they maintain their membership in NATO?

Griffin: Because it helps them. They can get something for very little, and they are getting it. They're getting a considerable amount of protection - Norway and Denmark. This is reflected also in the amount of contributions that they make to NATO.

While I was there I took occasion to take the percentage of the gross national product that the various countries would devote to their defense. I also took the percentage of manpower in the countries which they would devote to defense. And I added these two factors together. A pure mathematician would undoubtedly question me on just what this means. I'm not too sure what it means, except that in relativity you can get some relationship of what one country is doing in this particular field to what another country is doing. So I ended up with a final factor, and I listed all those in order of their size. I found that the United States was number one on the list. Number two was Turkey, number three was Greece, and Italy, if you included the carabinieri in their forces, was about number five. (If you didn't include the caribinieri Italy was right in the middle.)

This showed that in terms of what they had to give the people down South were giving more on a percentage basis and supporting NATO more on a percentage basis than any of the other countries. I found this to be very interesting and I gave it some publicity.

At the time of the major subordinate commanders meeting in Belgium General Bray of the British Army was CincNorth, General Crepin of the French Army was CincCent, and Admiral Hamilton of the British Navy was CincAFMED, and I was CincSouth. One of the subjects that we discussed there at this time was logistics.

I had already observed that as soon as one started asking questions about logistics, "Do you have the logistic support to back up these emergency plans?" and so forth, the ready answer was, "Logistics is a national responsibility, and we just assume that the countries will provide it."

I directed my logistic people to get on the ball a little bit more than that and actually get into some nuts and bolts in these various countries to try to dig them out and make doggone sure that they were in fact going to provide the logistics that was required.

It was about a year after I got there that Admiral Kidd, who now is the Chief of our naval material command, came over as a brand new Rear Admiral as my assistant Chief of Staff for logistics. He took this bull by the horns and really took it to town, and we improved NATO logistics I think about a thousand percent during that period.

Each of us in our area, when we were asked to report to the Supreme Allied Commander, gave a rundown on the weaknesses and strengths and problems of the area. In so many cases this is the type of a meeting that you have - you tend to highlight your problems and soften up a little bit on your places where you may be a little fat - it's the name of the game.

In summarizing the situation in the South I highlighted the fact that the great problem of the South at that time was the problem of Cyprus. Cyprus of course as we know is the source of much of the difficulty down South in the arguments between Greece and Italy. This proved to be one of the most important points that I had to keep under constant consideration during the entire time that I was CincSouth.

Eighty percent of the people in Cyprus are Greeks, and twenty percent are Turks. They had been on that island for hundreds and hundreds of years. They never had gotten along too well, but had managed to live without getting into much of a war.

I'll just comment very briefly at this time on Cyprus, but I will get much more in detail on it later on.

The period of trouble over Cyprus started when Archbishop Makarias was brought back from an island in the Indian Ocean wher[e] he had been sent by the British, was brought back to Cyprus. Then Cyprus was given its independence as part of the British decision [to] get rid of practically all of their overseas possessions. This l[eft] a very unstable situation on that island. It proved to be one of [the] most difficult subjects which occupied much of my time during the entire time that I was CincSouth. I will comment on this in deta[il] much more later on.

Q: There was a certain amount of fishing in troubled waters on t[he] part of UAR and others too.

Griffin: Yes.

Makarias was a very positive individual. He's one whom I co[uld] never get around to trusting too much. I know also that he was, shall we say, in the hair of the Greek Prime Minister all the ti[me] no matter who the Greek Prime Minister happened to be. This fina[lly] became became very much the subject of my attention for the next few years.

Q: Admiral since you were talking about logistics in Paris - wha[t] portion of the defense planning by NATO at this time placed reli[ance] on atomic weaponry?

Griffin: Not too much of it. I would not characterize it by any specific percentage, but not very much.

We considered atomic weapons at that time to be very much of a fallback position, so to speak, and did not contemplate use of these weapons in the early stages of an emergency. The atomic weapons that we had available were of course under complete U. S. control. The ones that we figured we would use first would probably be ADMs, atomic demolition munitions, because these could be used very profitably in many of the approach areas to the South, for example, in the approaches to Northern Italy and the approaches to Northern Greece particularly, and would delay any oncoming land force a considerable period of time. These in combination with tactical weapons from guns would be undoubtedly used first.

Once you start using atomic demolition and other atomic type of weapons it's awfully difficult to stop their escalation.

As a result of this situation where the United States had the atomic weapons and their control and use and custody very carefully delineated by U. S. law, the United States found itself in a peculiar situation over there.

We had the weapons, and they were located in the countries in the South in barricaded places that were provided by the host country. The United States, of course, also with agreements between the countries assured the other countries that our plans for use of atomic weapons in all-out war would be compatible with the plans of the NATO Alliance. But that was about as far as the United States would go. The other countries were not privy to the specific plans of the United States for atomic war in Europe, nor could they be under the terms of our law. Therefore the countries there had to accept the word of the United States that these would be available as a backup. The United States, in other words, was providing an atomic umbrella under which the NATO Alliance could operate, principally in the conventional field.

Q: Did that not represent a change in thinking from an earlier period?

Griffin: No, I think that this was generally what was true all along.

The U. S. Sixth Fleet, for example, has plans and has had plans for use of atomic weapons. The Strategic Air Command has had plans for use of the atomic weapons that they have. The U.S. Second Fleet has plans, the Polaris Submarine Force has plans. All of these plans, of course, are dovetailed at the headquarters at Offutt Air Force Base under the Joint Chiefs of Staff. But it has always been understood that the U.S. would provide the strategic deterrent umbrella under which NATO could operate.

This particular situation however got to point where other countries were quite insistent upon knowing more about what this was all about. Some of them considered that this was tending to be an infringement of their sovereignty and so forth. As a consequence of this feeling the United States took the initiative in the NATO field of recommending, and it ultimately resulted in the setting up, of a nuclear committee on which the United States would be a permanent member and other countries would rotate membership. In the South we would have a Greek on it at one time and a Turk on it at another time. This was a sub-committee of the Military Committee of NATO.

Considerable work proceeded in that field largely in accord with instructions contained in a McNamara's memorandum on that subject. It resulted in a feeling within the Alliance which was good. It tended to give to the countries concerned a feeling that they were in fact participating in the total nuclear planning bit of the whole Alliance. In fact I think that practically everyone understood that they weren't, but nevertheless it was enough of a facade in that direction to be successful.

My next visit was a most interesting one, it was my visit to Turkey. I had visited Turkey only once previous to that, when I was Commander-in-Chief U. S. Naval Forces Europe and made the visit there principally for the purpose of visiting the naval commander. (I must back up on that because I had been to Turkey before, in the 1930-31 period.)

This time I left Naples and landed first at Izmir. The purpose of that was to meet the various dignitaries in the Izmir area and then have General Michaelis, ComLanSoutheast, join my party and continue my visit to Ankara.

The Turks have a very unusual type of honor ceremony. They are the only country that I've ever seen in the world, of course I haven't seen them all, where the inspecting officer has a direct conversation with all the troops that he's inspecting - not to the individuals, but to all of them. The inspecting officer stops when he starts to pass the guard and says, "Mer haba askir." That in Turkish means, "Greetings men." Then he says, "Nasil suniz - how are you?" And then all the troops reply, "Sagol - long life."

I called on the various dignitaries in the Izmir area including the senior Turkish Admiral there, the Governor of Izmir, and of course Lieutenant General Michaelis who was ComLanSoutheast, and Major General Box who was Sixth ATAF Commander.

I also called on the Mayor of Izmir. He's a very interesting individual, spoke English beautifully, had lived in the United States for many years, very pro-American. He went back over there and proved to be a very adroit politician and has been elected Mayor of Izmir for several terms and has everything really under control.

This was largely a ceremonial series of calls. I have a summation of my talks with all of these people which is available

Q: I take it you didn't go near the Russian border.

Griffin: Not on this visit. This was not out to East Turkey. This was to call on the high command, so to speak, in Turkey.

We were entertained as usual by large receptions. The next day, accompanied by General Michaelis, we flew to Ankara.

I had an opportunity there to talk with U. S. Ambassador Hare for only just a few minutes. I had met Ambassador Hare before, and I saw him during the first part of my visit at Ankara because he was under prior commitments to leave Ankara and would not be there during my visit.

One of the first things that is done when you make an initial call of this sort at most all of the capital cities - in Rome it the tomb of the Unknown Soldier, in Athens it's the tomb of the

Unknown Soldier, in Ankara it's Ataturk's mausoleum where you lay a wreath. They're all very similar as prescribed ceremonies, and you're well briefed on what you have to do in carrying this out.

The first one I called on was General Sunay, who at that time was the Chief of the Turkish General Staff, a very popular man in Turkey. He is now the President of Turkey. I had a very interesting conversation with him.

Much of the conversation during the early stages of my visits to these countries, particularly Greece and Turkey, had to do with either forthright statements or veiled statements about the situation in Cyprus - the other side is always wrong, and why can't they see our way of doing it, and so forth.

I called on the Minister of Defense Dincer. Then I called on the Chiefs of the various services. General Tural was Commander of the Turkish Land Forces. General Tansel was Commander of the Turkish Air Forces - a very interesting individual, spoke English fluently which very few of the Turks did, and actually in thinking was a much more Europeanized individual than most of the high commanders in the Turkish forces that I met. General Tansel had had some education on the continent. He also had served as the Commandant of the NATO Defense College. He was married to a woman who had had practically all of her education in Europe.

All of the various calls were made with the usual protocol. We were put up at the Ordu Evi, which really in Turkish means officers club. They have an Ordu Evi, at each one of their major cities. They insisted that we stay there, although the plumbing was not too good. We were warned to be very careful about the water. We had small pills with which we would purify the water, or at least take enough impurities out of it so that we could drink it. We stuck to, generally speaking, not drinking any water or as little as we had to, and drinking beer or a soft drink or something like that. However, we shied away from even that when some soft drinks came up to our room with just a little piece of lead foil over the top of them, so obviously they had not been filled in a very sanitary manner.

Interview No. 15 with Admiral C. D. Griffin, U.S. Navy (Retired)
Place: His home in Washington, D.C.
Date: Thursday morning, 6 January 1972
Subject: Biography
By: John T. Mason, Jr.

Q: This morning, Sir, I think you want to continue with your remarks on your visit to Turkey, your first visit to Turkey.

Adm. G.: Perhaps the highlight of this visit was my opportunity to meet and talk with General Sunay, who was the chief of the Turkish General Staff. At this particular time in history, the government of Turkey in reality was at the sufferance of the armed forces and the individual who controlled the armed forces was the chief of the Turkish General Staff.

Q: Do you mean that the political setup was so weak?

Adm. G.: The political setup was weak and this type of democracy was so new to Turkey as a nation that they were feeling their way into modern democratic principles of government. A major factor that made it possible for them to proceed in this way was the control that the Turkish Army -- they were by far the greater in prestige, manpower, and influence than any of the other armed services -- was the power that the Turkish armed services had over the country. It produced a stability under which the introduction of democratic principles could be achieved in an admitedly slow but yet a positive and reasonable degree.

Q: And was the military at that point in agreement with the development of democratic principles?

Adm. G.: Yes, they certainly were, most assuredly, and General Sunay, as the chief of the Turkish General Staff, was in fact the most powerful man in Turkey at that time.

General Sunay had been in this job for several years. He was an elderly man of great prestige in the country. The president of Turkey, President Gursel, had been sick for quite some time and it was quite apparent that he probably didn't have too long to live. There was little question as to who would relieve him as president of the Turkish Republic, and that would be General Sunay. So he had the prestige not only to command the armed forces but also to move into the job of president of the republic. In Turkey the transition would take place in this manner.

When President Gursel would die, then General Sunay would be retired from his job in the Army and would be given one of the life senatorial jobs. They had a certain number of life senators, who were appointed, and from that job he could move to the job of the presidency. He could not go directly from the job in the Army to the job of president, but he could from his job as a life senator because the president had to come from the parliament. I mention this because he was a powerful man and also a very good man for his country. He was not a wild-eyed individual. He was a very calm and moderate individual, and very forceful, and yet an individual who was very, very strong. I'm sure that all of us who knew him thanked our lucky stars that Turkey and NATO had someone as stable and as good as General Sunay to fill these very important jobs.

My talk with General Sunay on this particular occasion, as was the talk of almost everyone there in Ankara at that time, had to do with the recalcitrance of the Greeks in the Turkish-Greek affair over Cyprus. You had no halfway ground here at all. If you agreed with the Turkish view, then you sided with them. If you disagreed, you sided with the Greeks. It was just that simple. In addition to it, the Greeks had in the recent past taken some actions which had not helped the situation at all. I think that the Prime Minister, Papandreou, probably was too much under the influence of Archbishop Makarios and forced some of these things on the part of the government, things that stuck in the Turkish craw at this time were, oh, such items as the Greeks refusing overflight clearances for Turkish aircraft that were proceeding, say, to Italy on NATO business and had no intention to land in Greece at all.

Q: Just as an annoyance?

Adm. G.: Just as an annoyance, that's right. Also, the Greeks refused to permit any NATO inspection teams, multi-national inspection teams, to come into their country which included any Turkish personnel. Things like this, which I will cover in greater detail later on, were very irritating and didn't help the situation at all. But, suffice to say that much of the attention of all of the senior people in the Turkish armed forces at this time had been taken up with their antagonism toward Greece which had been rekindled as a result of the very unsatisfactory situation on Cyprus. I think that's about all I'll say now on that particular visit, because this was pretty much of a makee-learn visit for me, and it was good to have the opportunity to meet all these people.

Now, before we go on to my next visit, which is of significance, and that is my visit to Athens, I do want to mention a few things about the Cyprus problem. Cyprus was so much a part of our difficulty in the south that I think it's well to comment briefly on this.

The Cyprus problem, as of this time, was basically one of communal frustration arising from the attempts of the majority Greek and the minority Turkish communities to live together on an island where the rights and privileges of both were rigidly defined by the terms under which independence was granted. You will recall that the British, as part of their over-all policy of granting what had formerly been members of the British Empire their independence, extended independence to Cyprus and the precise terms of this granting of independence were contained in the 1959 Zurich-London agreements, and the Cypriot constitution which resulted from that agreement and which ended five years of intense fighting on that island -

Q: And this was proving to be a strait jacket now?

Adm. G.: Yes. Well, let's put it this way. It presented the Cypriots with a Hobson's choice. It was a take it or leave it proposition, so far as they were concerned, and none of them wanted to live that way. And to complicate matters further, of course, Cyprus is very close to Turkey and much farther from Greece, so the immediate disputants in the matter included the Cypriots, the mainland Greeks, the Turks, and also the British, as the guarantor nation under the Zurich-London agreement, and, of course, extending into the outer perimeter, we had the U.S., the U.S.S.R., the United Arab Republic, and NATO and the United Nations as interested in this particular island.

As I think I said before, the island is about 80 percent Greek and 20 percent Turk. The basic trouble is that, as you indicated, it put the Cypriots in a strait jacket and provided them with little flexibility to meet changing conditions. The compromise effected at Zurich and London created an independent Cyprus protected by the United Kingdom, Greece, and Turkey. The British, who initially wanted to retain full sovereignty, ended by keeping only their military bases. The Greeks and the Greek Cypriots had wanted enossis, which is unity with Greece, but instead got only an independent political entity. The Turks and the Turkish Cypriots wanted to keep the British presence as a buffer between the two ethnic communities, and when this seemed to be impossible due to the basic policies of the British government at that time to withdraw from outlying areas, then the

Turkish policy became that of partition of the island. It can be seen therefore that no one was happy under these circumstances.

We see in the general Mediterranean area this type of thing many, many times, and the immediate cause of the difficulties here was the decision of the British to withdraw. The Greeks and Turks had been at each other's throats for many centuries. Everything was all right so long as the British were there, but neither country would accept the other in a dominant role on the island. I could see this very clearly and so often in the command structure of NATO, and this is the reason why we had to put an American officer in command of the Land Forces, Southeast, and why we had to put an American officer in command of the 5th ATAF, Allied Tactical Air Forces, both at Izmir. Neither the Greeks nor the Turks would accept either a Greek or a Turk in any overall command position. So, if it was an American, ok, if it was a Britisher, ok, but that ended it. They would not accept an Italian. It created a considerable problem for us both in command relations and, of course, that's exemplified by what happened on that island.

The question of enossis, or alignment with Greece - becoming a part of Greece, was not something that was new. Actually, long before Cyprus became independent whoever stood in the way of enossis was considered by the Greek Cypriots an enemy. When Greece fought for her independence in the 1820s, leaving Cyprus under occupation, the enemies were the Ottoman Turks, but after 1878 when the Ottoman Sultan ceded the island to Great Britain, the British became the enemy. So whoever is put in a position of preventing the island from becoming a part of Greece is the enemy.

As long as Cyprus was under Ottoman or British control, Turkish Cypriots were not concerned about their minority relationship with the Greek Cypriots because they realized that there was the Great White Father sitting up above who would prevent any injustice being done.

Q: But at that point the Greeks wanted the British out, didn't they?

Adm. G.: They wanted the British out because with the great majority on the island they felt that their chances then of achieving their long-sought goal of enossis could be accomplished. When the British decided to withdraw, the Turks became extremely worried about their security on this self-governed island and demanded that extensive guarantees be provided in the Zurich-London agreement.

As I say, this whole thing was really kicked off by the decision of the British to withdraw, and the pitched battles between the Greek and Turkish Cypriots began in late 1963 and were really an inevitable consequence of the day-to-day irritations, the historic animosities, and the extreme nationalism of the two communities. This was not something that was spontaneous as of that time. In fact, the thing had been in the making for many, many years.

The salient characteristic of politics in Cyprus at the

time of which I am speaking is the absolute breakdown in Greek and Turkish intercommunal relations. I don't know whether I mentioned it or not, but under the agreement the Greeks would provide the president, the Turks would provide the vice president, and the parliament would be divided on a 70-30 basis, Greek and Turk, but the minority would have certain veto powers. In effect, this type of arrangement prevented anything from happening and it gradually deteriorated into, as I said, a complete breakdown of intercommunal relations.

I'd like to mention just briefly one other aspect of this, too, because it crops up every now and then. The Greeks and the Turks - the Cypriots, that is - were so engrossed in battling each other that they practically ignored the issue of communism on the island. Now, the communists had been there for some time -

Q: Largely in what part of the population?

Adm. G.: They were largely in the Greek population, but they were a very small group, but very hard core and they were operated on by the Kremlin because the political and strategic aims of the Kremlin in regard to the eastern Mediterranean had been pretty clearly revealed by several Soviet announcements. Cuba had provided the Soviet leaders with one example of the revolutionary opportunities available when outposts espousing the communist cause can be established in politically sensitive regions. The Soviet Union had always opposed enossis, although from time to time it gave lip service to self-determination. But the Russians figured that there was a much greater possibility of communism gaining additional strength and influence in an independent Cyprus than there would be if Cyprus was a part of Greece. Therefore, they insisted that the Cypriots be left to work out their own affairs. In the meantime they had a small group on that island that continually stirred the pot and kept it going. Sometimes we have a tendency to forget that this was taking place there. The Russians were anxious to increase their naval presence in the Mediterranean at this time, and in fact they were increasing it year by year. If they could have an island such as this which would be available to them for occasional basing and for support and so forth, it would be very advantageous for them.

Moscow, therefore, insisted that the Cypriots be left to work a settlement of the internal conflict out by themselves, and of course this was an approach which could very well dissolve the Zurich-London agreements and jeopardize the British bases in Cyprus. It would further divide NATO and could very easily cause a war between Greece and Turkey.

I think that's about all I'll say about it now, but I thought it best to comment on this particular problem because it was so much a part of so many of the various things that were happening in the Southern Command.

Now let me turn to my trip to Athens and my calls. This took place in May of 1965 - 14-16 May. The purpose, as in the case of other visits, was to pay my respects to the government leaders and the military leaders of the NATO countries of the southern region.

I had heard much about the prime minister of Greece, Mr. Papandreou - Mr. George Papandreou. He has a son who is Andreas Papandreou, who at one time was a college professor in California. He gave up his Greek citizenship and I understand contributed rather heartily to many of the difficulties and unrest on the college campuses in California. Anyway, when his father became prime minister he persuaded Andreas Papandreou to come back to Greece. Andreas Papandreou was a very clever individual. He came back and was given a minor political position in the government by his father, the prime minister -

Q: Does this imply that the prime minister was in agreement with the philosophy of unrest?

Adm. G.: Not necessarily, but he respected his son's mental ability and I think that his son was clever enough so that he was able to pull the wool over his father's eyes. I think that the old man was very much a Greek patroit, whereas I don't feel that that was the case with Andreas. I don't want to get ahead of myself here but I mention this relationship because at the time I made this call, George Papandreou, the prime minister, was getting along in years; he was approaching eighty years of age at the time, and his son Andreas had a minor position in the government, something comparable to assistant secretary of state or something like that, and he had re-assumed at that time his Greek citizenship.

As I think I've indicated in all of these calls, at the time I called on the Greek officials, Cyprus, of course, was very much on everyone's mind, and on the particular day that I called it happened that Archbishop Makarios was in Athens and he was in conference with the prime minister. However, the prime minister received me shortly after I arrived there and interrupted his talk with the archbishop in order to receive me. I did note that he appeared to be very nervous. I got the impression that the archbishop was not being too helpful to him. As you possibly know, the Greeks have strings of beads, which they call worry beads, and the prime minister had a set of these and he was really giving them a good workout during the entire time! He was perspiring, he was quite nervous, and the worry beads were really going back and forth that day.

He seemed to want to impress me very strongly with the fact that Greece was trying to do everything within its power to keep the peace, but that provocative actions on the part of the Turks and of the Turkish minority on Cyprus were making his position most difficult.

I might say here that in both Turkey and Greece at this time there was probably more irresponsible newspaper reporting than had been seen in any country that claimed to have anything near a free press. When articles would appear in a Turkish newspaper, the Greeks would - the Greek officials would hang onto those promptly. They had whole offices that had nothing else to do but examine the Turkish newspapers, come up with articles that were detrimental to Greece, and feed them back into the government press. The same thing happened on the other side. So what the two governments were doing was reacting to newspaper accounts in the other country, and it was perfectly apparent to me very early in the game that this was what was happening, and I told both General Sunay and Mr. Papandreou that I quite frankly considered most of the newspapers in both countries to be highly irresponsible and I thought that they'd be a lot better off if they didn't pay so much attention to what appeared in the other country's newspapers.

Q: How did they react to this bit of advice?

Adm. G.: Well, they seemed to - Mr. Papandreou, I think, was so occupied with his own thoughts that it sort of went off his back like water off a duck's back. General Sunay took it a little more seriously, I felt. However, he was not about to budge from the stand he took that all the trouble was on the part of the Greeks, nor were the Greeks prepared to move at all because in their opinion the Turks were causing all the difficulties.

Let me finish my talk with Mr. Papandreou. He repeated time and time again that Greece would do everything within its power to keep the peace. He also asked me if I would help him in this, and I assured him that I would, I would do everything I possibly could. He also went on to say that he would do everything he possibly could to keep Makarios in Line. He said it was highly important and, as I said before, he reiterated that we must keep the peace because, in his opinion, he said, if a war between Greece and Turkey ever started that would mean that Bulgaria would help Greece and Yugoslavia would help Turkey and therefore World War III would be inevitable.

He was appreciative of the role that President Johnson had played in trying to head off a war over Cyprus. I was a little surprised at the positiveness of some of his statements regarding the ends that Greece would go to to keep the peace, but I was frankly inclined to the thought that he overstated his case and quite possibly would not be in a position to live up to it.

I next called on General Pipilis, who was the chief of the general staff. His job corresponded to that of General Sunay in Turkey. General Pipilis had been in this job for some time and was a very fine gentleman. I took up with him various questions that had been bothering me because I didn't feel that on this first visit it would be proper for me to take them up with Prime Minister Papandreou.

Q: Because you hadn't established a rapport with him?

Adm. G.: Because I hadn't established a rapport with him. However, I felt that - I had met Pipilis before at a change in command in LanSouth up at Verona and had a chance to talk with him briefly there. He had had duty in Washington at one time. So I felt that I could take up with him some of the things that were bothering me quite a bit at that time.

As a consequence of the situation in Cyprus, the Greeks had withdrawn from the LanSoutheast and the Sixth ATAF headquarters in Turkey most of their Greek personnel - that is, from the combined NATO headquarters. The rationale that they gave for this was that they were afraid that the Turks would take overt action against their personnel. They were unprepared to accept this unless the Turks were willing to give them positive assurances to the contrary. The Turks weren't about to do this and quite frankly said, well, we have done absolutely nothing to these people and, quite frankly also, the Greeks could not come up with any specific evidence. Nevertheless, the personnel were withdrawn. The only time we had any significant number of Greek personnel in those headquarters was when we were planning for or conducting a major NATO exercise. This was a subject of great concern to me because, as I told the Greeks, it's absolutely necessary to have Greek personnel in that headquarters, not only for the over-all good of NATO but, I stressed, for your own good because you must have someone in that headquarters who can represent the Greek viewpoint on all the various subjects that come up. I also said, "And I'm sure that when you have occasion to call that headquarters, you would also like to talk to someone in that headquarters who speaks your own language." The answer that I got for a long time was, "Well, the political situation is not quite right for it at this time. We understand your position and we will do what we can."

In addition to that, another factor that entered into it was overflight privileges by the Greek government for Turkish aircraft which were, as I have indicated before, proceeding on NATO business. And the third major irritant at the time was the clearance for multi-national inspection teams. I insisted that every inspection that was made should be made by a multi-national team, that is, a team which was comprised of people from Italy, Greece, Turkey, the United States, and the United Kingdom, and I would not permit an inspection team that had certain nationals denied access to go into a country. So, in many cases, some of these inspections were called off.

Now, I didn't actually threaten either one of the countries, but I saw to it that they understood just exactly what the NATO regulations were at that time, and one of the regulations was that if they did not have these inspections made by NATO inspection teams over a certain period of time, then they would lose NATO support for all of their activities in this field, including financial support. So they could see what I was driving at by not permitting them to have an inspection made. If no inspections were made for a period, say, of a year, they would lose some of their NATO financial support and this would hurt them.

I stressed these points very considerably and the Greeks would say the political situation is not right, and the Turks would say the political situation is not right. The Greeks would say, the Turks are threatening us, and the Turks would say, the Greeks are threatening us.

I also intimated, I must say very carefully, that the Greeks should take it very easy in this field because the Turks had overwhelming armed forces so far as the two countries were concerned.

I might inject here that as time went on I continually

stressed to my Greek friends that it was most important from their point of view not to take any overt action which might tempt the Turks or give them a national excuse to take military action against Cyprus -- because if they did I was sure that Turkey would move and, with the overwhelming military superiority they had over Greece, the results would be disastrous for Greece.

Q: In making these strong representations to these several governments, how closely did you tie in with the American diplomatic representatives?

Adm. G.: I kept them advised as to what I was doing and the gist of my conversations. In each country I would call on the American ambassador. In Turkey the ambassador there at that time was Parker Hart - Pete Hart. He had just relieved Ambassador Hare, who was an old-time Middle East expert. Pete Hart had been ambassador to Saudi Arabia, so he was well equipped for that job and did an absolutely splendid job. At the time of my original call in Greece, Ambassador Laboise had just been recalled - he was just in the process of leaving - and no ambassador had been nominated at that time to replace him. I thought this was rather strange that he should be taken out of there at that particular time because the situation over Cyprus was so tense. Ultimately he was replaced by Ambassador Phillips Talbot.

Q: I imagine that they were able to give you some insights into the local situation that you might not have had otherwise?

Adm. G.: Oh, yes. I leaned very heavily on their information which they furnished me. I must say that during the time I was in my job in NATO there, I was very much impressed with the strength of our U.S. representation in Turkey. On the other hand, I felt that our representation in Greece was fairly weak. I thought that Pete Hart was very, very strong, and Talbot was not so strong.

I called on the minister of defense, Mr. Garoufalias. He's a very intelligent man with strong convictions and a willingness to speak his mind. He was an extremely successful Greek businessman, a very wealthy man, and Greek right to the core, but he was smart enough to know that the worst thing that could possibly happen to Greece would be to have a military confrontation with Turkey, because he appreciated fully that the Turkish armed forces were just simply too strong for them. But, he said, they were not going to step back from their responsibilities and they were not going to permit the Turks, for example, to take over Cyprus.

Q: There was a certain amount of bravado, then, in their attitude?

Adm. G.: A certain amount, yes. At the end he apologized for the strength of his remarks, saying that he possibly had been carried away by his emotions!

Q: Was this a tendency you noted among Greek officials?

Adm. G.: No, just in the case of Garoufalias. The others tended to be very quiet, except Papandreou who talked quite a bit but, as I say, he was an old man, he'd been under very severe pressures, and was trying to figure out how in the world he could deal with this guy Makarios. That was his Number One problem. At the time I was there I did understand from our own people that Mr. Garoufalias probably more than any one single individual in the Greek government was handling the Cyprus affair. Incidentally, in both Ankara and Athens, I had an Allied Forces Southern Europe liaison officer, a colonel in the U.S. Army in each place, and both of these officers were extremely helpful to me. They had entree to practically any office in the respective cities and were very valuable to me over the years.

I took up with Mr. Garoufalias the headquarters at Izmir problem and the overflights for inspection teams without expecting to get any answer from him at that time. I just merely wanted to acquaint him with the problem as I saw it from my own point of view, and some of the irritants that were taking place. At this time, Mr. Laboise, as I said, had been detached as the American ambassador so they had a chargé there and I had nothing in the way of extraordinary conversations with him.

I did have a chance to see the King. I made a call on him and he received me. It was a very pleasant call. This was the first time, of course, that I had seen the young King. He was a very pleasant individual and although we discussed no very deep problems at this time we did later on. He did comment on the Cyprus problem, saying that, oh, it will be handled in time and he commented rather caustically on the point that politicians often make an awful lot of trouble for themselves, which I thought was rather good. He was very much of a Navy-oriented individual and, as you probably remember, he won a gold medal in the Olympics for sailing. He was tutored by his father, King Paul, who used to take him to important governmental meetings when he was thirteen or fourteen years of age to give him some flavor of how to handle things and how the king acted. At the time of much of King Paul's reign the relationship between Greece and Turkey was probably as good as at any time in history because King Paul had a prime minister named Menderes who was a very smart individual, not too emotional, and he could talk straightforward with the Turks and King Paul could see that his own prime minister and the people running Turkey pretty much arrived at a detente and, in his opinion, there was no reason why that shouldn't continue. But things started falling apart after the Menderes regime was defeated.

I was particularly interested in talking to the King as to whether or not I could detect any signs of his being controlled by his mother. This of course was one of the big - and I'll say this - stories that existed at that time, that he was very much under the control of his mother Queen Frederica, who was a very powerful woman, no question about it, and many of the Greeks used to call her "that German," but she and her husband, King Paul did a lot of good for Greece. In my conversations with King Constantine, my impression was that he was handling himself quite well. He was learning. He didn't pretend to know all the answers. And he was participating in as many governmental activities as he could without actually giving the impression of forcing himself in. He gave me the impression that he was also quietly, but rather effectively, laying to rest the charge that he was under the domination of his mother. I found him a very attractive and confident young man. At this time also, he was in the process of traveling about the country with his queen, letting his people see him and his queen.

I say "at this time," but earlier he had been doing that. He was not doing it at this particular time because this was in May and his first child was expected in June, so the queen was not doing very much traveling.

I think that completes the coverage on that particular visit to Athens.

I came back to my headquarters and after a short while made an inspection trip to northern Italy. The purpose here was to take a firsthand look at the border areas of the NATO command, and these included the normal briefings from all the military commanders in the field and in their headquarters, and observing the stationing of units in northern Italy obviously directed at guarding the various passes through which troops might come in an attack from the north.

Generally speaking, I thought the performance of the people in the field was good. There was certainly a very noticeable lack of up-to-date equipment on the part of many units, but generally speaking, recognizing the economy as the reason, I was satisfied with what was shown me.

Q: What would your estimate be of their capabilities to

withstand the onslaught of the enemy, should that happen?

Adm. G.: My thought was that they could hold for an appreciable period of time. Of course, this would depend entirely on the number of troops that would be put against them. However, in most of these cases, one of the things that entered into the equation very strongly was the question of atomic demolitions. In mountainous areas and where you have very narrow defiles and passes, you can do more good with atomic demolition to closing off passes than you can in most any other way. Now, if we had authority to use atomic demolitions, then there would be no question about the ability to hold these border areas for a long time.

Q: And the wherewithal to do that was available?

Adm. G.: The wherewithal to do that was available, right, but not under NATO control. It was under U.S. control as required by U.S. law.

I returned to my headquarters and shortly thereafter received the news that Prime Minister Papandreou had been fired. Well, I happened to know quite a bit about the background of this and what took place on this particular occasion. I've commented on Prime Minister Papandreou and on his son, Andreas Papandreou. Andreas was very much of a revolutionary at heart, but also, I think, supremely confident of his own ability. I don't believe at this particular time that he himself was actually a communist, but I felt that he thought that he could get in bed with the communists and then, later on, after they had served his purposes, he could disengage himself from them and go on to have a tight Greece that he wanted, very, very socialistic and very, very liberal. In my opinion, this was sheer idiocy, because I don't think anyone has ever accomplished this particular technique with the communists. You lose every time, if you try something like that.

Now, when he came back from the U.S., from his professorial job in the U.S. and became part of the Greek government, he started an outfit called "Aspida." The purpose of this organization was to recruit people in the armed services who would in turn be used to undermine the position of the government and the position of the armed services and particularly the Greek Army. As in the case of Turkey, the Greek Army was by far the strongest of the armed services and provided much of the stability for the Greek government. His actions finally came to the attention of Defense Minister Garoufalias and, after a thorough investigation, the defense minister determined that the charges in fact were true and ordered - this had been a sub rosa investigation - and he ordered an official investigation within the Defense Ministry of these charges, obviously with the thought of bringing all the individuals who were responsible before a court of law. This, of course, would include Andreas Papandreou if it could be tied to him and the evidence was rather overwhelming that it could be.

When Prime Minister Papandreou found out about this, as he did because this was an official investigation and major elements of the government knew it, he went to the king and asked permission from the king to fire Mr. Garoufalias and assume the defense portfolio himself. This obviously would have put him in the position of investigating himself or his own family. The king refused to do this and over several hours of conversation, culminating in an evening meeting between Papandreou and the king, about nine o'clock at night, Mr. Papandreou said, "Well, Your Majesty, if you will not permit me to assume the Defense portfolio, I will submit to you tomorrow morning my resignation as prime minister," and the young king, who was about twenty-six said, "Mr. Prime Minister, I accept your resignation now," and within an hour it was on the wires. And it was just as well he did that because it came to light afterwards that Andreas Papandreou had set up demonstrations in various parts of Athens and in other cities in Greece which were to take place, ostensibly spontaneously, with the announcement the following day that the prime minister, who could deliver an announcement in a very emotional tone of voice, was resigning because of the opposition of the king to certain of his practices and so on.

So, it was just as well that he did it at that time, because these things were all set up to happen the next day. Now, in this particular incident, I think the king handled himself extremely well. You may say that he cut off his nose to spite his face because this started a series of very unstable governments in Greece which continued until the take-over of the government by a coup later on. On the other hand, what was the alternative at this time? The alternative would permit Papandreou to take the Defense portfolio and that immediately would have the effect of having all the charges in the investigation withdrawn, the Greek Army would be infiltrated, and that was the one thing that provided stability within Greece, so that any government could function. In essence, the alternative to the thing would have been anarchy in the country - complete anarchy. I'm convinced of that. Therefore, I say it was a good thing for it to happen. I thought the king handled himself quite well. Unfortunately, later on, he didn't measure up quite as well as he did on that one occasion, but on that one occasion he did extremely well.

As I say, this started a series of governments in Greece, all of which were very weak and all of which were unable to accomplish anything of a decisive nature. As a consequence, the Cyprus situation just boiled along and really nothing could take place regarding that situation until a more stable government was possible in Greece.

My next visit out in my parish, as we sometimes called it, was for the purpose of conducting an inspection out in eastern Turkey. This visit was made between the 6th and the 9th of September.

Q: Out to Armenia and that area?

Adm. G.: In the vicinity of Erzurum, although actually I went all the way out to the Soviet border.

On the way out there, I stopped at Ankara for the purpose of briefing General Sunay on this particular visit. I was quite certain, of course, that General Sunay had been completely briefed on the thing, but just as a matter of courtesy and protocol since I was going on an inspection trip to his country and to inspect one of his armies, the Third Army, headquartered in Erzurum, I felt that under the circumstances it would be better and more politic to stop by Ankara on the way and just tell him myself what I was doing. This type of thing paid big dividends when you were involved with the Turks.

Q: This meant that you had to be utterly open and frank about the whole thing because your verbal report had to correspond with the report he had already received?

Adm. G.: Oh, sure, that's right. And there was nothing that I would hold back about his own country from General Sunay if he asked me in the way of factual information.

General Sunay had just concluded an inspection around all of the three Turkish armies. He'd just completed an inspection trip, and these are done in August as a matter of routine in Turkey - or they were at that time - for the purpose of inspecting the Turkish military units in the field, and also to give the chief of the Turkish general staff and other senior officers a look at the senior officers, generals, in the field. This particular trip was always used as an important ingredient in determining what general officers were to be promoted. They didn't have a selection board that came in and sat down, as we do, and fitness reports. They'd go out and inspect them in the field, and look at their commands. In the case of a brigadier general, they talk to the major generals and lieutenant generals over him, and get all the firsthand information right then and there. General Sunay had gone to eastern Turkey, northern Turkey, and to Turkish Thrace to get individual detailed reports on the candidates, and they also had an opportunity to see and talk to the candidates themselves.

I also had an opportunity to brief him in a general way about our Operation Deep Furrow. Deep Furrow was the code name for one of the standard NATO exercises which we had in the southern region on an annual basis. I extended an invitation to him also to ride in my helicopter which I would have sent over there and it would be available to go to the various observation points. I'll give more information later on in this dissertation on the two types of exercises that we had, one was the Eastern Express and the other the Deep Furrow.

I also took this opportunity to give him a short report on my understanding of the Greek political crisis and express my pleasure to him at the statesmanship and patience which the Turkish authorities had displayed in connection with this crisis.

Q: Tongue in cheek!

Adm. G.: That's right. General Sunay appreciated this very much. He said that he was sure having a lot of trouble with

Makarios. At this particular time, Makarios had demanded a detailed inspection of the Turkish rotation group. You see, the Turks kept a Turkish force on Cyprus and they rotated them, just as we rotate the Seventh Fleet and the Sixth Fleet, and Makarios had come up at that time with a demand that this rotation group be subjected to detailed inspection on its arrival and on its departure. This made the Turks mad as the devil and, frankly, I agreed with the Turks on this.

Q: The objective being what?

Adm. G.: The objective being to make sure that they knew precisely everything that the Turks were bringing in.

Q: You mean in the way of ordnance?

Adm. G.: They didn't want it to be possible for them to stockpile a lot of ammunition and other ordnance and to give excess ammo to the Turkish Cypriots on the island, so as to arm them.

One of the items that I also mentioned to General Sunay on this occasion was that the Turks are not very good at the business of public relations and they tended to be rather truculent in this field. In connection with Deep Furrow, part of which would take place in Greece and part would take place in Turkey, I suggested to General Sunay that it was my understanding that the Greeks had already prepared a very polished presentation for the benefit of the press and I had been informed that the Turks didn't have anything like this. I strongly urged that they have a presentation ready for a press briefing, which would be of great assistance to Turkey and NATO. He took that aboard in a hurry and about two days later I understood that they were working furiously on a presentation and actually came up with a pretty good one.

Well, we left Ankara and proceeded by air to Erzurum. We landed on a new strip there which had just - well, it was really not yet finished. It was built by NATO infrastructure funds. The field had been under construction for a couple of years, but construction work is slow because of the short construction season. It's only about four months -

Q: You mean the climate is so severe?

Adm. G.: The climate is so severe. You have eight or ten feet of snow there for five or six months.

Q: What mountains are they?

Adm. G.: They're out in eastern Turkey, actually a part of the Caucasus mountains. Mount Ararat was not far away to the east.

We arrived there and were greeted by the commanding general of the Third Army, General Tagmac, who, incidentally is now, I think, the chief of the Turkish general staff. This trip out there was extremely interesting. As in practically all of the outlying areas of the country, it's the Turkish Army that's doing things. They are the ones who are building the schools. They are the ones who are bringing in people to assist the locals in agriculture, engineering, mining, and things like that. For example, a college was built in Erzurum and they had at that college a group of about thirty-five American professors who were assisting the Turks in not only basic education but in how to take advantage of local conditions for agricultural development.

Q: By what program would that be financed?

Adm. G.: I'm sure it was financed under AID. It was the University of Nebraska, I believe, that had the sponsorship for this particular one. Other universities had other places in Turkey, but this was very much of a going affair.

In Erzurum you see a little bit of everything except the very modern. Much of it is back in biblical times. The Third Army stretches over that whole area, and this area was one that had been used by the Russians to invade Turkey on several occasions in the past.

We had the usual briefings and parties, entertainments, in Erzurum. We had one dinner party that happened to be on Mrs. Griffin's birthday, so they had a birthday cake for her.

Q: Oh, she was traveling with you?

Adm. G.: She was along and enjoyed it tremendously. However, she remained in Erzurum while I made various inspections. We used little L-19 aircraft, reconnaissance aircraft, to fly from Erzurum out to a small field about 15 kilometers from the border, the Russian border -

Q: You must have been mighty certain of your -

Adm. G.: Oh, it was a good day!

Q: Was this before or after the American colonels were lost?

Adm. G.: This was September 1965. I think they were lost after this.

Q: But it was during your time?

Adm. G.: Yes. We went out to about 15 kilometers and landed at a small field there, and then took vehicles from there out to the border. I noticed the same types of regulations at the border there as we had in Italy and at the Bulgarian border. One is not supposed to point toward the communist sentry because the Soviets in the one case and the Bulgarians in the other case consider this to be a provocative act. So you're asked not to point at the other country and you're requested not to take any pictures, any photographs. I actually did take some pictures through the slit window of the command post.

Q: What was your purpose in going directly to the border?

Adm. G.: To see the provisions the Turkish Army had made to 1) detect any incursion of attack, and 2) to get an appreciation of their ability to handle an incursion or attack.

Q: How alert they were.

Adm. G.: How alert they were to this? They rotated people from the rear areas up front. The great weakness that I saw there was the lack of effective equipment and particularly communications equipment. I visited a division headquarters that was way out in the boondocks and asked regarding their ability to communicate with higher headquarters in the rear. "Oh, yes, there's a communication van over there." Much to their surprise, I said I'd like to see it, so we went over and before they really had a chance to say no I got in the communications van and found that the total amount of communications in that van consisted of one radio transmitter and receiver which was about an early World War II vintage, and that was it! It was really pathetic and it opened my eyes.

These people were putting up a good show but the amount of modern equipment they had was negligible. They were willing to fight. They proved that in Korea.

Q: Were the Russians at the border aware of the fact that such a high-ranking official was present?

Adm. G.: I'm sure that they were. It's difficult to keep open movements secret. Further, I was not trying to keep my movements secret. There was some advantage to having the Soviet know. At each one of the places where we stopped we got very good briefings, and I got the impression that the Turks, while lacking equipment and most of the equipment they had, of course, was obsolete or obsolescent U.S. Army equipment, were in there pitching and they were doing a good job. They put on a good show.

Q: Were there any specific U.S. bases in that area?

Adm. G.: No. The only U.S. bases - that's probably not correct -

Q: U.S. installations?

Adm. G.: The only U.S. installations would be the units, the custodial units, for our atomic weapons.

Q: These were the units that were in contention with the Russians, were they not? The Russians were aware of this?

Adm. G.: Oh, yes, they were aware of it, very much so.

Q: Did you inspect any of those?

Adm. G.: I inspected those, but after one or two inspections I decided that it would be better if I did not inspect them myself, but rather had some of my staff who were specifically qualified for that work do it incident to my own visit there. The reason I did that was that I'd be accompanied by the senior people in that area. We'd drive up and we'd get to a gate of an installation, the gate would be opened, and I could go in but the Turkish general couldn't go in and the Greek general couldn't go in, and this created a very embarrassing situation. So I thought it was just another little irritant. This was so because of our own atomic energy laws.

Q: In addition to that, your presence, your inspection, of these units would tend to underscore them too prominently?

Adm. G.: It would, and also there was another factor, too. I was NATO commander, not a U.S. commander. These were strictly U.S. and in accordance with bilateral arrangements between the United States and Turkey.

Q: And one other question in this area: in such a remote part of Turkey and such an isolated part, did this create any morale problems with the U.S. units?

Adm. G.: Very little. They didn't particularly like this duty but their rotational policies were such that it didn't create too much of a problem. Everybody in the armed services had some unaccompanied tours in various places in the world, and this was their turn to have an unaccompanied tour.

Q: You mean devoid of family?

Adm. G.: Devoid of family, right. And you would either come to a place like this or go to Vietnam or some other place. So it was accepted in that light, and the tours were not too long. They were comparable to what we have had in a one-year tour in Vietnam or something like that.

The spreading of the troops in that area was rather thin, but at the same time we did feel that the nature of the terrain was such that there were very definite avenues through which any enemy would have to come, and therefore those were covered well, since the chances of their coming by any other routes were minimal.

Q: What was the over-all Turkish attitude towards the fact that they are on the front line?

Adm. G.: Let me say this. I think that they - and this is a very good question and one whose answer I had occasion to highlight on many occasions during my tour over there, and it's something that really it not too well understood by a great many Americans, particularly in the Defense Department, and some of our politicians and people in Congress.

The Turks feel that for years they have been sitting there, so to speak looking at the tonsils of this great big bear and defending the free world against it. They have stood up to them, they participated in Korea on the front lines. They had taken political actions from time to time - this was some years ago - which were not calculated to make them very friendly with the Soviet Union. They had been adamant on their right of inspection, of prior notification of any ships going through the Bosporus. They had done all these things and they felt "we deserve to get the help that we're getting because we've earned it." It wasn't just largese from a powerful friend, but we have earned it, and they felt very strongly about this. So when people talk about cutting foreign aid or cutting aid to Turkey, this was in the nature, to them, of cutting or reducing a salary which they had earned, and they'd worked for. It's this approach that must be understood in this country and on the part of many it's not understood at all.

I know on one of the occasions when I came back here to the States I had a series of talks with Senator Russell and Senator Scoop Jackson about destroyers for Turkey. I had long talks with them and these talks resulted in getting a couple of destroyers for Turkey that had been held up largely by Senator Russell. I think this argument was first presented by me to members of the Congress, that the Turks felt that they had earned and deserved help, that it wasn't gravy, this was something they'd earned - a salary, so to speak.

Q: That's very interesting. Now, it seems to me, as you relate it, that there was a very level-headed attitude on the part of the Turks. Why were they incapable of applying the same factual point of view to the Turco-Greek situation? They live side by side with them also.

Adm. G.: That's right, they live side by side with them also, but over the years there has developed very much animosity between the two. I recall that later on, in a visit to Greece, I called on General Tsolakas, who had relieved General Pipilis as the chief of the general staff. General Tsolakas had been in command of the Greek army up in the Thessalonica area. I pressed again for a return of the Greek personnel to the Izmir headquarters, and General Tsolakas said, "Admiral, you're absolutely right. I agree with everything you say. We should have our people there. I like Izmir, as a matter of fact. I was born there. Furthermore, it was at Izmir where the Turks hanged my father."

That little item was just dumped in my lap. All my intelligence had never turned that point up! It just hit like a dull thud. Well, you have animosities like this that go back centuries and you can't apply logical measures and yardsticks to relationships such as this.

Q: Yet the other situation you related seems logical enough!

Adm. G.: That's right. Oh, there are contradictions all over the place.

One of the observations that I had out there was that most of the dinner parties that we were given had local entertainment. These almost invariably consisted of a group of men dancers, and I thought to myself as one of them was dancing this particular evening - Mrs. Griffin's birthday - how well they would do on an Ed Sullivan Show! They were really very good and we enjoyed it.

Q: You didn't try to promote that, however?

Adm. G.: No, I didn't!

Q: Just a bit of color which you might add. How in such an outlying area was a dinner party conducted? With what degree of grace and finesse?

Adm. G.: Not bad at all. Actually, as was the case at most parties that were given for us in Turkey, they were conducted under the auspices of the Ordu Evi's, the officers' clubs, and they were all just about the same.

Q: Oh, I see.

Adm. G.: It didn't make a great deal of difference - oh, it certainly did in the types of food that you had - whether you were in Ankara or in Erzurum. As I say, out in this area you're back in biblical times, as you can see all around you. On our way out to Erzurum we stopped and refueled at Diyarbakir. This was a big Turkish Air Force base, about halfway from Ankara to Erzurum. The reason that comes to mind - and I'll comment on it later because one of our exercises was held in the vicinity of Diyarbakir - is that the old city of Diyarbakir was on the camel route to the Far East and all the caravans went through there. The old walled city of Diyarbakir, as is the case with the old city of Erzurum, dates back to some 3,000 B.C., so you've got an awful lot of "old" out there.

This whole trip, as I say, was extremely interesting and it was part of my education to see just what the situation was way out in the field, and that was part of my basic plan for my inspections of my command.

After returning to my headquarters in Naples, I had time out for a very quick trip to Washington. I borrowed an aircraft from U.S. Air Forces, Europe, under General Bruce Holloway at the time, to come back to Washington for a short visit which included my son's wedding. He was married on the 15th of September, I think it was, in Annapolis at the Naval Academy -

Q: And that was in 19--?

Adm. G.: That was in 1965. It was on a Saturday and Navy was playing Syracuse that afternoon. The temperature was 93°. I was my son's best man at the wedding and we had perspiration just pouring off us. I must admit that I shifted into a shirt for the game afterwards, and just as soon as the game was over I went right to Andrews and took off from Andrews for Naples.

Q: You had no other purpose? You just came back for the wedding?

Adm. G.: Well, I had one or two things to take up with the

authorities in Washington and they had been set up for this particular time so it coincided very nicely for me and made it possible for me to get back here, but I must admit that the large reason for it was to get back here for the wedding. But I had to get back to my headquarters in time to leave early Monday morning for Exercise Deep Furrow, so for a period of several days I was in the air considerably more than I was on the ground.

Exercise Deep Furrow took place in Turkey and Greece and involved an air drop in Turkey. These exercises were NATO-sponsored and their basic objective was to determine the readiness of the forces which had been made available by the national authorities to the NATO commitment. This involved the use in many cases of considerable U.S. equipment. For example, this Exercise Deep Furrow included an air drop and land operations in Turkey and amphibious operations and subsequent land operations in Greece. These exercises were also fully covered by the press. We had briefings and, as I commented earlier, by the time this exercise actually took place the Turks had prepared good briefings for the press and I sat in on the briefings for the press by both the Turks and the Greeks because I thought it might be a good idea to have the commander in chief there, and also to answer any questions that might be asked by the press because, quite frankly, the people, particularly in Turkey, were not too adept at fielding press questions. So I took most of the questions myself.

Q: Was this an international press?

Adm. G.: Yes.

Q: Were the Russians permitted?

Adm. G.: If they wanted to, yes, and quite often we did have some communist press there. They rarely asked any questions but they were present.

The exercise went off quite well despite the fact that we had considerable fog. I made a big hit with the Turkish authorities because my helicopter was the only one that landed at the landing area for a matter of about an hour and a half. The others couldn't find it, and my helicopter's pilot had gone out the day before and gone to the landing areas and taken a couple of cross bearings of the beacons and radio stations, so he knew precisely where the landing area was and we were the only ones that got in in this morning fog. That made an impression on the Minister of Defense.

Incidentally, General Lemnitzer was down there for this exercise, too. So we had the Minister of Defense and General Lemnitzer and a couple of his officers with him.

The exercise was very good and, as I say, fully covered by the press. I don't think it's necessary to go into any great detail on it. This time I went on over to the Greek part of the exercise. It was almost entirely necessary to have done it this way at this particular time, to split the exercise into two parts, one in Turkey and one in Greece, because neither side would permit the other to come in and participate on their soil.

Q: And officialdom was giving equal attention to both?

Adm. G.: That's right.

Q: In the case of an exercise like this, which you did witness, then did you write a critique on it?

Adm. G.: Yes. We would have a full critique for each one of these exercises which would be prepared by my staff, cleared by me, and sent up to General Lemnitzer.

The exercise over in Greece was also very good. Our same group included General Lemnitzer and also the Assistant Secretary of Defense Hoopes, who happened to be a friend of mine, Tim Hoopes. He was at the National War College in the same class I was in. He later became Undersecretary of the Air Force, but he is now not in the government. On this occasion I had another opportunity to talk to the King because the King was there, and he asked me to join him for lunch because, he said, "I get tired of eating alone."

Q: That's protocol with his own people?

Adm. G.: That's right. I purposely centered all my conversation around the exercise.

Q: Did your assessment of him continue to be that of a level-headed young man?

Adm. G.: Yes, it did. I stressed the fact that the only time we could have any Greek personnel in the Izmir headquarters was when we had an exercise such as this. During the exercise there were Greek people in the headquarters so I used this occasion to stress to the King how beneficial it was that those people were there and it was too bad they couldn't stay. I urged him to go ahead and send them back as rapidly as he possibly could.

Q: Did you get a reaction from him on that point?

Adm. G.: Yes, indeed. He said he felt very strongly about it himself and he agreed that the time was appropriate now for permanent assignment to Izmir of the Greeks. It was then that he continued on a reminiscence of his father and the Prime Minister at that time, Menderes, and according to him, King Paul had told Menderes that while the troubles between their two countries were deeply rooted, he still felt that it should be possible for the two of them to work out all their problems. King Paul said that obviously when you've got a large percentage of the population of one nationality, it is only logical for that nationality to have more control than for the minorities, and King Paul had told Menderes that if the situation in Cyprus could be worked out profitably to them - which meant the Greeks taking over! - he would offer NATO a base any place on Greek soil that it wanted, including Cyprus.

Constantine himself said that there was no question in his mind but that his father's views were correct and this business of partitioning really never worked any place. He pointed out Germany, Korea, and Vietnam, and said it wouldn't work on Cyprus. Constantine said that his father had been optimistic about reaching an agreement on Cyprus until the United Kingdom disrupted everything by their own selfish interests, and that the political situation deteriorated sharply thereafter.

Q: What was this disruption?

Adm. G.: When the United Kingdom decided to give Cyprus independence and get the hell out. At this particular time in our conversation I made a note that things really hit the fan. The conversation was interrupted by an aide to the king who reported excitedly that the Turks had just taken action to deport twenty-five Greek citizens of Jewish faith, giving them twenty-four hours to leave Turkey!

I subsequently learned from our Consul General in Istanbul that the report was essentially correct.

This, of course, gutted any further discussion about returning Greek military personnel to Izmir! This is the way it went during much of my time over there. I made a note that I believed that any further effort by third parties with regard to Greek military representation at Izmir would have to be deferred at least until after the elections in Turkey, which were coming up.

That finished our Deep Furrow exercise.

Interview No. 16 with Admiral C. D. Griffin, U.S. Navy (Retired)
Place: His residence in Washington, D.C.
Date: Thursday morning, 20 January 1972
Subject: Biography
By: John T. Mason, Jr.

Q: As usual, it's a pleasure to see you, Sir. Last time, you had us journeying in eastern Turkey, in an ancient province of Armenian Turkey, I guess. You went to the Russian border and then you made a very quick - brief - trip back to the United States and that's where Chapter 15 concluded. Do you want to take up the story from that point?

Adm. G.: Right. As you said, I did cover the Exercise Deep Furrow both in Turkey and in Greece, and also Exercise Eastern Express in Diyarbakir. I would like today to go through several other what one might call the routine visits in this command. As you recall, I said before that one of my efforts was as quickly as possible to see all parts of the command and especially the border areas in the far reaches of the countries involved.

I reported earlier on my going out to the eastern border of Turkey and also going to the northern border of Italy. My next trip - and this was in late September and October of 1965 - was to the Thessalonica area of Greece and the northern border of Greece with Bulgaria, Yugoslavia, and Rumania. This was a standard type visit in which I saw the troops in the field, the defensive positions which were strategically placed insofar as the defiles in the mountains were concerned. This particular border and particularly the Bulgarian part of the border was characterized by a mountainous area to the north. The border itself, however, was on the south side of the mountain peaks and therefore the Bulgarian territory really was in a commanding position. Furthermore, if the Bulgarian armed forces were to come through the several passes which were readily available to them - at one point they were less than 75 kilometers from the Aegean sea - this simply highlighted the necessity to be very alert to any possible action on the part of the Bulgarian forces to move from the north. It highlighted also the necessity of having very carefully prepared plans, especially for demolition of the routes through which their armed forces would have to come.

The Greeks were quite well aware of this and so far as I was concerned I felt were prepared for any eventuality. It was quite apparent to me, however, that atomic demolition charges would be extremely useful in this area. As usual, I felt that the troops were short of equipment. I guess that we had a natural tendency to compare these troops with well-equipped American troops. Nevertheless, the equipment was very meager, however, I felt that they would do a good job with what they had.

Q: How were the Bulgarians equipped?

Adm. G.: The Bulgarians, from our best information, were pretty well equipped. The Soviet Union had been giving them cast-off equipment. It was given to the Bulgarians in considerable quantities. They had quite good aircraft. As a matter of fact, the aircraft that the Russians were giving the Bulgarians at the time were aircraft of a more modern vintage than the ones that the Greeks had.

Q: What was the state of tempers at the border?

Adm. G.: It was almost exactly the same as in every other border area that I'd seen. There was no dialogue between the two sides at all. Careful look, watch, waiting attitude on the part of all. The type of attitude which was true out in eastern Turkey was true here and, again, as in the case of eastern Turkey, we were asked not to photograph the communist side of the border or make any motions with our hands or otherwise that could be interpreted as being a hostile action. We were very careful about these things and it was, as I said, essentially the same type of procedure as we had out in eastern Turkey.

Q: I take it, then, there was no ease of passage for civilians over the border?

Adm. G.: No, indeed, not at all. It was most difficult to go across and I think that any of the natives who lived up in that area who went across, the chances are that they would go across at some place in the mountainous area pretty far from the road system. The road, of course, was open for people with legitimate business to go across the border and they would be permitted, provided they had the necessary papers.

I don't want to spend too much time on this because I think the facts are pretty well documented otherwise.

My next visit was to Malta, and I'd like to spend a little bit of time on this because Malta is a very interesting Island. I think we're all familiar with the history of Malta in World War II and, as a matter of fact, the early history of Malta and particularly the Malta as depicted in the Book <u>The Great Siege</u>, which is one of the most interesting books that I've read in some time.

Malta had been granted independence by the British government and, in line with their basic political policy of turning over to the various countries of the former British Empire the right of self-determination - so they had been granted independence. The British, however, did keep a governor general there, although his authority had been curtailed considerably and, of course, the ties with Britain remained very, very close. One of the first things that was noticeable, however, was the effect of granting independence and the British cutting back in the Mediterranean on the economy of Malta. This was especially noticeable in the shipyards. An island such as Malta with magnificent harbors had long lived on the revenues which came to the Maltese from the shipyards. These shipyards were run, of course, by the British for many, many years and they employed many thousands of Maltese people. They were very good. When independence was granted there were several companies in Britain that consulted with the Maltese government in regard to continuing management of the shipyards. One of the companies, a Scottish company, had a contract for management of the shipyards. However, the number of British forces and participating naval forces, in the Mediterranean was being cut back steadily, which resulted in less work in the shipyards.

One of the other sources of revenue for the shipyards had been the cleaning of oil tankers following passage through the Suez Canal. With the Suez Canal closed to all traffic, this source of revenue was almost completely eliminated. It was during this period that the United States, in an effort to help a bit, sent ships of the Sixth Fleet to Malta for routine maintenance. This would give a little bit of work to the shipyards and also would further help the economy of Malta when crews of these ships would go ashore on liberty and purchase various and sundry things that one could get in Malta. There was plenty of very-well-done brass things that could be gotten in Malta, brier pipes were made in Malta and, actually, many of them with high-price tags on them were sold in England and in New York -

Q: Dunhill?

Adm. G.: Under the Dunhill name for about ten times what you would have to pay for them in Malta, but they were made in Malta. There was considerable in the way of cloth work that was done in Malta.

On this particular visit I met Mr. George Feldman, an American businessman who had been active in the political field for many years. He was the first American ambassador to the island of Malta, and also this was his first ambassadorship, his first job of any kind in the State Department. He had been associated with the government in various categories, largely in the logistics field, and I might say that he did, on his own, quite a bit for Malta because he persuaded a few American companies to come in there and establish places of business, all this designed to help the economy of Malta. Naturally, it also was an outlet for American business.

Strategically, the island of Malta was a very valuable piece of real estate. I think everyone has of course heard about Malta being an unsinkable aircraft carrier in World War II and it's quite true. The airfields on Malta were very valuable to any country or coalition of countries that might have the use of them. The value of Malta was enhanced also by the conditions in Cyprus. Another factor which entered into this equation, as far as I was concerned in looking at it from a U.S. point of view on the training side but in a total NATO point of view, was the precarious predicament that we were in in connection with North African bases. The Americans and the British had bases in Libya. The American Air Force used the Libyan air base as a training area. Most of the Air Force, as we know, was in England and in Germany, known as U.S. Air Forces, Europe, and in those countries in that area there were very few places where they could train with live ammunition, shooting at drones or sleeves or anything like that, or doing bombing. Training areas were very few and far between.

However, in Libya you had the training areas. Practically

the whole country could be used as a training area and the Mediterranean Sea was right there and could be used. So American units rotated down to the Libyan base for their training, their live training, which kept their military effectiveness and readiness at a high level.

At this particular time, one of the individuals, in our opinion, who was holding to the status quo in Libya was King Idris. He was getting along in years and was in not too good health. It was quite apparent also that he was not going to live too much longer, and from all that we could gather the total prospect of continuing the current arrangement after his death or deposition, whichever would first take place, would be rather small This would mean that having a place such as Malta where you actually could fly in your aircraft squadrons and let them train there - because there were excellent bombing ranges at Malta on some of the uninhabited small rocks and islands, and also the Mediterranean Sea was there where you could shoot.

So the prospect of losing North Africa as a training area was a very live one and this, in turn, enhanced the relative importance of Malta.

Conditions, of course, in Cyprus and the probability of not being able to use the British bases there also enhanced the relative importance of Malta. So from the viewpoint of the airfields and the harbor and the shipyards, Malta was a very important piece of real estate.

Now, at this time, the command CinCAFMed, Commander in Chief, Allied Forces, Mediterranean, was in existence and Admiral

Hamilton, a British naval officer, was the CinCAFMed. CinCAFMed was originally set up by Admiral Mountbatten and had been in the hands of a British admiral ever since. At the time of my visit, however, it was quite apparent that rumblings were going on in connection with this command. One of the basic principles that had been applied in international relationships, and particularly NATO, was that the country that provided the forces would get the command. This is a very much oversimplified statement and there were slight modifications from this, but generally speaking, if you provided the forces you'd get the command. Now, the British had this command for many years, ever since it was established by Lord Mountbatten, and properly so because they were providing very large naval and other forces in the Mediterranean. However, they were cutting back these forces at this time, while at the same time the Italians were building up their naval forces very considerably, and the Italian naval forces were good. They were quite different from the ones that existed in Italy before and during World War II. They were very good.

A case in point, which I will comment on a little later, is the missile systems that they had in some of their ships. These were American missile systems - missile systems that the Americans were having a great deal of difficulty handling and managing and making them work. The Italians put them in their ships and made them work. They were actually working for the Italians much better than they were for the Americans. The answer to that was quite simple as soon as you got into it.

They put some of their best people in this field and kept

them in there. They weren't being transferred every two or three years. They kept them in there, their systems were well documented, which was one of our difficulties. We put the systems in our ships, made little changes in them, and it would be six months before those changes went into the place where the missiles were being built and came out in the form of blueprints and documentation back to the ship. So, if you didn't have a factory representative aboard who knew all about these, or an enlisted man or a chief or an officer who knew what the score was on it, you were lost. This was one of our difficulties, but I won't go into that because I'm afraid it would take a book to write about that. It wasn't very good.

Anyway, the subject of what do to about CinCAFMed was rapidly becoming a very current one. The British realized this, the Italians were unhappy that they had not had any more in the way of high commands in the naval field. Yet there were certain things that were possible and certain things that were not possible in this area. I've already commented that neither the Greeks nor the Turks would accept an Italian CinCAFMed, neither the Greeks nor the Turks would accept one of the other in that job, and they were becoming unhappy that the British were holding on to it, while at the same time the British forces were almost being cut out entirely. So the net result would be that about the only nationality they would accept would be an American. However, this would be awfully awkward, too, since the Americans already held the top command in Naples. Because of local international politics, the Americans also held the Land Southeast Command

and the 6th ATAF Command, so this would make the whole thing topheavy so far as the Americans were concerned.

Well, the solution to this became apparent to many people. Do away with CinCAFMed and create a Commander, Naval Forces South, put him under the command of CinCSouth. Then you would have a clear-cut command - a Naval Forces South, you had Air Forces South, and then you had the two Land Forces South, one in Italy and one over in Greece/Turkey. So I was directed to prepare a staff study on this by General Lemnitzer, and I started this, and this was one of the things I discussed with Admiral Hamilton on this visit, because I very much wanted to include him in this staff study and to get an input from him as to the desires there.

I won't say anything more about that at this particular time, but I wanted to give this background on Malta. Our visit there was a very pleasant one. They had had elections in the not-too-distant past and the Conservative Party had won despite a very vigorous campaign that was put on by the Labor leader there, Dom Mintoff. I made routine calls on the various people on the island, including the archbishop, an old gentleman who was in his middle eighties at that time. One of the things that was quite noticeable about the government there was the age of the various ministers. I would suspect that the average age of the ministers at that time was certainly in the seventies, and I saw very little indication of any tendency to bring younger people into the government.

I commented on this to Ambassador Feldman, who, incidentally, presented his papers to the government the first day that I was there, so we were on hand when he actually became the American ambassador. This, of course, gave me an opportunity, which he had sought, to brief him on the total situation in the Mediterranean and in NATO. This was a splendid opportunity for me. I spent several hours on this subject with Mr. Feldman and I'm sure he gained a lot of information which he had not had before, and during the time that I was in the CinCSouthFlt he remained very close to me and did not hesitate at all to send me messages asking for information on various and sundry things. I satisfied his requirements to the best of my ability.

My next visit was to CinCCent at his headquarters at Fontainebleau - Commander in Chief Central Europe. We had Commander in Chief Northern Europe, Commander in Chief Central Europe, Commander in Chief Southern Europe, and Commander in Chief Allied Forces Mediterranean. They were the four major commands under Lemnitzer.

This officer was a French general, General Crepin. This was purely a courtesy visit to pay my respects to my associated chief, shall we say. General Crepin was one of the senior of the French Army officers and was doing a fine job, from all I could see. We had briefings there and we stayed at his quarters. His chief of Army staff, who was General Graf von Kielmannsegg, a German general who, in fact, later on relieved General Crepin when de Gaulle withdrew the French people from the Joint and Allied staffs. The Air member of his hierarchy was Air Chief Marshal Sir Edmund Huddleston.

This visit did not include any visits to troops in the field, merely the headquarters for briefings and get-togethers, dinners, and so forth. While on this trip, after visiting CinCCent, I took advantage of the proximity of two other U.S. commands to drop in and see them. One was U.S. Air Forces, Europe, at that time under the command of General Bruce Holloway of the U.S. Air Force, an old friend of mine. As a matter of fact, he was a classmate of mine at the National War College. He had his headquarters at Wiesbaden. I also saw the Commander in Chief of the U.S. Army in Europe who was General Andy O'Meara at that time, with headquarters in Heidelberg.

Much of the visiting between these headquarters took place by train because it was too foggy to fly or to drive in many of the local areas.

Q: This was wintertime?

Adm. G.: This was wintertime. I also took advantage of this trip to attend a board of directors meeting of the North Atlantic Council of the Girl Scouts, which was held in Heidelberg.

Q: And why that?

Adm. G.: I had been on this council ever since I had been in London, and when I went down to Naples they asked me to continue serving on the board of directors and so I did. I found it very interesting to keep up with the activities in the various areas.

This was something that the Navy wasn't doing too much about because there were very few naval forces over there which included the families. Most of it devolved upon the Army and the Air Force, who were shore-based and had their families with them.

I next returned to my headquarters in Naples and later made a very interesting trip, a very short one, to the Italian missile range on Sardinia at Salto di Quirra, where they gave us a briefing - this was just simply a one-day trip covering the total installations they had and their ability to handle all the various types of drones and their ability to check the missile-firings of their ships. While we were there, they put on a demonstration of shooting at a drone, a demonstration which proved to be completely successful. It's a very fine missile range and the U.S. Navy was anxious to use it. At this particular time the Sixth Fleet was using a missile range, a French missile range, but the capacity of that range was rather limited and arrangements had been made for units of the Sixth Fleet to use the Italian missile range.

I made several other visits to local areas, for example, Rome and Caserta to see the Italian artillery and armory schools, and then another visit to Turkey and Greece. In Turkey I called on Prime Minister Suleiman Demiral and on the Defense Minister, on General Sunay, and on Ambassador Hart.

With General Sunay I took up the question of ComNavSouth, the overflights of Greece, and reported to him what the Greeks had told me earlier - that they would do everything in their power to prevent any further embarrassment to Turkish planes proceeding on NATO business.

In Greece I saw Ambassador Talbot, Prime Minister Stephanopoulos, and Defense Minister Costopolous, and General Solakis who, by this time, had moved down from command of the Army in northern Greece to become the chief of the General staff. I pled with all of these, as I did every time I came to Greece, to please return their personnel to the headquarters at Izmir. I think I've already mentioned that General Solakis said that he would do everything he could because he just loved Izmir, that's where he was born, and that's where they hanged his father.

Q: Tell me, how did the British react to this proposal for ComNavSouth? And the demise of the command which they had?

Adm. G.: The British didn't, of course, like it. Giving up high-command jobs, prestige jobs, they didn't like at all, but they recognized fully that they had no case at all and were quite prepared to accept it. One of the things that I had in the back of my mind at this time was to insist that initially the Italian admiral who would become NavSouth with headquarters in Malta would have a British chief of staff. This was somewhat of a departure from normal practice because normally the commander would have the right of selecting his own chief of staff and it usually would be someone from his own country. But in this case I felt that the expertise of the British in total planning work, for that matter, in that particular area and knowledge of the Mediterranean, having been there so long, plus, quite frankly, a little sop for losing the high command. So I determined that I would take a hard-nosed position on this and insist that the chief of staff be a Britisher. And this was accepted.

I had plans to go up to Berchtesgaden over Christmas, but they came to a grinding halt when I suddenly came down with a very severe case of hepatitis. I really don't know where I got this, but this particular year hepatitis was rampant in Italy. They had had several children's schools closed in the Rome area. I had been under the assumption that for this disease it's a thirty-day incubation period, which seemed to be accepted by the doctors. During this period I'd been out into the Aboukir area and had had luncheon out there. I'd been careful but you can't tell. When you have luncheon under primitive conditions, you can't tell what you're going to get. I'd been in Greece where hepatitis was quite rampant and, of course, in Italy. But most of the time in Italy I had been eating in my own headquarters, except for dinners that we'd been invited to. Quite frankly, I never did pinpoint precisely where I got this contaminated food. Anyway, I got it and for some two months I was on the second floor of the Vila at Naples and ran the headquarters from there. After the first couple of weeks, people would come over - every day I'd get a briefing, but when the doctors would let me sit up for a while I would have briefings and staff discussions and make decisions. I ran the headquarters from the second floor of the Villa Nicki.

Q: After an attack of hepatitis, are you immune?

Adm. G.: The doctors will not say - will not give you a flat answer on that. They say that the probability is that you are immune from then on. This is a very debilitating disease and a nasty one. I can assure you that for a long time you have no desire to eat anything that contains any fat or grease because it will nauseate you. What happens when you have hepatitis, a severe case of it, is cells in the liver are destroyed, physically destroyed and chemically destroyed. The human body, however, can function reasonably well with about one-third of a liver. So the destruction of the liver is probably in the order of half. In other words, you have some cells still functioning a little bit. You're on a very, very rigid, bland diet, and one of the things that affects the liver, as we all know, most readily is alcohol. The worst thing that you could do shortly after recovering from a bout of hepatitis is to consume alcohol. The doctors say at least a six-month period for the reconstitution of the cells of your liver. The cells of the liver have an ability, with proper diet and rest, to reconstitute themselves. However, if you take alcohol, it directly hits the liver when it goes into your system, that's one of the things that it hits first, if you put alcohol in there and those cells in the liver are destroyed while they're trying to reconstitute themselves, that finishes the reconstitution process. If they are destroyed at that time, they're gone and they can never be reconstituted. That's why it's so very important not to have any alcohol during that period.

Well, the doctor said six months, I doubled that and made that a year, and actually in fact tacked on three extra months because I thought it would be good. Some British friends of ours and we got together in the South of Spain at Soto Grande to have a little celebration at that time. I might just go on and say that we did this and I made myself a martini on that occasion. I had had no alcohol of any kind, nothing, for fifteen months, and I made myself a martini and had all the proper ingredients and everything and I tasted it, and it just tasted awful, absolutely terrible! So I threw that out and mixed another one. I thought I'd undoubtedly made a mistake, and the next one was very bad, so I ended up having a thimbleful of Scotch in a great big glass of water and that was that. Perhaps I should have left well enough alone at that time!

Q: You'd been successfully weaned!

Adm. G.: Yes, that's exactly right.

Well, after getting clearance from the doctors to continue my normal work, I made a trip to Oslo, Copenhagen, London, and Lisbon. This was a courtesy visit again. To Oslo, of course, to visit CinCNorth and to get briefings from him. CinCNorth was a British general and our American ambassador in Oslo was Miss Tibbetts, an American lady and a Foreign Service officer.

Q: A career girl?

Adm. G.: A career girl, yes. On this trip two of our ambassadors were women, Miss Tibbetts, a career Foreign Service officer and in Copenhagen, Mrs. White. Mrs. White was a very spectacular individual who had been the mayor of Red Bank, New Jersey, for three terms, the first in the history of the city ever to have been elected to more than two terms as the mayor, and she was quite a gal. She understood politics from A to Z and was tremendously popular throughout Denmark, because she'd go around and see all the cities and call on the mayors. She spoke their language and knew what their problems were and so forth. The only thing that was rather humorous about this whole thing was that in practically every place, of course, for protocol, arrangements would be made to take care of the Ambassador's wife while the ambassador was making a call, and along comes a lady ambassador and they'd say, what do you do with her husband! Mr. White had been a very successful businessman in New York and he was somewhat at a loss as to what to do so he took over running the embassy residence. He kept all the books and he ordered all the food and he directed the staff of servants. In addition to that, he got mixed up in amateur theatrical work in Copenhagen and ended up having a wonderful time and being a very popular individual.

Of course, in London, David Bruce, an old pro, was absolutely terrific, and in Lisbon, George Anderson, who was my classmate and a very close friend.

Now, I think it might be well at this stage of the game to have a little bit of a review as to just where we stood.

There were basic differences, of course, throughout this entire area. The Greeks and the Turks most assuredly were not getting along too well. I had been unable, except in the instances where we had major NATO exercises, to get any Greeks back into the Izmir headquarters. Neither the Greeks nor the Turks, and especially the Greeks, were fond of the Italians because the Greeks, of course, remembered the Italians and Germans coming down into Greece during World War II. The Italians were not enamored of the Greeks and Turks, rather tending to friendship and sort of superciliously, to the east.

However, I must say this about the Greeks and the Turks. They did support NATO. I'm not sure whether I covered this in an earlier talk or not. From the viewpoint of the percentage of gross national product, the percentage of manpower, and so forth, the Greeks and the Turks were right up there next after the U.S. in contributions to NATO.

Q: They were on the firing line, too.

Adm. G.: They were on the firing line. They were right there. They bordered communists countries. They had been invaded many times in the past, both of them, and they understood it and were quite prepared to take the consequences now. But they also expected that NATO and particularly the U.S. would recognize the fact that they were providing a holding operation on the frontier against communist countries and that by doing this and by participating as heavily as they did in NATO, they actually had earned much of the equipment and aid they were getting from the U.S. and from other NATO countries. The other NATO countries were very, very short on this. Only Germany could give them hardly anything at all.

Q: Isn't this an illustration of the fact that a threat of hostilities or of at least danger of hostilities is the thing that really makes an organization like NATO viable?

Adm. G.: Yes, and as you go along in years, of course, the actual threat tends to fade from memory and it has to be revived every now and then by psychological moves.

Q: But the potential enemy isn't always that obliging!

Adm. G.: That's right. That is most assuredly so. In some cases you have to provide a little bit of it on your own. Usually the communist countries, particularly the Soviet Union, have a tendency to make mistakes themselves, enough so as to avoid the necessity of bringing something in yourself. By that I mean on many occasions just before our Congress, for example, here in the United States has been about to address itself to the defense appropriation bill for the coming year, the Russians have done something. On many occasions they have done something that was very blatant. Czechoslovakia is a case in point. This has tended to keep the value of NATO in the forefront of the minds of people and also the necessity to maintain adequate armed strength within the country. This has been true over in Europe also.

But sometimes you have to provide your own input to this equation and this, quite frankly, was one of the reasons that entered into the business of having NATO exercises in the southern region, and particularly the Eastern Express exercise wherein the allied command, Europe, mobile force was brought down from central Europe - practically all the airlift provided by the U.S. and usually included at least a battalion of troops from the U.S.. And also because of the nature of the exercise the thing was held out in the countryside which gave a maximum exposure of the people in Greece or Turkey or Italy to this particular NATO exercise and kept it at the front. Also, NATO being the subject of this gave an opportunity for NATO authorities, including myself, to have talks in addition to the private talks with the chiefs of state of the countries concerned and remind them, for example, that ever since NATO had been in existence not one square inch of NATO territory had been taken over by the communist forces. So it provided a psychological springboard and, quite frankly, that was one of the reasons in addition to the very obvious reason of demonstrating to the people that NATO would come to their help when needed and also to train and test the training of the troops that were involved in these exercises.

I have commented on the political differences between these countries. The situation in regard to CinCAFMed was a very awkward one but we were under way with the solution to that by ultimately forming a ComNavSouth. It was quite apparent to me that there were other things that had to be done in order to get these countries together. Of course, the Number One question was to get the Greeks and Turks together. It was perfectly clear that Cyprus was merely a sort of a catalytic point, that the differences between Greece and Turkey had extended back hundreds and hundreds of years since the days of the Ottoman Empire -

Q: How did the State Department feel about the prognosis of this thing, the possibility of them cementing their relationship?

Adm. G.: I think that the general feeling at the time was that this was something that's going to take a very long time to work out and anything that can be done, even seemingly in a very small way, is a step in the right direction. We had at that time, I felt, very strong ambassadorial leadership in Turkey. We had Ambassador Hart there who was a splendid individual. I felt that our ambassadorial leadership in Greece was considerably weaker, Ambassador Talbot at the time. Of course, he had a very tough job because at that time Prime Minister Papandreou having been fired, the Greeks were going through a series of what can only be characterized as very, very weak governments and they were fortunate if they could just hold their own.

Under these circumstances, I cast around in my mind as to what things I could do to help the situation, and one of the things that I decided early in the game was, after having had a chance to see pretty much all of what some people call my parish, I thought that it would be a good idea to have a southern region conference on a periodic basis. We had conferences with SacEur, Supreme Allied Commander, Europe, General Lemnitzer, at his headquarters on a periodic basis. I thought if we could all sit around a table in a conference that I would chair with the senior people in the three countries there -

Q: This was Italy, Greece, and Turkey?

Adm. G.: Italy, Greece, and Turkey - and with key people from my staff, key staff people from these other staffs - we'd all sit around in a room together and discuss basic problems in what I hoped would be a situation of get-togetherness, so to speak. So often, it has been my experience, difficulties between people and between countries are so much the result of a lack of communication at all levels. I felt that if we could get together and clear up any misunderstandings, discuss problems quite frankly face to face, we could do an awful lot of good for each other, for the southern region, and for NATO as a whole.

I broached this idea with my own staff and sort of floated a feeler about it to the senior people of the various countries represented on the staff. The result of this poll, if you want to call it that, was favorable. I had in mind, of course, rotating the location of meetings at the various capitals of the countries concerned, and because of the nature of the problem in our southern region, most assuredly had thought that we must have the first meeting in Rome in order for everyone to get used to talking to each other.

To make a long story short, this thing did take hold and we did have our first meeting in Rome, and this particular meeting was a very profitable one. I also succeeded in establishing the principle there that I would chair the meetings. There was a tendency in the southern region, particularly on the part of Turkey, that anything that took place in their own country they would provide the chairman. I recognized the danger of this because if the host country would provide the chairman the thing could get out of control very, very rapidly and it could result in situations developing where I would be in the position of being embarrassed and the whole thing would fall flat on its face and we'd be worse off than if we hadn't even started it.

So, I got agreement that I would be the chairman, and, as I say, this was a very important thing because I didn't want some of the leaders chairing a meeting. I had in mind particularly General Tural, who was going to relieve General Sunay as chief of the Turkish staff. I by no means wanted to have him chair one of these meetings because General Tural was a very tough old Turkish soldier of the old school and had none of the astuteness or the likeableness of General Sunay. Anyway, I arranged the meetings so that the representative of the host country, and that would generally be the chief of the general staff, would make a welcoming address to all the participants in the conference, make any administrative announcements and arrangements he cared to, or say most anything that he wanted to say at that time, and then would ask me to chair the meeting.

This was understood and this worked. General Aloia, the

chief of the Italian general staff, who was a very smart, very suave individual, carried out his part of the job very well and then turned the meeting over to me and I ran the meeting from then on. We had a very successful meeting that year. The following year - I'm getting, of course, out of calendar scheduling now because I think I ought to handle this by subject - in 1967 we had the second annual meeting in Ankara. I was pretty much on tenterhooks for this one and had applied a great deal of pressure on the Greeks to be sure that they would accept, and the Greeks did accept and did come to the meeting. The only difficulty that I had at this particular meeting in Ankara was that General Tural, who started the meeting, made his remarks, welcomed everybody and so forth, turned it over to me and I started running the meeting and he started jumping in and making decisions. I had to suggest to him that he was out of order. We got over that rough spot and after that the meeting went all right. It at least accomplished the purpose of getting us all together and accomplished further the purpose of having a fairly significant number of senior Greek officers in Turkey at Ankara. They were treated perfectly fine. The host country had several receptions and parties for us and the meetings went off okay.

I was detached before the third meeting in Athens so I'm not in any position to report on that.

Q: Did it go on?

Adm. G.: So far as I know, it's still going on, and I certainly hope so because I felt it was a very good thing to have.

There were several other things that we did along this general line. I decided that it would be a good idea to have in Naples a NATO ball on an annual basis. We would all dress up in our best finery and have a very formal NATO ball. This was accepted with a great deal of enthusiasm by the ladies and, in this connection, we had a very active NATO Wives Club which my wife had had an awful lot to do with sparking. There had been a NATO Wives Club there at the headquarters but my predecessor's, Admiral Russell's, wife was in the hospital in Washington during much of his tenure there and, as a consequence, lacked any direction really on the feminine side from the commander in chief's point of view.

This NATO Wives Club was very instrumental in accomplishing a lot of good work between the various countries. The wives of the officers from Italy, Greece, and Turkey were completely unaccustomed to anything such as a wives' club. They didn't have anything like that in their countries -

Q: This is peculiarly American, is it?

Adm. G.: This is peculiarly American. The wives in these countries do not play anywhere near the role that they play in America, nor do they have the influence on many things that they have in America. American is something quite unusual in this respect. It took a lot of education and understanding on the part of the American wives to get these other girls accustomed to the various procedures, the get-togethers, how they ran the club, and, of course, one of the things that we had to watch constantly at the headquarters was if you assigned a Greek something to do you had to assign a Turk something to do that was comparable. You could never leave either one of them with the idea that the other was getting a little bit better deal than they were getting. This, to a limited degree, applied to the Italians also, but not very much because this was their country. They were the hosts, and they had a lot of important jobs which had been given them, so they watched a lot of this other stuff rather casually. I had an Italian aide who would be relieved by an Italian, whereas my Army aide one term would be a Greek and another term would be a Turk. So the Italians didn't feel too strongly about this particular thing because there was no question that they were getting their fair shake of everything. But with the Greeks and the Turks you had to be very careful. I could never have a dinner party, for example, and invite only one and not invite the other representatives. This was something that had to be very carefully thought out all the time.

Our wives at NATO, American wives, were very good at this business and did a lot of wonderful educational work insofar as the other wives were concerned, the Greeks, Turks, and the Italians. The two that played the predominant role in this were my wife and the wife of General Hardy, Virginia Hardy. General Hary was the ComAirSouth, a lieutenant general in the American Air Force, whom I had incidentally gotten down to Naples. ComAirSouth when I got there was Lieutenant General

Webster, U.S. Air Force, and after about six months or so he informed me that he was going to retire early from the U.S. Air Force in order to be in position to take a job as the Air Guard commander under the governor of Hawaii. Hawaii was his home and this was a plum of a job and he very much wanted to take it.

At that time General Hardy was commander of the Third Air Force up in England and by this time also Bruce Holloway, who was an old friend, was back as Vice Chief of Staff of the Air Force, and McConnell was chief of staff of the Air Force. I wrote back to them and said - told them in effect that, while I didn't want to put myself in the position of being accused of doing any Air Force detailing, if they could see fit to send John Hardy down there and promote him from major general to lieutenant general, I'd be very happy to have him. Well, in fact, this is exactly what happened. He was sent down. So I got John, who's a splendid fellow and also another War College classmate of mine and Virginia, who's a terrific girl and she took over and ran the NATO ball for us that year.

These girls did a wonderful job and we had this NATO ball which was the first one that had ever been held. It was tremendously successful. All the high dignitaries, of course, from the Naples area plus several from Rome came down for it. We had a number of the ambassadors there from Rome and, as I say, it was a tremendously successful thing.

In a job such as CinCSouth I felt that you had to do things like this. These, what you might call extra curricular activities in some areas of business, provided the - a - means of communicating where in some cases none others were available. As a consequence we stressed this type of thing. The ball was very successful; it received a lot of publicity and NATO benefited greatly from it.

We also set up something else that the Italian, Greek, and Turkish ladies had undoubtedly never seen, and that was a NATO debutante ball! This was done obviously under the sponsorship of the American ladies, and also worked really very well because several of the - this wouldn't have worked, it would have fallen flat on its face had we not had several young ladies, daughters of the various -

Q: Eligible daughters!

Adm. G.: Eligible daughters of the various officers. If there'd been nothing but a bunch of American daughters, if would have fallen flat on its face. But we did have some very cute eligible young ladies involved in something like that and they will talk about it continually in their homes and, believe me, the fathers got the news! We had the fathers bring their daughters in and present them to Mrs. Griffin and me at the end of a long, very formal walkway with red carpeting and everything. Then they went over and they had the first dance after all of them had been presented, they had the first short dance with their daughters and then they turned them over to their escorts for the evening. All of the older folk sat at tables around, and it turned out to be a most interesting affair. Whether they're continuing that, I don't know, but it takes a lot of participation and understanding and direction -

Q: And tactfulness?

Adm. G.: Oh, absolutely, no question about it. We had the wife of one of the brigadier generals in the U.S. Army who was an Italian and who had lived in Naples before they were married, and she was an absolutely brilliant woman. She spoke about five languages, was an accomplished musician and - you mention it, and she was good at it. She had this Italian temperament and she'd go off sometimes half cocked and, boy, either Mrs. Griffin or Mrs. Hardy would have to grab hold of her and quiet her down because, Italian or not, she was an American wife and she could get us into an awful lot of trouble real fast.

It was very, very interesting to see how all of this went on, and I must say that during the time that we had these various things, all the very active Wives Club, the debutante ball, we really had a much closer rapport in the staff than we ever had before, because this stuff rubs off. We had been doing quite well in the Officers' Club there and, as a matter of fact, before this NATO ball had finished about eight months of construction work and had built a big ballroom that could handle about 500 people, and that's where we had our NATO ball and that's where we had the debutante ball. As I say, these things did a tremendous amount of good for the command.

Now, I think there's very little purpose to be served by going any further into the details of routine trips, but rather we might just as well get into the business of the Greek situation. I don't know whether you want to start that now or wait until next time.

Q: Admiral, I know that Israel wasn't in the cognizance of the NATO command, but nevertheless you were - the Sixth Fleet was involved in the whole picture and the Sixth Fleet as an American fleet was involved with Israel. So, would you tell me about your position in all this?

Adm. G.: You're certainly correct. NATO had nothing to do with this except to be intensely interested in what was happening of such an important nature as this on the southern flank of NATO. The participation by U.S. forces in this was through the Sixth Fleet. Now the Sixth Fleet, of course, the commander, Sixth Fleet was double-hatted. He was Commander, Sixth Fleet, on strictly U.S. business, and he was Commander, Striking Force, South, with the Sixth Fleet for NATO business, but these particular activities were outside the cognizance of NATO. However, I did have on my staff a small communications detachment which was put there for the purpose of keeping me advised as to critical developments insofar as the U.S. was concerned - by that I mean developments that would be of interest to me as CinCSouth. Also within the headquarters compound at Naples I had the headquarters of the command of Submarine Flotilla 8, who also had a NATO job under me. He was kept completely informed and I would get daily briefings at his headquarters on developments in that particular crisis.

We had been, of course, following this very closely for a long time because it was quite obvious that something was going on. I had had occasion to brief a group of American businessmen about it. About thirty-five American businessmen came through and we briefed them at the headquarters. This was a customary thing. We had unclassified briefings which we gave to those people who were not qualified to receive classified information, and the subject of the Arab-Israeli conflict, which was a continuing one for a long period of time, came up in the question period after that briefing. I was asked quite bluntly by one of the American businessmen, "Are you concerned about this?" and I said, "I certainly am." So he said, "Well, do you think this is liable to result in any hostilities there?" I said it had all the ingredients that are required for a conflagration and, "I see very little evidence at the present time to suggest that either side is about to pull back, take any departure from the rather severe positions which they have taken."

He said, "You think it's possible that they'll have a war, then?" I said, "I certainly do. I think it's quite possible." "Well, Admiral," he said, "if they do have a war, what do you think the outcome of that will be?" I said, "From the information that's available to me, I think the answer to that is quite clear. The Israelis would win it and win it very easily, very handily." He said, "What do you mean by that?" I said, "Oh, about a week to ten days or something like that and it might possibly be all over. That's purely speculation on my part. I haven't been down there to actually see in detail on the spot what they have, but that would seem to me to be rather the order of magnitude that's correct."

Actually, it was about three weeks later that the Arab-

Israeli conflict did take place in 1967 and, as we all know, it lasted about a week.

Q: Six days!

Adm. G.: That's correct, and it was during this time, of course, that the USS Liberty was pummelled by the Israeli forces, which was a very distressing thing, but here we are again with lack of good communication, which was clear there. She was brought in to Malta for voyage repairs prior to being returned to the States and one of the officers on my staff, Rear Admiral Kidd, the American authorities asked me to release him for the purpose of conducting the investigation in connection with the Liberty affair. This he did to the complete satisfaction of all concerned, as I knew he would do. He's an absolutely tremendous officer in all respects and he now is a four-star admiral.

Q: Yes, I know.

Griffin #17 - 755

Interview No. 17 with Admiral C. D. Griffin, U.S. Navy (Retired)
Place: His residence in Washington, D.C.
Date: Monday morning, 31 January 1972
Subject: Biography
By: John T. Mason, Jr.

Q: Well, Sir, I'm looking forward to chapter No. 17, which has more to do with the happenings in the Mediterranean area. You were there until 1968.

Adm. G.: Right. At this time, I think it might be well to comment very briefly on some of the ancillary things connected with the more important aspects of my duty there, but things which, all together, fitted into the total pattern of this particular job that I had. As I said before, although the job was presumably a military one, it in fact was probably about 85 percent political, and there were many opportunities to conduct business in connection with something not actually part of the job - sort of, in principle, like many business deals are completed on the golf course. In my own case, we had at the CinCSouth headquarters an honor ceremony which was probably one of the nicest affairs of this kind that I've ever seen. It was highlighted by mounted carabinieri. I think it's the only honors ceremony that I've ever seen in my life in which mounted troops were used.

Anyway, between the Italian carabinieri and the U.S. Marines, we managed to have an extremely colorful ceremony which all visiting dignitaries accepted with the greatest of pleasure.

Q: It sounds a bit like a rival to Buckingham Palace!

Adm. G.: Very much so, except I think it was somewhat more colorful than at Buckingham Palace. Needless to say, this created a good impression on VIPs who were calling at the headquarters.

Another element along this same line were the formal dinners which we gave. I think that we probably entertained as much as any Class 1 embassy did around the world. We constantly had visitors at the headquarters and visitors at Vila Nicki, at our residence. During the last year that I was there we had between two and three house guests per night year 'round. Our formal dinners were done extremely well. Mrs. Griffin was very adept at coming up with very colorful place settings, and table decorations. She was aided in this by our stewards and in particular one steward who was extremely artistic. He would have ideas and Mrs. Griffin would have ideas and the net result was that our table decorations were commented on all over Europe.

This might seem to be a very small item but nevertheless it had a very beneficial effect on our relationships with the authorities in connection with NATO.

Q: Well, it's very closely tied in with a statement you made a few minutes ago - that 85 percent of your duties consisted of political aspects.

Adm. G.: Yes, that's right. Another element -

Griffin #17 - 757

Q: Before you go on to something else, tell me what sort of entertainment you'd provide for the evening, when you had a big formal dinner.

Adm. G.: We normally had part of my band which was made up into a string group and they played music during the cocktail hour. Our formal dinners were always, as the British say, 8 for 8:30. People were invited for 8 and they knew that we would sit down at 8:30.

Q: How many did you seat at one time?

Adm. G.: We averaged about twenty-four in our dining room. Entertainment in the summer would be on a more casual basis, out on the terrace, and we would have up to about fifty seated out on the terrace. Usually we had a string group playing music throughout the entire dinner and sometimes they put on a musical performance during the evening after dinner. Quite often we had what turned out to be a very popular form of entertainment: after dinner, the ladies would usually go to our living room for their coffee and liqueur, and the men would gather in part of the entrance hall for our coffee and liqueurs. During the entire time that I was in Italy I had been pressing the Italian authorities on the subject of a golf course in the Naples area, and I found that having a putting contest after dinner turned out to be something that was very popular. I had a strip of Monsanto carpet that had been given to me by a friend in England who represented Monsanto and, unrolling that and having several putters, we would usually divide into two groups and we had a prize for the man who won the putting contest and a prize for the woman who won the putting contest. Although most of the Italians had never had a golf club in their hands, they fell into it very nicely and seemed to get a lot of pleasure out of it.

This type of thing proved to be very enjoyable, and we had other games that we played afterwards. Normally, the dinners would break up by about 10:30. They were not the prolonged dinners that are held in some places. People got there promptly on time and knew that they would get away about 10:30, and this was what they liked to do. They liked to make it a short evening. Of course, the dinners were always characterized by various toasts appropriate to the occasion and they were responded to by the senior guest of honor.

All in all, we found these formal dinners to be very beneficial in our conduct of business and the people in our headquarters and the people in Naples, the senior civilians in Naples, enjoyed very much coming to the villa- being invited to the villa- to attend these parties. We had, of course, as I mentioned before, to be very careful in our guest lists. Sensitivity on this subject was at a very high level, particularly the Greeks and the Turks. If you had Greek individuals who were invited to dinner, you had to have Turks at the same dinner.

Along the same line, also, was included the barge. This proved to be one of the best instruments I had for conducting extracurricular activities in connection with my job. The barge was not a normal Navy-type barge, but was a twin-engine Chriscraft, about 45 feet long, slept six people plus a crew of five, cruised very nicely at fifteen knots, was very comfortable, and we used it very extensively. It was put in the water about the first week in April and stayed in the water until about the second week in November, and during that entire period was used practically every weekend and quite often during the week for trips to Capri, to Ischia and other islands in the vicinity of Naples. We also made several weekend trips on it, leaving sometimes on Friday afternoon and returning either Sunday afternoon or early Monday morning. We had ship-to-shore radio so I remained in contact with my headquarters and maintained a schedule with my headquarters whenever I was away so I could be contacted almost immediately at any time.

Quite often, when it was impossible for me to make a barge trip, I would send someone on my staff to host the trip. We normally would put food aboard and over the weekends, starting from June through September, we would normally go into some of the lovely coves in the vicinity of Naples and anchor and go swimming from the barge. The water in the Mediterranean is like water I have never seen any other place. It doesn't appear to be very salty, but you can float on it, I could float on it hour after hour. I could, in fact, stand up and maintain a vertical position just by moving my head back and forth. The water would come up to about my chin. I've been in water that's quite salty, such as the Salt Lake in the United States, but there when you dried off you would have a film of salt on you.

When you dried off up on the deck of the barge in the Mediterreanean, there was no salt, which meant, of course, that the salt itself was in solution, completely in solution in the water, and it was just velvety - that's about the best description I can give of it. I think it's the finest swimming in the world - the Mediterranean.

Q: Tell me, Sir, was the barge exonerated from the prevailing rule of the Navy - no liquor?

Adm. G.: Yes, it was exonerated and I served liquor aboard the barge.

Q: The guests you entertained on the barge, were they foreign people or were they largely VIPs from the U.S.?

Adm. G.: All types. For my weekend visits I would normally take, in addition to house guests we might have, people from my staff, and during the year I would have enough opportunities so that I pretty well covered most of the senior people of the staff, and they all got a tremendous kick out of it. During the week sometimes I would let senior staff members use it themselves, and also during the week I made provision to have the members of the band, the members of my Marine guard, and the families of the barge crew make a trip on the barge. I'm sure that Mr. McNamara's cost-effectiveness boys would have taken a dim view of it, had they known that it was there, how much it cost, and so forth!

Q: That implies the fact that you never entertained any of them on board!

Adm. G.: That's correct. They were not there. But it was an absolutely wonderful thing to have and we certainly got a tremendous lot of pleasure out of it, and it also did an extremely good job in letting people relax. For example, one time I recall Senator Symington came through and spent two or three days with us. He had just finished a round-the-world trip in which he had spent about a week in Vietnam, he had spent four days in Israel. This had been a fact-finding trip for him as a member of the Senate Armed Services Committee and Foreign Relations Committee also, and he was genuinely tired when he got there. I said, "Well, rather than give you any formal briefings here, I think it's best that we just go out and make a little trip over to Capri and relax and I can brief you personally on my barge on the way over." So we did this and it made all the difference in the world to him. That's just an example of how the barge could be used very much to our advantage.

I also want to comment on another aspect of life in Italy. I'm not sure I haven't covered this before, but at the risk of duplication I'll mention it. That is our trips to Verona. During the summer some of the finest opera in the world is held at the Arena in Verona. The Arena is an old ring that had been used in the Roman era for some of their fights, gladiators, and it had been converted into an open-air opera house. It was an oval and the stage was erected at one end of the oval in such a position that the center of the stage was at one of the focal points. Each oval has two focal points. The stage was there and with the seating that was left they could seat about 25,000 people for the opera. At night people would come in with candles and, on a signal, all lights would be turned out and they would light the candles and it created an absolutely magnificent view for everyone.

We were usually invited up there for each season and I timed my trips so that we could take in two successive nights at the opera, getting a different opera each night. In 1966, for example, we saw "Tosca" one night and "Aida" the next night. "Aida" had just under a thousand people on the stage at one time, and it was absolutely fantastically beautiful.

Q: Were these the LaScala people who performed?

Adm. G.: They were experts from all over the world. To get an invitation to perform at the Arena was considered a high honor. They had the stars of La Scala, the best that we had in the United States, and the musicians came from all over Europe and the United States. It was perfectly magnificent. I'll never forget the performance of "Aida." During the second act of "Aida" a full moon came up right over the middle of the stage, came right on up with some very white fleecy clouds floating by. The whole scene was absolutely indescribable.

Q: Like some fantastic vision.

Adm. G.: Yes, and as I say the construction of the theatre there was so well designed that the acoustics were just magnificent. You could hear just absolutely beautifully. This was something that we looked forward to every year, going up there and taking in this. It lasted for about five weeks in the summertime and fortunately every year that we went up there we happened to hit it when the weather was good. We had no performances rained out, so we saw the Arena at its best.

We always stayed at the Hotel due Tori which is a fascinating hotel. Each room was decorated differently and depicted a particular time in European history and, quite often, would also represent an individual such as Napoleon. Down in a little room off of the lobby they had colored slides and you could be shown what your room looked like there, so you'd look over all these slides and say, I want that one, and rather than go in and say I want a double with a bath or something like that, you'd actually pick out your room from these colored photographs.

Q: I want to be projected into this historical period!

Adm. G.: That's right! And the rooms were done in exquisite taste. So, Jack, when you get over there, be sure and go to that hotel.

Q: I'll make a note, yes.

Adm. G.: Let me now comment on a trip that I made which was of great interest to me.

As we are aware, there was no formal relationship between the NATO organization and the CENTO organization. This was largely because the northern, or Scandinavian, people in general felt that there should be no relationship between CENTO and NATO. However, the people down south, particularly the Turks, felt that there should be some relationship. From my point of view, it seemed quite obvious that there should be something more than just a casual relationship because, in case of any armed conflict, we must assure ourselves, for example, that there is no conflict between the courses of military action taken by NATO and by CENTO. These would have to be correlated in such a manner that there would be no conflict. That's what I'm trying to say in a very roundabout way.

So, the way this was handled by General Lemnitzer, SacEur, was to delegate to me, as CinCSouth, the responsibility for maintaining this NATO-CENTO relationship and for adequate correlation of our military plans. As a consequence of this, I invited the military representatives of CENTO, the permanent representatives, of each country in CENTO had a lieutenant general, a three-star general officer who was a permanent representative. As you know, the United States is not a member of CENTO. However, they maintain an observer status in CENTO. Turkey was, of course, a member of CENTO and a member of NATO, both.

Q: Who are the other nations in CENTO? Iran?

Adm. G.: Iran, Turkey, Pakistan, Great Britain -

Q: And France?

Adm. G.: France, with the United States in an observer position. This was orginally known as the Baghdad Pact. Iraq was a member of it and then when the government of Iraq was overthrown, they got out of it and the headquarters shifted from Baghdad to Ankara, and that's where the permanent staff of CENTO was and where the permanent military representatives maintained their offices.

In this position as the delegated authority to maintain relationships between CENTO and NATO, I set up a trip to Iran, and this was an extremely interesting one. I went over there in October of 1966 and had a splendid visit which also gave me an opportunity to have a visit with the Shah. I had last seen the Shah just after World War II when I had visited there in company with Admiral Connolly and had always remembered the Shah as, at that time, of course, a relatively young man who had recently come to the throne but who demonstrated a remarkable knowledge of the war in the Pacific, and in particular of the carrier actions in the Pacific. In fact, I recall that he knew considerably more about that than I think most American citizens did. He was a young flier, very good-looking, rather impulsive at that time, so I was very interested to have a chance to see him again.

This time, of course, he was much older, but still an extremely interesting man. I had about an hour and a half talk with him, just the two of us - he speaks fluent English - and we discussed most everything from the field of grand strategy to his own particular problems there at home. He, in my opinion, had always been a very enlightened monarch who did an awful lot of good for his own country. He had established systems, for example, for individual soldiers - the last six months of their active duty would be devoted to training them in skills that could be beneficial to the villages from which they came. If they needed carpenters in the village, they'd be trained to be carpenters, or metalsmiths, and so forth. He had set up many low-cost housing villages and was rapidly bringing his people from a completely backward position to one of some elements of modernity. He was very progressive and, as I say, almost completely wrapped up in the welfare and development of his own people and his country. And in that context he commented rather forcefully on many things that were happening worldwide. Although a Moslem country, he was not Arab and he took a very dim view, for example, of Nasser.

He felt that Nasser was being used by the communists and he didn't have the faintest idea he was being used and therefore was probably as wicked a man as there was in the entire world, according to the Shah. He felt that the British were, unfortunately, not playing their cards very well and he was very much concerned about what was going to happen when the British finally withdrew from the Persian Gulf area. He was in a position where he would have a lot of pressure put on him from the north by the Soviet Union, with the Soviet Union using Nasser as a tool, it was quite apparent that considerable pressure could be put on the Gulf area from the south. So he was looking ahead at just what could be done about this.

Q: In that connection, did he express himself at all on the oil situation? He has most recently expressed himself in an interesting fashion. I wondered if he had anticipated this stance?

Adm. G.: Yes, indeed. He was quite aware, no question about it, of all the things that were happening. I don't know how much detail you want me to go into on this. I have a complete memorandum of my conversation.

Q: Why don't you let me have a copy of it as an appendix?

Adm. G.: Sure. This is one of the longer ones that I have here, as a matter of fact. What he was aiming for, of course, was a situation where there would be stability in his part of the world. He wanted to receive help from the United States, he was quite willing to pay for it, and he felt that in many parts of the world the United States was not being very knowledgeable. Only on one thing did he agree with the United States. He agreed that the action which the United States had taken in Vietnam was the correct one. Up until that time, however, he had the impression that the United States was simply not knowledgeable as to the dangers of communism in the world and was somewhat inclined to hide its face in the sand.

Q: Did he express any confidence in his ability to withstand the Russians and to handle that situation?

Adm. G.: Yes, he said that - he indicated that with United States help, partially in the field of military equipment which he would buy, but more importantly in the political field, he could hold his own. One thing that had happened in Saudi Arabia strengthened his hand somewhat.

The Saudi Arabian government under the old king had been a very weak one but when Faisal took over -

Q: Not under Ibn Saud but Ibn Saud's son?

Adm. G.: Ibn Saud's son, that's right.

Q: Saud?

Adm. G.: Saud. When Faisal took over from Saud, the Shah felt that this was a move very much for the good because he had a lot of respect for Faisal. Faisal was much more competent to run the country than Saud was, and he felt that Hussein of Jordan was an extremely fine ruler and was doing a good job under very difficult circumstances. So he strongly supported Hussein and Faisal, and just a look at the map can show why, of course, because they were very good buffers from any actions to be taken against his country and the Persian Gulf from the south. By this time, of course, the Russians had been moving very strongly in Yemen and Somalia and, with their relationship with Nasser giving them harbors and ports on the Red Sea, their infiltration was moving along very well.

At this time, of course, the French were not in CENTO.

Q: And Britain's world position had deteriorated.

Adm. G.: Britain's world position had deteriorated very considerably. At this particular time he was very much interested in getting some modern aircraft for Iran. He wanted to get the F-4 aircraft.

He was quite laudatory on many aspects of the things that the United States had done, however. He pointed out that the world had never seen such magnificent unselfish philanthropy as had been practiced by the United States after World War II to aid countries to restore themselves after the devastation of the war to help the economies of the countries and to aid the people of the countries. He also recognized that it was not possible for the United States to continue to be the safeguard of the entire world indefinitely. There had to be a time when this would be taken over by other countries to share the effort. He was inclined to get a little bit philosophical from time to time. He indicated that he felt the United States too often tried to change things overnight. For example, he commented on the African countries. Do we expect some of these countries in Africa to be run exactly the same way as the United States is run? We seem to feel that all countries must be made over into our own image, and suggested the U.S. might take another look at this.

Many of these comments reminded me of a magnificent book

which I had read by Bob Murphy, the warrior diplomat, which certainly highlights many of these points.

Very little of the conversation that we had really dealt with military hardware. Most of it was the Shah's thoughts on important aspects as affecting the world community and on himself. He had recently made a trip to several Eastern European countries and I gathered that the principal reason for this particular visit - or series of visits - to these countries was to sort of line them up in a loose relationship in case things might develop in the future wherein the countries close to Russia might be better off if there was an understanding. This would have to be an extremely loose type of relationship to have included Iran in this, and I thought it was awfully interesting to get his reasons for this. He would not be specific at all. I reported this entire conversation to Ambassador Meyer, who was the American ambassador at Teheran at that time. He's now over in Japan, just about to leave Japan.

Anyway, I'll have a copy of this memorandum conversation.

The whole trip was a very, very fascinating one and it was extremely good from the viewpoint of Mrs. Griffin, too, because she's quite an antique collector, particularly glass, and at this particular time I gathered that it was fairly well known around the world among antique collectors that one of the last of the few places - a few good places - left in the world for this type of buy was Teheran. I ended up by being taken around to a number of these places, and I must say that we walked into one of them and my wife would look over a crowded room packed with what I called junk, and if there were five pieces there that were darned good, why, she'd spot them practically with one glance. And we actually did get quite a number of very fine pieces. We have upstairs a Limoges clock, which I think she got for about $40 or something like that and the thing's still running. We also picked up some Baccarat crystal and some other very fine things.

All in all, it was an extremely fine visit. I must comment on one thing, however. I had stressed to my aides that when we left Iran I wanted to have plenty of good caviar aboard the airplane. So they had left orders at the airport for - they have a place there where you can order and then have it delivered to your aircraft when you're leaving, and when we were about to leave and the aides had gotten all this caviar, about five kilos of caviar -

Q: I take it it's not sixty dollars a pound over there!

Adm. G.: No, but it was still pretty expensive. It wasn't sixty dollars a pound, but it was rather dear there as well, but not that much. Then, very much to my surprise, two kilos were delivered to the airplane from the Shah and two kilos were delivered from the office of the chief of the Iranian general staff. So we ended up with a planeload of caviar. Fortunately, much of it was in 100cc and 200cc packages, so if we could keep it chilled it would last a long time. But I must say that we had caviar with our cocktails for a long time and it was really good. I really had plenty of fine caviar.

Q: Beluga?

Adm. G.: That's right. It was the real McCoy!

Now, I think it well to cover next the Greek situation. It's probably best to start off at the time when George Papandreou was fired by the king as the prime minister. Both he, George Papandreou, and his son, Andreas Papandreou, primarily Andreas, from that time on continued their activities in Greece, their what I would call subversive activities in Greece. Also, it was most difficult for the king to get a government that was a strong government and would be a stable government because of the unrest that was being created by the activities of the Papandreous. There were several Greek governments, all of them weak, and this of course, added to the unrest in the country.

Q: By whom were they financed?

Adm. G.: I believe that they were financed largely by the communist elements.

Government after government was formed in Greece, none of them strong, all of them weak. At the same time, all of them would say no, we cannot send our staff members back to Izmir to the NATO headquarters there, the political situation is not right for it. So I was being thwarted at every turn to really bring this headquarters back to its proper staffing level.

It became apparent that the election that was coming up in 1967 in Greece contained the possibility of the Papandreou party winning and, I'm quite certain that as a consequence to this, there was very considerable plotting being done at all levels with a view to taking over the government. I'm quite sure and I have every reason to believe, for example, the Greek Army would never permit an election to take place that could possibly be won by the communists. Rabble-rousing had been going on all over the country and, in the absence of a strong, effective government in Athens, was being pretty successful. Therefore, as I indicated before, the Army, the king, were all involved in planning for an ultimate take-over of the government.

I have reason to believe that, for example, the king and the chief of staff of the Army were one group planning for this. Another group that was planning at the time was the group ultimately known as The Colonels. Their activities were quite widespread and they had representation on the staff level in practically every important staff agency connected with the Greek armed forces.

Q: This was the younger element, wasn't it?

Adm. G.: The younger element. Right. It was led by Colonel Papadopolous, who is now the prime minister. They knew the proposed timing of these other groups and so about two weeks before they were quite sure that the king and the chief of staff of the army were going to move - that is, the chief of staff of the Army with the knowledge and approval of the king, about two weeks before they expected them to move, the young group moved and took over the government in a bloodless coup.

Q: What was the divergence in point of view between the colonels and the chief of staff?

Adm. G.: The Colonels didn't think that they were moving fast enough. Also that there were quite a number of reforms that they felt should take place in the government and they were, shall we say, less than confident that the existing hierarchy would accomplish the reforms that they felt were necessary.

As a consequence, they moved military elements, particularly tank battalions, into the Athens area and took over the government in a bloodless coup. It was really not until some time after this successful coup took place that the depth of this organization was realized. By that I mean the number of people who were in it and the extent of their internal intelligence activities in the government of Greece. The king was left in a position of being well out on a limb at this time. Martial law was put into effect in the country and the colonels - I use that phrase because it probably is as good as any - told the king exactly what their platform was, shall we say, and in effect asked the king to accept their group as the government of Greece. Negotiations between the king and the colonels took place on a continuing basis for quite some time, and the king simply refused to accept any diminution of his own constitutional powers.

Q: Is this what they were demanding?

concerned at some of the activities that took place in the government when Queen Frederica was operating. I think a characteristic of succeeding Greek governments had been an element - I won't go so far as to say that they were all loaded with elements of fraud and so forth, but there wasn't probably a single Greek government that was completely trustworthy. There were always some elements of fraud in succeeding governments. The colonels knew about this and they were determined that they, when the situation was a correct one in their viewpoint to take over the government, would take it over and would eliminate these unsavory elements from the government and have a real, fine, honest government of Greece.

So they moved, as I said before, about two weeks before the king and the Army would have moved. They did it in an extremely capable manner and took over the government. As you know, that government still is in control in Greece and my observations of it during succeeding visits over there it was quite apparent that this was, in fact, a good government. It had produced stability in the country, it was providing the people of Greece with a good, honest government. It's still in power. How long it's going to be before they permit a revised constitution, before they permit a vote to be taken by the people of Greece, I don't know. The king, as you know, left the country and went to Rome, where he still is. I have been greatly surprised by the fact that he has not gone back. This government has made overtures to him time and again to come back. He would, of course, have to accept the fact when he goes back that it will be without the powers that he formerly had - without all of them, however, he would have many of them. From what I have been able to gather, I think the offers that have been made to him have been rather fair. One thing they will not permit, however, would be his mother to come back and occupy any position in connection with the government of the country at all. They will not permit her, which leads me to think that since he has left Greece, I would guess - and I'm not sure of this, this is just an estimate of mine - but I would guess that she has played a somewhat bigger role in his life than she was at the time that I first met the king over there and at the time he fired Papandreou, because I think that he was moving rather well in the direction of getting away from that mother complex that he had had as a younger man. But I will say that I've been very surprised and very disappointed that he has not gone back.

They keep pictures of the king and queen in their offices in Greece and I think it's well known that they made overtures to him to come on back, but just simply became hardheaded on this subject and personally I think he's making a great mistake.

Q: What sort of popular support does the colonels' government have?

Adm. G.: I think that they have widespread popular support in the country now. Some of these very leftist people to the contrary. The statements of Andreas Papandreou I wouldn't believe for a minute. Melina Mercouri, who has popped off on the subject of no liberty in Greece, is a rather famous drunk, as a matter of fact, made famous by an extraordinarily good moving picture. Her father is a card-carrying Communist. Now she's around popping off about these people in Greece.

Q: And the latest one, Lady Fleming!

Adm. G.: That's right. But so far as I can see, the alternative to the good government that they have now would have been chaos and ultimately a communist take-over of the government in Greece. That was the alternative, in my opinion. And I think these people are doing a good job. They are improving the economy of the country to a greater percentage than the economy has been improved in decades, and while there is a diminution of civil liberties and also of the press, such things appear to be necessary for the time being. If they are gradually relaxed, many of the rather stringent rules that they put in when they first took over and people that I have contact with over there tell me that the people of Greece are quite happy with the way their country is moving now, the way it's being governed.

The socialist countries up north in NATO take a dim view of it, as might be expected. They would much prefer to have a communist take-over than to have anything approaching a dictatorial type of government. I think they have a government which is good and it's sound and it's honest, and that's what Greece needed at this particular time. So I do not share the view that Miss Mercouri or Andreas Papandreou and people like that have about the current government of Greece at this time.

As I say, I'm very disappointed that the King has not gone back.

Q: I often wondered, Sir, if he felt that this colonels' government would be a short-lived one and consequently he didn't want to identify himself with it and its image as something of an anti-democratic government, that this would jeopardize his long-term prospects.

Adm. G.: Oh, I think undoubtedly at the outset he thought that it would not be too long before this particular government would fall, and therefore his best chance of retaining all the power would be to not associate with this particular government. But it seems to me the time has long passed when it has become quite apparent that this particular government of the colonels is in power and will remain in power for an indefinite period of time.

Q: What is your prognosis in terms of U.S. support for the colonels' government? This indication of opposition within the Congress to open support and certainly the press is opposed to any move on the part of the administration in this direction.

Adm. G.: My feeling is that the United States government should support this regime. I commented earlier on the fact that, on a percentage basis, Greece and Turkey have provided more for NATO than any other country in NATO except the United States. That continues to this day. The United States is liked by this government of Greece and I think it's a shame that any aid that normally would be given the government of Greece is being withheld. My prognosis is that, short of having a government headed by somebody like Fulbright or McGovern or someone of that ilk, I certainly feel that the United States government should support the regime militarily, economically, and politically, because I think it's by far the best course of action.

What we want to have in this world are good solid governments that are not trying to subvert other governments. We want stability in the world, and we get that by supporting governments such as the one that's in Greece now. They're there, they have control of the country, they are aligned firmly with the West, they believe in democratic principles, and I'm sure, as soon as the situation is correct, they will re-establish constitutional government and permit free elections and no restrictions on the press, which they have at this time. As I say, I'm very disappointed that the King has not gone back but remains in Rome. I'd like very much to have a chance to go over there and talk to him because I think I could probably find out some of the reasons!

Well, one good aspect of the new government in Greece had to do with my perennial problem, the relationship between Greece and Turkey. This government showed rather early in the game that it was much more pragmatic than some of the other governments in Greece. It indicated that it wasn't about to permit any stuffy attitude with regard to Cyprus to get out of hand and prevent the establishment of more friendly and normal relationships with their neighbors. They were quite aware of the fact that the two countries were there next to each other and felt that it was rather absurd to be sitting there arguing sometimes on what was considered to be very small points time and again when they could be living in peace to the betterment of the whole relationship in that part of the world. As such, this government, the government of the colonels, made pretty much a new approach to this.

Before this rumor had gotten very far, however, we had our second Southern Regional Conference. As you will recall, we had the first one in Rome and that came off extremely well. I was very pleased with it. Our second one was held in Turkey and I had my fingers crossed on this one all along, but things went along normally. The Turks agreed to let the Greek representatives attend the conference and they didn't come up with any minor irritations or anything like that.

Q: And you were to chair the meeting?

Adm. G.: I was to chair the meeting. It was set up for the middle of October 1967, 17 to 19 October, in Ankara. Our hosts were the Turks, of course. General Tural, chief of the Turkish general staff, hosted a reception the first evening that we were there. It was very fine and, of course, members of the staffs of Italy, Greece, and Turkey were there. All of us - by all of us I mean General Aloia, who was the chief of the Italian general staff, Vice Admiral Abgares, the chief of the Greek national staff, and I - participated in a ceremony of laying a wreath to Ataturk. We did this as co-participants, all three of us marching together and laying a wreath. This is a standard procedure over there when you make an official visit to Ankara, that is, laying a wreath at the tomb of Ataturk -

Q: At the shrine of shrines!

Adm. G.: At the shrine of shrines - and the procedures for this are explicitly laid down and everyone knows exactly what he has to do at every particular minute.

The whole meeting went along very well. I was really pleased, right at the beginning of the meeting General Tural made some opening remarks welcoming the people there and then promptly started to chair the meeting and I had to remind him as diplomatically as I could that I was the chairman of the meeting. We got over that little rough spot extremely well. There was only one other time when I felt that things might have gotten out of hand, and that was at the time for each of the representatives of the countries concerned to make their final remarks. At this particular time the subject of formation of ComNavSouth was very much up in the air. It was just before the change was accomplished, and I had spent quite some time talking to General Tural on the subject because it was the Turks who were holding up the final ratification in the NATO Council of this organization change. And what the Turks were holding it up for was the subject of the naval boundaries in the Mediterranean.

At the time CinCAFMed was formed by Admiral Mountbatten, naval boundaries were delineated in the Mediterranean with Greece being given a big slice of the water all around it and going over almost to the coast of Turkey. The Turks took a very dim view of having all these islands right up practically to their coast being in a Greek-controlled area. So they wanted all naval boundaries eliminated in the Mediterranean. Actually, I shared this view and I had had a long conversation with General Tural with that as my principal point. I had pointed out to General Tural that I shared his view, however, he must recognize the fact that, with the current organizational setup, the Turks had been unable to get their thoughts approved over the past ten years. Therefore, if he was continuing to block this change, we would continue with the same organization that had refused to give them what they wanted for ten years, and he would be much better off if we had a new organization because, then ComNavSouth would come directly under me and I tended to share his view. I also made it quite clear to him that it was perfectly obvious that I couldn't move too rapidly on this particular point because I could not just tell the Greeks, well, the hell with you, I'm going to go ahead and do it. You don't work things out that way, but since I did share his view that the boundaries should be changed or eliminated entirely, he would stand a much better chance of - the Turks would stand a much better chance of getting what they wanted under the new setup than they had under the old one.

So, with this argument, he accepted finally, and I have a full memorandum of the conversation on that one because I think it is a very important one, and I'll have that available if you like. The memorandum of that conversation plus a memorandum which was prepared by my assistant chief of staff for intelligence, who was a Turkish brigadier general who attended that meeting with me and wrote his own minutes. Afterwards I asked him to write his own minutes so I made sure what I had was correct. And it was well that he was there because General Tural's interpreter was missing some of the points that I was trying to make and he was also missing some of General Tural's points getting across to me. So communication was evidently not too good, and the Turkish brigadier general finally took over from the interpreter and did the interpreting himself, which was very good from my point of view because later on the relationship between General Tural and myself was rather strained, largely, I think, because he felt that I was not carrying out my promises which he thought I'd made to him at that time for changing these boundaries.

Anyway, that's a little background there leading up to the final talks which were being given by the individual members of the conference. As I say, everything was going very fine, then in his closing remarks Admiral Abgares felt compelled to take the Turks to task for raising the subject of the revision of the naval boundaries in the Mediterranean, which actually had nothing to do with this particular conference. Of course, this had been a bone of contention between the Greeks and the Turks, and it was quite obvious that the Turks who had just mentioned it in their remarks without taking any firm stand on it had struck a very sensitive nerve, and he was adamant in his position that the Greeks would not even consent to a discussion of the subject.

Fortunately, General Tural, who spoke next, did not reply in kind. This was one of the few times that I have seen him really hold his temper nicely, and I was very pleased because I thought with him coming up next, being the host country, they were the last to speak - I felt that with him coming up next he could just blow the conference wide open and maybe put all the Greeks in jail for all I knew! However, he was well aware of my sympathy with the Turkish position on this matter, and I think that plus the fact that they had had no chance for his staff to prompt him on it; let him go ahead and comment without taking the Greeks apart.

I was, as I say, very pleased with the results of that conference and felt that it was actually accomplishing quite a lot that would be of much value to NATO as a whole.

Following the second Southern Region Conference, I, of course, was planning on all of my farewell calls because within two months of my being relieved we had an Allied Command, Europe, commanders' conference up in Belgium from the 23rd to the 26th of October -

Q: This was 1968?

Adm. G.: This was 1967. This was the first main conference that we had in the new headquarters in Belgium. By that time, NATO had approved the formation of ComNavSouth, so now we had three major commanders in NATO - CinCSouth, CinCCent, and CinCNorth.

The trip was largely one of familiarization with the new

headquarters and it was an opportunity for me to make a report to General Lemnitzer and to the other CinCs on my observations, having completed about three years as CinCSouth, and so actually my presentation was made with that in mind, on giving a summation of my stewardship for this three-year period. I felt that much progress had been made in stabilizing the situation in Europe and in continuing to provide a base on which no further incursions of communism on the continent was taking place. I did emphasize, as I had at the beginning, the importance of the Mediterranean and the growing awareness of that importance on the part of the Russians by improving and updating the status of their forces in the Mediterranean not only from the quality point of view, but from the quantity point of view. I felt that Lemnitzer had a very fine handle on this particular subject, and it was quite apparent to him that this was rapidly becoming the area of greatest interest insofar as his job was concerned.

I had a copy of my presentation that I gave, if you'd like to have that.

In November of that year I was invited over to Madrid to attend an East Coast regional meeting of the Navy League of the United States, which was held in Madrid at the invitation of the chapter there, of American businessmen in Madrid. I was asked to come over and make a speech there. This was an opportunity which I very much appreciated because I felt that this was a good chance for me to get in another crack at the growing Russian influence in the Mediterranean and to point out again that, in contrast to what many people had said that the Russians lost in the Arab-Israeli war - in contrast to that, the view that I held was that actually, instead of losing, they had gained, and all one had to do was to go through a country-by-country analysis of the countries on the Mediterranean littoral and it was quite apparent that in total influence they had gained very considerably.

This gave me an opportunity, as I say, to do that in a speech which I did not have cleared. As you are aware, I was in a NATO position and I didn't feel that I had to have my speeches cleared.

Q: You mean cleared by the U.S. Navy?

Adm. G.: The U.S. Navy or the U.S. government. A copy of my speech was taken back to Washington by the chief of information, the Navy chief of information, who, unbeknownst to me, sent it over to the State Department for clearance and it came back all chopped up. But by the time I got it back, the speech had been delivered some three weeks before that.

Q: Who was that, Admiral Miller?

Adm. G.: Miller, It was really chopped up and some childish changes had been made in it, really funny. The substance of my speech appeared in U.S. News and World Report a couple of weeks after it was given.

Q: Did you get any flak on this?

Adm. G.: No. I just told them quite frankly that I had no intention of having my speeches cleared by the U.S. government, and there was no difficulty there. I have a copy of that speech here, too.

In addition to giving me an opportunity to make a speech, I also cherished the thought of going back to Madrid because there were some old friends there and I had felt ever since France withdrew from NATO that we should make it possible for the Spanish to get into NATO, but I guess this was a dream which was almost impossible of accomplishment in view of the stand that the Labor governments take against any form of what they considered dictatorship in government. Also, being a NATO officer, I really had under those circumstances no logical or legitimate reason for going there on business, but this gave me a reason so I took advantage of it and paid calls on General Munoz-Grandes and others in the government there. Also, it gave my wife an opportunity to do a little shopping. As a matter of fact, I have an oil painting that was done by a young Spanish painter called "The Dream of Columbus." It's a very fine painting and I'm happy to say that the painter has increased greatly in stature in recent years, and of course that always increases the value of a particular painting.

We started our farewell calls in the latter part of November and they continued into December. I called in England and Belgium from 29 November to 5 December, Germany 11 to 14 December, and then stopped the calls for the holiday season. We went up to Berchtesgaden over New Year's and had a perfectly delightful time. This was one of our favorite places to go over a holiday, particularly during the winter -

Q: You could say that Hitler knew how to select a site!

Adm. G.: He sure did. He really picked it, or the people picked a good one for him and then built that place for him up there. I made several visits to Greece and Turkey, 8 to 12 January, and the Turks were very embarrassed at the behavior of General Tural, who saw fit to make an inspection trip down in the south part of Turkey during the farewell call. He still felt that I had not treated him too well, but the minister of defense and the prime minister went out of their way - and President Sunay - went out of their way to be especially gracious to me.

The government of Greece, Prime Minister Papadoupolos, presented me with a decoration as Supreme Commander of the Royal Order of George I.

Q: He had taken this over from the King?

Adm. G.: He had taken over this function from the King. This ceremony was attended by all of the senior people in the government, and it's one of the highest decorations that they give to a foreigner. I believe that our Vice President got this same decoration last year. They had an account of this in the Athens newspaper.

I left the farewell calls to Rome as the last and I made

those from 15 to 17 January. While there, the Italian government was kind enough to give me one of their high decorations.

So this concludes my visits. I never will forget some of those rides in Rome accompanied by an escort of about a dozen carabinieri on motor cycles. They were about the wildest rides I have ever had in my life! The two Italian aides that I had, one succeeded the other, both were Italian Air Force officers, both jet pilots, both admitted to me that they were never so scared in their lives as they were riding in that automobile, going right through the center of Rome with thousands of automobiles all over the place, and going about sixty miles an hour! It was really something. I'll never forget.

Q: You gave over command, when?

Adm. G.: I turned over the command on the last of January, the last day of January, to Admiral Rivero. As a matter of fact, I have a copy of the speech that I made on that occasion and also have a tape of that ceremony. The thing that always gets you there is when, one of the last things when you get in the car and start to go away, and they play "Arriverdci, Roma"! Everybody's crying.

Q: I wonder if you'd conclude with a statement on your prognosis of the NATO organization and its effectiveness, its role in Western Europe?

Adm. G.: Well, I might say that the proof of the pudding is in the eating, and the fact remains that since NATO came into existence better than twenty years ago, not one single square inch of free territory has been taken by the Russians, by the communists. Therefore, NATO has most definitely proved itself as a very successful alliance and all we have to have from time to time is a little bit of a blow-up some place to make people remember. We have a tendency to be very, very forgetful. We also have a tendency, I think, to underestimate or mis-estimate the character of our principal opponents in the globe on which we live. We tend to think of them in terms of ourselves, and these people don't think that way, and they don't have any intention of thinking that way.

Therefore, as much as we would love to see countries disarmed, as much as we would like to see moneys - the huge amounts of moneys - that are spent for armament go to other purposes, I can't see that this will happen, certainly in my lifetime and for possibly a very long time in the future. We must continue to operate under an umbrella of military strength which gives us the capability of preventing a forced take-over of countries of the world by what now is our major enemy, and that is communism. As a part of this umbrella, I think we very definitely need a NATO.

Now, I think, therefore, that there will be a continuing requirement for NATO through the indefinite future, perhaps with not as much U.S. contribution to it as we presently have, because I think a very fair question can be asked, why should we as taxpayers of the United States pay a lot of money to provide forces to protect European countries when those countries with strong economies are unwilling to provide adequate forces to protect themselves? This is a very difficult question that any administration we might have in Washington has to answer.

Therefore, I would anticipate that there would be through the years a gradual reduction in the U.S. presence in Europe. As the economic capabilities of the various countries there continues to rise, they can better provide for their own defense and as a possible concomitant to perhaps more normalized relationships between the Warsaw Pact and the NATO countries. But this is a long-range proposition, I think. I hope that the visits of the President to Peking and to Moscow will have some beneficial effect, but we must always remember that it's absolutely necessary for us to provide the military umbrella under which we can conduct all these international relationships between other countries and the United States. We must remain strong militarily and strong politically and strong economically and strong morally, if we are to succeed in having a world in which any of us can take pride in living.

Q: I congratulate you, Don, and thank you for doing a fascinating oral biography.

Adm. G.: Thank you very much, Jack, it's been a great pleasure for me.

INDEX

to

Volume II (Chapters 10 through 17)

Reminiscences of

Admiral Charles Donald Griffin

U.S. Navy (Retired)

ABGARES, Vice Admiral: Chief of the Greek National Staff, p. 782; p. 785.

ALOIA, General: Chief of the Italian General Staff, p. 782.

ANDERSON, Admiral George: Chief of Naval Operations, P. 490; gives Griffin choice of assignments - becomes Op-03, p. 491; his differences with Secretary McNamara, p. 536ff the Cuban Missile Crisis, p. 551 ff; apparent plan of McNamara for his dismissal, p. 562; his appointment as Ambassador to Portugal, p. 563-4; the Rose Garden Ceremony, p. 564; his service with General Eisenhower, p. 618-9; p. 739.

ANTARCTICA: p. 543-4.

ASPIDA: an organization of Andreas Papandreou - to undermine the position of the armed forces in Greece, p. 700.

ASW (Anti-Submarine Warfare): developments in this area - the SQ-26 sonor, p. 524-5.

BALDWIN, Hanson W.: p. 542-3.

BRITISH POLICY - withdrawal from the Mediterranean and elsewhere, p. 626 ff; difficulty in Malta, p. 628-9; effect on the Royal Navy, p. 630-1; the RAF and British aviation in general, p. 631; emphasis on POLARIS SS's as deterrents, p. 633.

BROSIO, The Hon. Manlio - Secretary General of NATO: p. 664-5.

BRUCE, The Hon. David K.E.: U.S. Ambassador to the United Kingdom, p. 572-3; p. 596-7; p. 739.

BULGARIA: Griffin's visit to the Greek-Bulgarian frontier, p. 722-4.

CENTO: relationship with NATO, p. 764-5; Griffin's visit to Iran in the role of liaison, p. 765-6; p. 769; p. 772.

CINC AFMED (Commander in Chief, Allied Forces, Med.): status of this British NATO command, p. 728-31.

CINC NA SOUTH: p. 731; p. 734; Griffin insists that when this command goes to an Italian Admiral that he have a British Chief of Staff, p. 735; p. 783-5.

CINC NELM: p. 567; loses raison d'etre with the establishment of the STRIKE Command, p. 567-8.

CINC SOUTH: Griffin takes command from Admiral Russell, March, 1965, p. 651; a description of the command set-up, p. 651-5

Griffin institutes a series of inspections and visits, p. 657 ff; Italy, p. 657-664; Paris, p. 664-5; a stand-down situation for NATO forces - the question of morale, p. 666-7; laisee-faire attitude towards NATO in the north, p. 669; logistics and the NATO commands, p. 670-1; CYPRUS the number one problem of CINC SOUTH, p. 671-2; the possible use of atomic weapons, p. 672-4; visit to Turkey, p. 675 ff; CYPRUS - see entries under CYPRUS: visit to Greece, p. 687 ff; difficulties with Greeks over Greek personnel in NATO headquarters in Turkey, p. 691-2; multi-national inspection teams - difficulties in getting clearance, p. 693; inspection of the border areas (Northern Italy) of the command, p. 698; the Greek crisis and the resignation of Papandreau, p. 700-1; trip to Eastern Turkey, p. 702-716; visit to the Russian border, p. 708-9; visit to the custodial units for atomic weapons, p. 710-711; DEEP FURROW, p. 717-719; visit to Thessalonica and northern border of Greece, p. 722-725; border fortifications, p. 722-3; visit to Malta, p. 725 ff; visit to Cinc Cent, p. 732-3; the Italian Missile Base at Sardinia, p. 734; further visits - Norway, Denmark, Portugal, p. 738 ff; a recapitulation of the component parts of CincSouth command, p. 740-1; Griffin devises regional conferences of his command, p. 744 ff; institutes an annual ball, p. 747-8; other social activities, p. 749-50; p. 756-7; the navy barge, p. 758-60; NATO liaison with CENTO, p. 764-5 ff; Greek politics, p. 773-780; Second Regional Conference (in Turkey), p. 782-786; Griffin makes a summation of his three year stewardship at NATO Headquarters in Brussells (Oct. 1967), p. 786-7; as Cinc SOUTH Griffin speaks his mind on Russian advances in Mediterranean - Navy League meeting in Madrid (1967), p. 787; farewell calls p. 789-791.

CINC US NAVEUR: Griffin's command in London, p. 572 ff; his personal accommodations, p. 575-6; Romany at Virginia Water, p. 576-7; Griffin finds inadequate communications in his command, p. 579-80; his efforts to improve the physical headquarters and equipment of the command, p. 580-2; a program of meeting with European CNOs, p. 583; spreading the word about the 6th fleet, p. 583; Griffin's contacts with U.S. businessmen abroad, p. 584-6; Griffin's visits to nations in Western Europe, p. 596 ff; Holland p. 600-1; Morocco, p. 601-4; Turkey, p. 605-6; Greece, p. 606; Norway, p. 607; the Vatican, p. 608-10; Spain, p. 610-613; Operations Steel Pike p. 635-7; problem of "presentos", p. 638-9.

USS CLAUDE V. RICKETTS (ex BIDDLE): p. 634-5.

CONGRESSIONAL TESTIMONY: p. 509-514; McNamara's initial report
     for the entire Department of Defense, p. 519-521.

CONSTANTINE II, King of Greece: p. 696-8; p. 701-2; p. 719-720;
     p. 774-5; p. 781.

CREPIN, General (French): CincCENT (Commander in Chief, Central
     Europe - NATO), p. 732.

CUBAN MISSILE CRISIS: p. 550 ff.

CYPRUS: the number one problem for Cinc South, p. 671-2; problem
     increases with the advent of Makarias and withdrawal
     of British, p. 672; p. 681-7; inflammatory nature of
     popular press in Turkey and Greece, p. 689-690; conse-
     quences in Greek actions in NATO, p. 691-2; p. 721; the
     attitude of the Greek Colonels, p. 781-2.

DEEP FREEZE OPERATION: p. 543-4.

DEEP FURROW: NATO Operation - held on annual basis, p. 704-5;
     p. 717-19.

DeGAULLE, General Charles: fails to attend 20th anniversary of
     Normandy landings, p. 595-6; p. 597-9.

DEMIRAL, The Hon. Suleman: Prime Minister of Turkey, p. 734.

DENFELD, Admiral Louis: p. 561.

DENNISON, Admiral Robert Lee: p. 552 ff.

DIEM, Ngo Dinh: President of South Vietnam - Griffin's picture
     of him, p. 467-8.

DIYARBAKIR: ancient city in Eastern Turkey, p. 715-6.

EASTERN EXPRESS: NATO Operation - held on annual basis, p. 704;
     exercise held in vicinity of Diyarbakir, p. 715-6; p. 722;
     a primary reason for this exercise, p. 742.

EISENHOWER, General Dwight D.: President of the U.S. p. 497-8;
     his visit to London for the funeral of Winston Churchill,
     p. 615-620; the story of the General and the tablecloth-
     his visit to Hawaii, p. 648-9.

ENOSSIS: The Cypriot policy for union with Greece - see entries
     under CYPRUS.

USS ENTERPRISE: p. 534; around the world cruise with USS LONG
     BEACH and USS BAINBRIDGE, p. 640-2.

ERZURUM, Turkey: visited by Cinc South - headquarters of the
     Turkish Third Army, p. 703; p. 706; work accomplished
     there by the Turkish army, p. 706-8; p. 715-6.

F-111: Griffin's story on this, p. 535 ff.

FAISAL, ibn Abdul-Aziz, King of Saudi Arabia: p. 768

FANFANI, The Hon. Amintore: Italian Foreign Minister: p. 658; p. 662.

FELDMAN, The Hon. George: U.S. Ambassador to Malta (1967), p. 726; p. 731-2.

FISH, Lt. Paula: p. 621.

FLEET OPERATIONS AND READINESS: Griffin becomes Op-03, p. 491; p. 498-9; brings several of newest ships and several of oldest ships to Washington - demonstration for budgetary reasons, p. 499; influence of Mendel Rivers with shipbuilding program, p. 500; nuclear powered ships, p. 500-1; dealing with Admiral Rickover, p. 500-2; selling the new shipbuilding program within the navy, p. 506-8; Congressional testimony, p. 509-510; program authorization by the Congress and implementation, p. 515-8; question of best equipment for ships, p. 522 ff; establishment of SEAL Teams for Vietnam, p. 522-3; other developments, p. 524 ff establishment of SEAL Teams for Vietnam, p. 522-3; other developments, p. 524 ff; Griffin and his options after Op-03, p. 558.

FREDERICKA, Queen of Greece: p. 777.

GAROUFALIAS: Greek Minister of Defense (1966); p. 606; p. 695-6; investigates the ASPIDA and brings about resignation of Prime Minister Papandreau, p. 700-701.

GENDA, General Minoru: Japanese General, p. 465.

GETTY, J. Paul: (American oilman) Sutton Place, his castle at Guilford, England p. 644.

GILPATRICK, The Hon. Roswell: Deputy Secretary of Defense, p. 552; p. 561.

GREECE: politics in 1967, p. 773-4; p. 775-9.

GREEK-TURKISH RELATIONS: see entries under Cinc SOUTH and CYPRUS.

GRIFFIN, Admiral C.D.: personal recollections of the 7th fleet command, p. 459 ff; p. 479; p. 489; after duty in Op-03 his appointment to London with four stars, p. 559-560; apparent plan of McNamara on a shakeup in Navy's top command, p. 562; the scope of CincEur command, p. 566-7; sudden death of Mrs. Griffin in London, p. 578-9; Griffin remarries in Nov. 1964, p. 613-614; p. 623-4; alerted to the fact he would follow Adm. Russell as CincSouth (NATO), p. 625; succeeded in London by classmate Adm. Thach, p. 625-6; his friendship with J. Paul Getty, p. 644-7; his bout with hepatitis, p. 736-8; Mrs. Griffin role in NATO entertaining, p. 747-8; Mrs. Griffin in Teheran, p. 771-2; his farewell tours, p. 789-791; retirement, p. 791.

HART, Parker (Pete): U.S. Ambassador to Turkey (1967) p. 694-5.

HODDAIDO: p. 474.

HUSSEIN, King of Jordan: p. 768.

INONU, The Hon. Ismet: p. 605.

ISMIR: see entries under Cinc SOUTH: NATO Headquarters in Turkey - attempt to have Greek personnel assigned - attitude of Greek King, p. 720-1; p. 735; p. 775.

JAPANESE DEFENSE: p. 487-8.

JOINT CHIEFS OF STAFF: p. 496-7.

KEATING, The Hon. Kenneth: Senator from New York - his comments on the crisis building in Cuba, p. 554.

KENNEDY, The Hon. John F.: a friend of Admiral Anderson - names him as Ambassador to Portugal, p. 538-540; the Cuban Missile Crisis, p. 550 ff; Kennedy and Adm. Anderson, p. 563-4; p. 593-4;

KHRUSHCHEV, Nikita S.: Premier of Russia - the Cuban Missile Crisis, p. 550 ff.

KIDD, Admiral Isaac C. Jr.: his work as Assistant Chief of Staff Cinc South, p. 671. investigates the incident involving the USS LIBERTY, p. 754.

KINMEN - Island of: Chinese Headquarters on this offshore island, p. 465.

KOMBOKIS, Major C.A.: Greek Army Aide to Cinc South, p. 656.

KORTH, The Hon. Fred: Secretary of the Navy - p. 547-8; observations on his technical background, p. 547-8; Griffin's differences with Korth, p. 548-9.

LEMNITZER, General Lyman L.: p. 575; p. 577; p. 731; p. 665-6; present for DEEP FURROW Operation, p. 718-9; p. 787.

LIBYA: value of the air base there under King Idris, p. 728.

LUCE, Admiral David: First Sea Lord (1964), p. 574; resigns in protest over government decision to cut out carrier program, p. 630;

MAKARIOS, Archbishop: President of Cyprus: p. 672; p. 689-690; p. 696; his demand for a detailed inspection of the Turkish Rotation Group, p. 705.

MALAYA: p. 471-3.

MALTA: p. 628-9; increasing value of her airfields, p. 727-8; see also entry under CINC SOUTH.

McDONALD, Admiral David: the sudden news of his appointment as CNO, p. 565-6; p. 577; p. 579.

McNAMARA, Robert: Secretary of Defense—his influence in the Navy Department - The Whiz Kids, p. 491-4; p. 496-8; p. 504; his testimony on the Defense Department Budget, p. 518-521; more on his techniques, p. 533-4; McNamara and Research, p. 535-6, p. 541; his differences with Admiral Anderson, p. 536 ff; his attitude towards Hanson Baldwin, p. 542-3; McNamara and Anderson in the Cuban Missile Crisis, p. 553; p. 557-8; p. 560; his apparent plan to fire Anderson, Ricketts and Griffin - implemented only in the case of Anderson, p. 562; p. 570; McNamara and nuclear-powered attack carriers, p. 642-4;

MERCOURI, Melina: p. 778-9.

MEYNER, Robert B.: Governor of New Jersey, p. 473-4.

MICHAELIS, Lt. Gen. John Hersey: COMLANSOUTHEAST, p. 675-6.

MINTOFF, Dom: Maltese Labor Leader, p. 731.

MISSILE PROBLEMS: p. 527-8.

MORO, Aldo: Prime Minister of Italy, p. 657; p. 661.

MOUNTBATTEN, Admiral Lord Louis: Chairman of the British Joint Chiefs, p. 573.

MUNOZ GRANDES, Capt. Gen. Agustin: p. 610-611.

NASSER, Gamal Abdel: President of Egypt - the Shah's view of him, p. 766.

NASTY BOATS (Norwegian MTB's): used by the U.S. Navy in Vietnam with the SEAL TEAMS, p. 522-23.

NATO: Need to keep the organization viable, p. 740-2; Griffin's attempts to strengthen the Cinc South command, p. 742-3; the southern regional conferences, p. 744-5; first meeting in Rome, p. 744-5; second meeting in Ankara, p. 745-6; Griffin institutes an annual Ball, p. 747-8; other NATO social activities, p. 749-50; the liaison with CENTO, p. 764-5; NATO and its importance to Western Europe - a summary statement of Adm. Griffin, p. 791-3.

NAVY LEAGUE: Madrid Chapter invites Griffin as Cinc South to speak at regional meeting in Madrid, p. 787-8.

NEELY, Captain Guy Morton, Jr.: Aide to Admiral Griffin as CincNavEur, p. 565, p. 592.

NIETO ANTUNEZ, Vice Admiral Pedro: Minister of the Navy in Spain, p. 610.

NITZE, The Hon. Paul: p. 558.

NOMURA, Admiral Kichisaburo (Japanese): p. 479-80.

NUCLEAR POWERED SHIPS: p. 532-5.

PALMER, Arnold: p. 461-2.

PAPADOPOULOS, Colonel George: Prime Minister of Greece, p. 774; p. 790.

PAPANDREOU, Andreas: radical son of Greek Prime Minister, p. 688; p. 699-700; p. 773, p. 778.

PAPANDREOU, Georges: Prime minister of Greece, p. 606; p. 688-89; p. 690; p. 696; p. 699; p. 773.

PAUL I, King of Greece: p. 697.

PIPILIS, General (Grek): Chief of the General Staff, p. 691.

POLARIS: p. 530-1; Griffin discusses European bases, p. 587 ff.

POPE PAUL VI: p. 608-9.

RADAR Development: p. 525-6.

RADFORD, Admiral Arthur: Gen. Eisenhower's evaluation of him, p. 618-9.

RAHMAN, Tunka Abdul: Prime Minister of Malaya, p. 472-3.

REEDY, George: p. 616-7.

RICKETTS, Admiral Claude V.: Vice Chief of Naval Operations, p. 561-2.

RICKOVER, Admiral Hyman: p. 501-3; Griffin secures his cooperation, p. 503; p. 504-5. p. 641.

RIVERS, The Hon. Mendel: Member of Congress, p. 500.

ROLL ON/ROLL OFF Ships: development of, p. 525.

ROMANY at Virginia Waters, England: see entries under Cinc US NAVEUR.

RUSSIAN NAVY: p. 480; p. 483-6;

SARAGAT, The Hon. Giuseppe: President of Italy, p. 657, p. 662.

SARDINIA: CincSouth visits the Italian Missile Base at Salto di Quirra, p. 734.

SCHOECH, Vice Admiral Wm.: relieves Griffin as Cinc, 7th Fleet, p.479

SCOTT, The Hon. Hugh: Senator from Pennsylvania - in Hong Kong, p. 468; his accident, p. 469.

SEAL Teams: p. 522-3.

SEVENTH FLEET: Griffin's account of the scope of this command, p. 459-460; Griffin's efforts to keep wives informed on fleet activities, p. 464; reports sent back to Washington by C-in-C, p. 475-6; discussion of fleet communications, p. 476-7; intelligence gathering, p. 477: recommendations on flag officers, p. 478; performance of crew as ambassadors ashore, p. 482-3;

SHAH OF IRAN (Mohammad Reza Pahlavi): Griffin's talk with him in Teheran, p. 765-9 (copy of the record in appendix).

STEEL PIKE - OPERATION: An operation in Spanish waters under command of Cinc Lant (Oct. 1964), p. 635-6.

STRIKE COMMAND: McNamara sets up this command over the objection of the Navy and Marine Corps, p. 567-9; disestablished in 1971, p. 569; McNamara's rationale, p. 570-1.

SUNAY, General Cevdet: President of Turkey and former Chief of the General Staff, p. 605; p. 677; p. 679-80; p. 690 p. 703-6; p. 734, p. 790.

SUTTON PLACE: name of English Castle owned by J. Paul Getty, p. 644.

SYMINGTON, The Hon. Stuart, U.S. Senator from Missouri: p. 761

TAIWAN: Visit of Adm. Griffin - inspection of defenses, p. 465-6; mainland activities directed at Taiwan defenses, p. 469-70;

TANCEL, General (Turkish): Commander of the Air Forces, p. 677.

TAYLOR, General Maxwell: p. 496-7.

THACH, Admiral John S.: p. 625-6; succeeds Griffin in Cinc NAV EUR command, p. 650.

TURAL, C. General: Chief of the Turkish General Staff in succession to General Sunay, p. 745-6. p. 782-3; Griffin's problems with him on naval boundaries, p. 783-6; p. 790.

TURKEY: Government, army: see entries under CINC SOUTH, General SUNAY; Turkey on the front line with Russia and what it means to the Turks, p. 712-3.

VERONA, Italy: the summer opera, p. 762-3.

VIETNAM: Visit of Griffin, p. 466-7.

WARREN, The Hon. Earl - Chief Justice of the United States:

incident involving Mrs. Griffin, p. 623-4.

WILSON, The Hon. Charles: Secretary of Defense, p. 494.

YOKOSUKA: p. 461 ff;

ZURICH-LONDON AGREEMENT: by which Cyprus became independent - see entries under Cyprus.